KICKING & DREAMING

!t
itbooks
AN IMPRINT OF HARPERCOLLINSPUBLISHERS

A STORY OF HEART, SOUL, AND ROCK AND ROLL

KICKING & DREAMING

ANN & NANCY WILSON with Charles R. Cross

itbooks

A continuation of this copyright page appears on page 291.

HarperCollins books may be purchased for educational, business, or sales promotional use. For information please e-mail the Special Markets Department at SPsales@harpercollins.com.

A hardcover edition of this book was published in 2012 by It Books, an imprint of HarperCollins Publishers.

FIRST IT BOOKS PAPERBACK PUBLISHED 2013.

Designed by Paula Russell Szafranski

Library of Congress Cataloging-in-Publication Data is available upon request.

ISBN 978-0-06-210168-6

13 14 15 16 17 ID/RRD 10 9 8 7 6 5 4 3 2 1

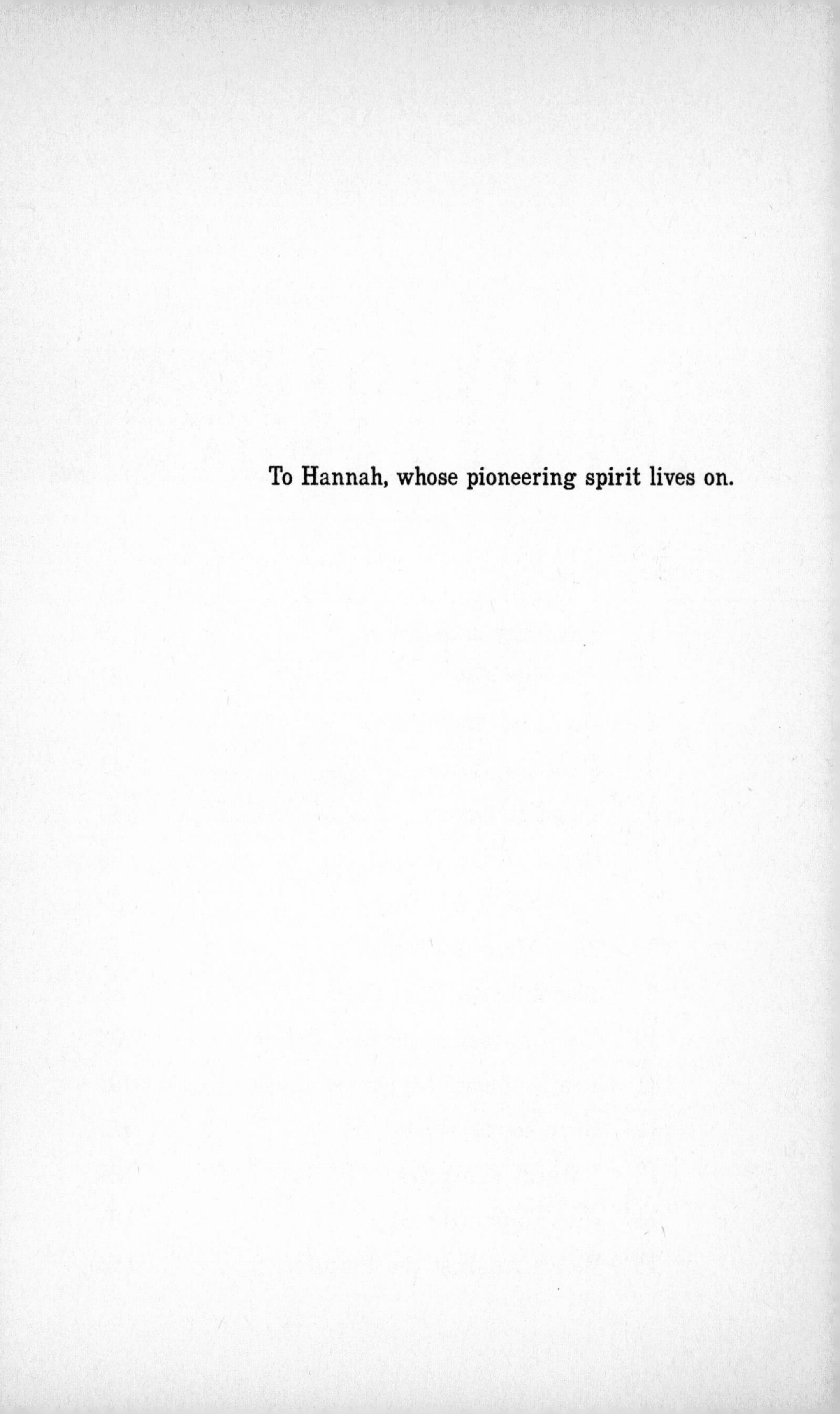

To Hannah, whose pioneering spirit lives on.

CONTENTS

PROLOGUE

L'homme magique, Calgary, Alberta, Canada

OCTOBER 18, 1975

Our journey starts with Ann's encounter with the Devil's nightclub and poisoned food. Nancy, meanwhile, battles the demons of disco, orange jumpsuits, and flames both good and evil. . . .

ANN WILSON

I never thought much about it at the time, but looking back it seems odd that our career came crashing apart and then came magically back together in a club named Lucifer's.

Robert Johnson, Mick Jagger, Keith Richards, Jimmy Page. You might have expected all of them on the bill at Lucifer's, in Calgary, Canada. But in October 1975, the red-flamed letters on the club's marquee read FROM VANCOUVER . . . *DREAMBOAT ANNIE* recording artists: Heart. Never mind that my sister Nancy and I were from the Seattle suburbs, temporarily transplanted to Canada.

The red letters in the sign, with a couple of burned-out bulbs, could have represented what was happening to Heart's career. We had been red-hot for a time, but our flame was suddenly flickering. *Dreamboat Annie* had come out two months before, and "Crazy On You" earned decent airplay in Vancouver. But the album had been released only in Canada, and with very limited distribution. Our label had a staff of two and operated out of a desk in the corner of Mushroom Studios.

We had come to Vancouver three years before with a plan for stardom. The plan had worked: Slowly, steadily, we had moved forward. As we joked among ourselves, we had become "the number-one cabaret band in Vancouver." That meant we played nightclubs six nights a week, five sets a night. Those gigs had paid off artistically, if not financially. If one believes the theory Malcolm Gladwell puts forth in his book *Outliers*, that if you spend ten thousand hours doing something you get good at it, Heart had become very good, indeed.

But we were also broke. Every Canadian dollar we earned went into instruments, amplifiers, speakers, or our van, which often collided with wildlife. At that moment our van needed costly repairs from a moose accident before it could make it back home from Calgary.

Our manager—and my boyfriend—Michael Fisher, aka "the Magic Man," was constantly pushing his "five-year plan," which was to build Heart from a nightclub act to an album band, to stardom in Canada, and finally to U.S. success. Everything had worked accordingly until our album came out and failed to take off immediately, and our career went into a stall phase.

Since we couldn't play Vancouver clubs every week without wearing out our welcome, we had to take any gig we could find. We played taverns, roadhouses, keggers, private parties. We played dozens of high school dances. We once played a prom in North Vancouver where Michael J. Fox was the student body president. He came back before the show to shake our hands.

"That kid is going places," Nancy said of the short, good-looking boy with a strong handshake. She was right.

We took the gig at Lucifer's in Calgary, a fourteen-hour drive from Vancouver, because it was the only offer we had right then. We were booked for a two-week run, five sets a night, six nights a week. That first night, we drew a packed house on a typically slow Monday. But after the show, the club manager lectured us that we had brought in "the wrong crowd." Our fans hadn't eaten enough food, and they drank beer rather than pricier hard liquor. He also said we played too loud.

As the week went by, it was more of the same. We played to big houses, yet the manager thought we should play more covers. Disco was big at the time, and he suggested we'd be more successful if we dropped our original songs entirely and played only disco hits. Playing in this club felt as if we could have been working at an insurance company with a demanding boss. This wasn't rock and roll.

On Saturday night, our sixth in a row at Lucifer's, with another week to go, the club treated us to dinner before the show. We were thankful for it, because we often ate brown rice cooked on a camp stove in our hotel room. But the food the club served had a suspicious odor. Actually, it tasted like Pine-Sol disinfectant. They had either washed the serving plates in Pine-Sol, or the cleaner had somehow gotten into the food. It was disgusting.

I began to wonder if Lucifer's was trying to poison us because we weren't a disco band.

NANCY WILSON

I had only joined Heart two years before, after dropping out of college in Oregon. It had always been Ann and my goal to be in a band together, but I joined somewhat reluctantly and transplanted myself up there. I wanted to play with my sister, and I, like everyone else in the band, had drunk the Kool-Aid and believed that we could be the best live band in Canada.

That belief was not shared by the manager of Lucifer's, who kept telling us to play disco hits. When I first joined, we would occasionally cover the Bee Gees "Nights on Broadway" or "Jive Talkin'" to get people on the dance floor during our opening set. But by 1975, we were trying to do more original material—*Dreamboat Annie* songs. It was our statement to the world that disco was not going to get us.

As the week went on, we got more criticism. The manager said we didn't dress well enough. The Stylistics had been there before us, and the manager pointed to a picture of them on the wall, with their matching suits, and told us we'd be more successful if we dressed like them. Another band was pictured wearing orange pantsuits. In that era we usually wore jeans with Kimono-styled tops. It was hippie, but it also had flair. It was our style, and not a fabrication by a record label, or a club manager. We wanted to look sexy, but we did not want to dress in a way that objectified us.

The fact that we were women, and sisters, always got a lot of attention, but there was a lot of male energy in Heart, as well. Onstage, Roger Fisher, our lead guitar player, would strut around wearing a little leather vest showing off his rock-hard abs, and he played a lot like Jimmy Page. He was a brilliant player, but he had a temper and could be a wild man. By Saturday night, we were exhausted, and we were sick of being ripped into for just being Heart. Before the show, Roger got a bottle of Grand Marnier from the bar. He poured it out on the dressing room floor. Then he lit it on fire. It was just like Jimi Hendrix at Monterey.

In the dressing room, the manager had posted a long list of "House Rules" that ran the entire length of one wall. They read:

No bad language.

No spitting.

No chewing gum.

No smoking.

No drinking.

No lighters.

No dungarees.

No groupies.

No drugs.

No dogs.

As I read this, I looked at our band. We were wearing jeans, smoking cigarettes and pot, drinking, and our guitar player had just set the floor on fire. But the regulation that bothered me the most was "No dogs." Dogs have always been part of the Wilson family, and any club that didn't allow a sweet dog backstage was just heartless.

Roger went up and at the bottom of the list he wrote:

"NO FUN. THIS PLACE SUCKS."

Because we were two women playing rock music, we had come against barriers at every step. "Is your guitar really plugged in?" I'd be asked many times. "You play pretty good for a girl," guys would constantly say. Our skill at doing Led Zeppelin covers had earned us the nickname "Little Led Zeppelin," but we also knew guys called us "Led Zeppelin with tits," behind our backs. We naively thought if we were good at our instruments, we'd be judged as musicians, and not by gender. We had no idea that being females in rock 'n' roll would be an issue we would face at every turn.

But that kind of struggle we were used to. Lucifer's represented a different kind of battle. It had less to do with the fact that we were women and more to do with a divide between what was then the disco-dominated music world, and anyone trying to do anything else. The club felt like the establishment, and the establishment felt like the enemy. It was the absolute low. I thought, "I left college for this?"

By Saturday, the tension was obvious. When we went onstage, I could see that something was off with Ann. She had that glint of anger in her eye. Ann has never liked anyone to tell her that she can't do something. She had struggled harder than anyone to make Heart happen, and things weren't working out. She looked scorned, and I had long ago learned that Ann Wilson scorned was a force of nature.

Ann started the set by asking Michael Fisher, who was doing the sound, to turn us up. She knew this would make the manager upset. Then she addressed the crowd:

"How'd your dinners taste? Mine tasted like Pine-Sol. I think they washed the dishes with Pine-Sol." And then she launched into "Crazy On You." It was the first time during that stand at Lucifer's that we had opened a set with a song of our own. The crowd, our beer-only fans, went bonkers. It was us, our song, our words, our chords, and not disco. The instant Ann started singing, I could see her fury had subsided, and she was back into the music, soothed by it.

Not that the owner noticed. When we came offstage for the night, he was furious. He hauled Ann, along with Michael Fisher, into his office.

ANN

I knew we were going to get yelled at, but what the club owner said surprised me: "You're fired. Clear out of your rooms tonight. And you won't be getting the rest of your pay."

"We have a contract!" Michael protested.

"Not anymore," he said, ripping the contract up.

We went back to the dressing room and told the band. The dressing room was made of wood veneer. Someone in the band kicked a wall, and his foot went right through it, leaving a gaping hole.

We'd come so far, and it had ended at this. Our van couldn't make it home. We were getting kicked out of our hotel. I had just been fired from a gig, and I had never been fired from anything in my life. My band, my life, had fallen apart in a club named after the Devil in the middle of the Canadian prairie.

Walking back to my room, I couldn't bear the idea that I would have to tell our parents as well. Our parents had always been supportive of music but they had been suspicious that I was corrupting Nancy, bringing her into an adult world of rock 'n' roll too fast, too soon. And here, in Lucifer's, their fears had come true.

As I was packing up my room, with no idea where we were going, the phone rang. It was Shelley Siegel, promotions manager for Mushroom Records. "Any chance you can get out of that contract in Calgary?" he said.

"The contract just got ripped up," I said. "We were fired."

"Great," he said, as if that were the best news he'd heard all day. "You've got a gig opening up for Rod Stewart for two shows, starting in Montreal. It's in four days, and Montreal is twenty-three hundred miles away. Do you think you can get there?"

"We'll get there."

The only way we could make the journey in time was by train. We carted all our gear onto a rail car and ended up having the car to ourselves for the three-day ride. It turned into a day and night jam, with everyone in the band grabbing acoustic instruments. We played all the songs we'd grown up on. It was "Here Comes the Sun," "Michelle," "House of the Rising Sun," and "Gloria" all the way to Montreal. At that point, the band was one big family. It was the sweetest, most innocent time Heart ever had. It was all joy and all possibility.

When we got to Montreal, I felt like I was stepping into a fairy tale. It seemed more French than Paris. The whole city was draped in romance. Every street corner dripped with poetry. It was like it was surrounded with torches.

The venue was gigantic. We'd played big nightclubs before, but the only time I'd even been in a venue as big as the Forum was when I saw the Beatles play at the Seattle Center Coliseum. At showtime I walked onstage, but it was so bright out there I thought the house lights were still on. I could see fans standing up and cheering. Every person who wasn't clapping was holding up a lighter.

I thought that Rod Stewart must have come onstage behind us. I turned around but all I saw were my bandmates, who looked stunned. Nancy was more astonished than I had ever seen her.

The fans wouldn't quiet down, so I walked to the side of the stage and asked Michael Fisher what was happening. "One of the French-language radio stations has been playing our album," he said. "It's a hit!"

Four days before, I had been eating Pine-Sol–laden food, had been fired from my first gig ever, and had been busted flat in Calgary. Now I was walking onstage in a sold-out arena of eighteen thousand people who loved us before I even opened my mouth. Michael Fisher later told me that the moment had been electric for him as well because it was "proof of concept"—that the plan he had come up with, which had been executed by everyone in Heart all those nights in those smoky nightclubs, had worked. It was one radio station, and one whose listeners weren't even English-speakers, but it was proof it was possible for us to find an audience.

I walked back to the microphone on the Forum stage and put both hands on it to steady myself. I paused to catch my breath. But I didn't start singing. Instead, I said the words in French that someone backstage had cued me with. "Cette chanson s'appelle 'L' Homme Magique.'" In my broken French, I was telling them the song was called "Magic Man." The crowd went absolutely bananas. As the guitar solo started the song, everyone in the place sang along.

It was only one city in the world, but for the first time we were stars.

1

THE LADY AXE KILLER

The secret family history of kidnapping, scalping, and revenge killing, and those pesky, annoying, irrelevant "Women who Rock" Questions. . . .

NANCY WILSON

In the four decades that Ann and I have been in music, we've been asked countless times what it's like to be "a woman in rock." This question is asked in virtually every interview we do, by men and by women. We sit politely and try to come up with an answer we hope will encourage others. But what I really want to do is scream questions in reply, like "What's it like to be a *human being* in rock? What's it like to be a *human being* on the planet?"

In forty years, we've never come up with the perfect answer to the "woman in rock" question or the other common question: "Why did you first think women could rock?" We have no perfect answer for the simple reason that we never thought gender was a barrier to picking up guitars. We started playing because we loved music. If we would have known how difficult it would be to be women fronting a band, it might have stopped us. But probably we would have done it anyway.

Yet there is a secret chapter in our family history that might explain our urge to fight against the norm, so to speak. The story itself is in American history textbooks, but our connection to it has never been revealed. It has long been part of our family lore, passed down to us. I've since passed the story on to my children, as has Ann, and my other sister Lynn. It is a story of murder, kidnapping, and revenge, with enough gruesome details to make any *Behind the Music* episode look tame. So imagine an alternative world, where Ann and I are sitting down with an interviewer who asks: "Why did you think you could be a woman in rock?"

Our answer: "Because we are descended from a notorious woman who murdered men with a hatchet, scalped them, and later sold their scalps for a reward."

My bad joke inside the Heart tour bus has long been that I am not the first family member to slay people with an axe. The original axe slayer was Hannah Dustin, our great, great, great, great, great, great, great, great, great, great grandmother. Dustin was our mother's maiden name.

I first heard Hannah's tale from my mother when I was five. Before I picked up a guitar, I must have heard the story a hundred times. Family gatherings were always important to the Dustins, and the tale would have slightly different shading whether an aunt, or uncle, or my mom was telling it. The basic framework was always the same, though, and always horrific and shocking. In some strange way, because Hannah's actions were so unexpected, and so rare for a woman, I always felt secretly proud of murderous Hannah.

Her infamy began in March 1697 in Haverhill, Massachusetts, not far from Salem. During King William's War, French emissaries bribed the Abenaki tribe to attack an English settlement. Twenty-seven colonists were killed and thirteen taken hostage. Hannah's husband escaped with eight of their children, but she and her newborn daughter Martha were kidnapped. The hostages were marched toward Quebec. On the way the Indians killed six-day-old Martha by smashing her head against a tree. Hannah had to watch as her newborn was murdered in front of her.

Six weeks later, Hannah was still being held hostage on an island in the Merrimack River. One night while her captors slept, she loosened the rope used to tie her wrists, grabbed a tomahawk, and killed one of the men who was watching guard over her. Seeing Hannah's actions, another hostage killed the other guard. Hannah then used her bloody hatchet to kill two Indian women and six of their children.

Hannah and the hostages climbed into canoes and began to head down the river, away from the carnage. But before they went far, Hannah had second thoughts—there was more venom in her. She went back to the island to scalp her victims. Holding the gory scalps, she climbed back into the canoe and escaped. It took her several days to reach Haverhill and her family.

Here's where the tale always really amazed me as a child: Once Hannah was back in civilization, she turned the scalps in for a reward. The Massachusetts General Court awarded her the princely sum of twenty-five pounds for the scalps. They paid her for her bloody act of murderous revenge.

I am not making this up.

Cotton Mather, Henry David Thoreau, Ralph Waldo Emerson, and others wrote about Hannah's story. In 1879, a bronze statute of Hannah was erected in Haverhill showing her holding a tomahawk and scalps. It is thought to be the first statue honoring a woman in the United States. In 1997, my sister Lynn and our mother traveled back to Haverhill to see Hannah's statue. Our mother was a voracious reader of history, and she really enjoyed this trip.

In 2008, I traveled there, too. I had my picture taken holding a guitar in the same pose as the statue of Hannah Dustin holding the axe. I went inside Hannah's house, which is now a museum. Some of the pictures of Hannah showed black cats in the corner. Because Hannah's acts were so outrageous, and so unusual for a woman, there has always been intrigue around her, and there have been suggestions that she was a witch. Some of the same things have been said about Ann and me!

Hannah had incredible pluck. There was a fire in Hannah's belly that we share. She went outside the norm of what people expected a woman to do.

Ann was born with the same pluck, and I've got a bit of it, as well. Ann and I have also gone out on adventures into the unknown, but we've used guitars not tomahawks. We've tried to make ours a message of love, but sometimes there has been anger, and people have been wasted along the way. There are even chapters when revenge is part of the story.

At the museum in Haverhill, I bought a Hannah Dustin bobble head in the gift shop. I mentioned to the woman behind the counter that I was a descendant of Hannah. She leaned over, and whispered in my ear, "What do you think really happened?"

"It's all true," I said. "Every word is true."

ANN WILSON

Hannah Dustin was not the only warrior in our background. On the Wilson side, we come from a long line of Marine officers. Their service, honor, and valor are also part of our legacy. If Lynn, Nancy, or I had been male, the family would have expected us to join the Marine Corps, and we would have probably ended up in Vietnam.

Our grandfather, John Bushrod Wilson Sr. was a decorated brigadier general. His unit of Marines was the first U.S. force in Europe during World War II. In July 1941, they were sent to Iceland to prevent Hitler from establishing a U-boat base. He brought back heavy arctic sleeping bags that our mom made into quilts. We slept under those quilts growing up. General Wilson was later in the Pacific, where he fought in key battles in Guam, Bougainville, and Iwo Jima. He earned two Bronze Stars, and a Legion of Merit.

The general was married to Beatrice Lamoureaux. Nancy's French middle name comes from that side of the family (we are also part Scottish, Celt, Irish, German, and Italian). Beatrice's first child was James Phillip, who would eventually go into the Marines and become an officer.

Our father John Bushrod Wilson Jr. was born at the naval shipyard hospital in Bremerton, Washington, on April 8, 1922. During my dad's youth, the family traveled from post to post, and spent many years in Taiwan and the Philippines. Our dad was a peaceful soul and a gentle man. He grew to be six-foot-three and dashingly good-looking, and girls adored him. He was funny and smart, and he hoped to become a teacher. He never told me this, but my guess is that although he knew Marine service was expected of him, he probably hoped a war wouldn't be going on during his time in the "family business."

The Wilsons were originally from Corvallis, Oregon, where their ancestors helped establish Oregon State University. And that was where our father began college, majoring in education and English. He was already in the Reserve Officers' Training Corps because it was destined for him to be a Marine. But he also took choir, and it was in choir he met our mother.

Lois Mary Dustin was from Oregon City, Oregon, a small town outside of Portland. Lou, as everyone called her, was only five-foot-two, but she was a blonde firebrand. She was an intellectual, but she enrolled in college to study home economics. That was just what girls did back then. One of her high school journals shows the mindset of many growing up in that time. "When Cupid shoots his bow," one classmate wrote, "I hope he 'Mrs.' you!" Another read: "When you get married and have twins, come over to my house for safety pins."

When John met Lou on that campus that day, Cupid shot his bow, and thus began a love story that would continue over many decades. But amid a backdrop of war, theirs would be a love constantly on the move. What started was an itinerant, almost-gypsy lifestyle that Nancy and I have always believed was passed on to us.

After Pearl Harbor, John Jr. finished his final credits at college and joined the Marines. Our dad was sent several places for training, but stayed in touch with mom through letters. They had already talked marriage, but John felt that would only be proper once he'd become an officer. He was nothing but proper. To assure her of his intentions, our dad wrote to mom in

March 1942 on United States Marine Corps stationery. To our mother, this letter was her single dearest possession, other than her children. It read:

Subject: Request and orders.

1. It is requested by this command that you comply in all respects with the wishes of said command concerning matters of close attachment and eventual marriage.
2. It is further requested that you enter in a state of relaxation concerning the matter of this command's deep feeling for you.
3. This command loves your command.
4. You are hereby ordered (Paragraph 908, Section 17, Article 3b, Landing Force Manual) to remain on active duty with your present organization and commandant. This command will absolutely not tolerate any evidence of lack of "esprit de corps."
5. The foregoing are hereby directed and ordered for immediate carrying out, barring the exigencies of the service within reason, at your discretion.

By order of,

J. B. Wilson, Jr. Pfc., USMCR., Commanding

Our mother, always a romantic, just melted. But the letter also said much about what their relationship would be in the years to come: They would share a sense of humor, an appreciation of sarcasm, but also a deep, underlying commitment. Yet, as the letter also suggests, it would be a marriage that would fall under traditional gender confines. He was "commanding," even when he did it as sweetly as his letter suggested.

Two years later, in October 1944, he wrote her again to announce he had completed the Officer's Training School in Quantico, Virginia. He was now a junior lieutenant in the United States Marine Corps. He requested she travel across the country to join him. He told her they could be married in nearby Fredericksburg, Virginia, upon her arrival. He couldn't come to her because he might be shipped out at any moment. She knew in accepting his proposal it would almost certainly mean she'd be alone waiting for him to return from the war, perhaps for years. In those days, there was also every possibility this marriage could mean a quick widowhood. It was a dark time. But she packed her things and took a train across the country. She told everyone about her upcoming nuptials, and there were several stories in the local paper in Oregon City. I can only imagine how mom swooned to see the headline: "Miss Lois Dustin to Wed Lieutenant in October Services."

That train ride back east was the most single romanticized story our mother ever told. She took a train three thousand miles to this little Civil War town to get married. "John was like a knight," our mom would tell us. "I was going to a fairy tale town to get married to a knight." She was leaving her blue-collar Oregon world for a Civil War wedding to a Marine officer. She had grown up a huge fan of *Gone with the Wind*, and the wedding must have seemed like she was having her Scarlett O'Hara moment. Always concerned with fashion, she wore a tailored peplum outfit, hose, and black shoes. In her luggage, she carefully packed a blue wedding suit, and a "second-day" suit for the day after the honeymoon.

You cannot overestimate the effect this tale had on us growing up. We heard of a romance deeply caught up in journey, in travel, as if movement itself was a powerful expression of desire. It probably informed my lyrics more than any other single influence. In a way, it was how I first learned about love.

The wedding took place in a Methodist church in Fredericksburg, just feet from a famous Civil War battlefield. Mom carried a small white Bible and a gardenia. Dad wore his Marine dress blues, with spit-shined black shoes that would have reflected the scene like mirrors.

But even that picturesque wedding had complications that I only grew to understand later. Our grandmother Wilson, whom we called Maudie, was present, and she never approved of our mom. Maudie was the wife of a general, and as such she had hung out with Cary Grant and met General George Patton. She never felt an Oregon City–bred gal was good enough for her son. Maudie's attitude didn't soften after the marriage, or ever. That disapproval toward our mother resonated through our entire childhood.

Just days after the wedding, John was sent to the Pacific. Getting shipped out after a wedding was a common enough occurrence back then that a popular cartoon of the era showed a soldier waving good-bye to his bride at the train station, "Have a nice honeymoon, dear." Our mom clipped that cartoon out and pinned it in her wedding scrapbook.

With John gone, she packed up her three suits and took another train across the country to Oregon City. She moved back in with her parents. For a brief period of time, she took a job wiring Liberty ships for the war effort but later got a job in a department store. And there she stayed, awaiting news of her knight.

NANCY

In 1945, a telegram arrived for Lou saying that her husband had been seriously wounded and would not survive. He had been on Guam, and his jeep hit a landmine. A similar telegram went to Maudie. At that point, all three of the Wilson men were Marines fighting in the Pacific, and Maudie immediately tried to get John Sr. to find out more information on her son's condition. It was slow in coming, even to a general. The first telegram our mom got from her father-in-law read, "No information in Washington other than that John is seriously wounded." Another telegram indicated he was near death.

Our mom was devastated. She traveled to the Oregon Coast, where she stayed in a little cabin. She did shifts in one of the lookout towers where civilians scanned the sea with binoculars looking for Japanese submarines.

At night, she walked the dunes and mourned her lost love. In my mind's eye, when I heard the story, I imagined her in a long black veil, willing her love not to be dead.

And then the most amazing thing happened. She got a telegram two weeks later saying John would survive.

I was the youngest of the three daughters, so by the time these stories got to me, they had been mythologized and were wrapped in a deep layer of romanticism. But even at a young age I understood that in these stories with the perfect wife, the perfect husband, the perfect gentleman soldier, some of the pieces were missing. The perfect soldier was only flawless because he was off fighting a war. The man who was actually present was never going to be as romantic as an absent one. That was a vision of love I saw and learned from.

Our dad was sent to Pearl Harbor for medical treatment, and then flown to the Marine hospital at Cherry Point, North Carolina, for rehabilitation. Our mom traveled across the county once again to be with him. It was yet another transcontinental train ride to her man. John recovered, though he carried shrapnel in him for the rest of his life. But he was well enough that fall that Lou got pregnant.

World War II had ended by then, but John received orders to transfer to the submarine base Coco Solo in the Panama Canal Zone, and my mom went with him. It was there in August 1946 that my oldest sister, Lynn, was born. Lynn had the blue eyes and fair hair of my mother, the same traits that I inherited. Only Ann would get our father's brunette gene.

Lynn, our tribal elder, can relate the story of Ann's birth best:

LYNN WILSON

In 1948, we returned to the states and briefly lived with Maudie in La Jolla. While we were living there, our grandfather, General John Sr., died. He had survived two world wars and the storming of Iwo Jima's beach with his Marines, but he died of a heart attack while hunting on Camp Pendleton.

After that we lived in Camp Pendleton base housing. Then John was transferred to Twenty-Nine Palms, and mom and I lived in a converted chicken coop near Barstow for six months, waiting for him.

In early 1950, we moved into a two-bedroom house in San Diego. It was the most domestic place we had for years, with a small lawn, a backyard swing set, and artichokes and olive trees in the yard. It was there that Ann was born on June 19, 1950. Ann would later make much hay about the fact that her birthday was a day after Paul McCartney's (although eight years later).

Ann was a darling baby. Our mom fed Ann condensed milk with a touch of Karo syrup in it, and she grew chubby. It was a time when mothers were being told not to breast-feed their babies. Ann always wondered if that bad advice played a role in her body issues.

Ten days after Ann was born, our dad was sent to Korea. My mom heard nothing for weeks. Then, months later, with newborn Ann on her hip, and four-year-old me on her apron, my mother received news that our father had been killed in action. Once again, she got unreliable news about dad. Eventually word came that he was seriously wounded and might recover.

Our father rarely talked about his time in Korea and it was only years later, when a Heart fan who had been a Marine researched some of the history, that I learned the grisly details. Our dad landed in Korea with the First Division, Fifth Brigade. He served under Chesty Morgan, one of the biggest names in Marine history. Our father was a platoon commander. The book *Colder than Hell* includes our dad's story, though his name has been changed.

The Marines took Seoul, but the Chinese snuck down and surrounded them. If you survived one battle, you'd most likely die in the next engagement. Of a starting force of two hundred fifty, only twenty-seven of my dad's men survived the war uninjured.

In one fateful engagement, John was shot three times. A dead comrade fell on top of his wounded body. He couldn't move, or fight, and he was bleeding to death. All night he lay there, hearing Chinese spoken as the enemy moved in and finished off all the wounded. He was spared only because he was hidden under a dead man.

Dad was found the next day by reinforcements and taken by air to Balboa Naval Hospital in San Diego. He later received the Purple Heart for his actions. It is pictured inside the sleeve of Ann's album *Hope and Glory*; the medal is shown held in Nancy's hand.

Two years later, he was transferred to San Francisco where we lived in officers' quarters. We were there on March 16, 1954, when Nancy was born. Four years separated her and Ann, just as it had Ann and me.

Our dad celebrated our growing family by buying a 1954 Plymouth station wagon. When Nancy was just a few months old, our dad was transferred to Camp Lejeune, North Carolina. It was three thousand miles of driving, with Ann, me, and baby Nancy in the backseat. We arrived in North Carolina and moved into a house on the Outer Banks, while we waited for base housing. When it came through a week later, we moved yet again. One week after that, Hurricane Hazel completely destroyed the Outer Banks house. I guess we were just a lucky family.

2

THE BIG FIVE

Nancy is a curly-headed baby tied to the railing of a World War II troop transport on a trip across the Pacific Ocean. Ann dodges flour bombs while trying to earn her Girl Scout badges. . . .

NANCY WILSON

Our dad always loved nonsensical names. When we went camping, and he saw a sign for anything historical, he'd say, "Look, another hysterical landmark." Squirrels became "Skaveerls." Our mom was "Feevee," or "Mammass." Ann was "Inz" or "Inzy-pinz." Lynn was "Nice." And I became "Nacey Pootoose."

We often called our mother "Mama," so we needed a nickname for our dad, too. We came up with "Dotes." It made no sense, but then neither did any of the names he'd come up with. It stuck.

Dotes took it in stride, but also decided he needed a nickname for our entire clan. He started to call us "The Big Five." It was the most normal name he ever came up with, and the best.

My mom also had a few of her own names for us, and mine was "curly-headed baby." It came from a song she sang to me when I was in the cradle.

"My Curly-Headed Baby" was a folk song first popularized in the thirties: "She's my curly-headed baby, she's more than all the world to me." I had blonde curls, and I was to be her last baby. Just a few years after I was born, birth control pills became available, and our mom was one of the first women to take them. There would never be a "Big Six."

Mama's family loved large gatherings, and they always included music and sing-a-longs. Our maternal grandfather, Jules Verne Dustin, called them "hootenannies." I loved that name when I was a kid, because he told me it came from when an owl married a goat.

Grandpa Dustin sang in the church choir, but he also loved ribald vaudeville songs. He'd play Spike Jones records for us. He saw Spike Jones perform, which our grandma never forgave him for because she felt it was too randy. We loved those Spike Jones records with their shooting guns, slide whistles, and banjos.

At the family hootenannies many of the songs our various aunts and uncles sang were bawdy drinking songs. One was "The Ballad of Lydia Pinkham," which probably shouldn't have been sung around a five-year-old. Since I was four years younger than Ann and eight years younger than Lynn, my age seemed to be forgotten by everyone around me for most of my childhood. "Lydia Pinkham" was based on a real-life character who marketed a highly alcoholic "woman's tonic" to cure menstrual pains. Sample lyric: "Mrs. O'Malley had a problem, she could not have a baby, dear, but after drinking a bottle of compound, she had a baby twice a year!" I loved it.

They also sang disaster songs like "The Great Titanic." That one had a light-hearted sound, but the lyrics, obviously, couldn't be more tragic. But I drank them in. I loved being around all of that singing.

Within our house, our dad always played the radio and had a very high-end stereo. He also owned a reel-to-reel tape recorder, and often you'd see him transferring his records to tape, hoping to get a perfect copy before his kids scratched them. I remember we had many classical recordings, the Hawaiian wedding song album, the soundtrack to *South Pacific*, and records by Ethel Merman. Even at a very young age, Ann could do a spot-on Ethel Merman.

Anytime there was a car ride, we sang. The radio was usually on, and our mother and dad sang along, as did us girls. It was never about being a great musician, or singing perfectly. We grew up in an environment where music was part of the family every day. It was an atmosphere where music was always fun, and fun always included music.

ANN WILSON

When Nancy was only a few years old, Dotes was transferred to Taiwan. It was 1956, and there was still a real fear that China would invade Taiwan. Our dad was a major by then, big brass. The promotion did not make his life easier, though. He had more responsibility, though many of his fellow Marines would say he "was born with a silver spoon in his mouth" because his father had been a general. His promotion had nothing to do with his dad's rank, but Dotes lived with that attitude during his entire service career. He hated Corps politics, but it was his life.

We gave him a tearful good-bye, and then spent a few months in Oregon City with the Dustins. But my mom decided this time she wasn't going to wait for a telegram to announce Dotes was dead. Instead, she decided we were going to follow him. We left San Francisco on the USS *General W.A. Mann*, which was a troop transport that carried five thousand men, and had seen service in World War II and Korea. There were giant guns, and it was no place for a mom in high heels and three little girls. As we left under the Golden Gate Bridge, our mother had us stand on the deck and wave good-bye to the States. Nancy was wearing a tether harness tied to a railing on the ship to keep her from falling into the sea. She pretended she was a wild horse.

We were in Taiwan for three years, from when I was six until I was almost nine. It was an innocent time, but also one of tension. A week after we arrived, a typhoon hit, and we were trapped in our quarters for many hours until our dad came to rescue us. Eventually, we were moved to a former three-story department store that had been converted into housing.

Our mom was expert at making the abnormal seem normal. Wherever we lived, she draped cloth on the windows to make them appear elegant, and she used our trunks as coffee tables. She even made our department store home look habitable.

In Taiwan, she organized the Girl Scouts. Nancy was a Brownie, while Lynn and I were regular scouts. We earned our merit badges, and Mom sewed our patches and sashes. We would go on Girl Scout jamborees, though occasional artillery shelling from mainland China scuttled a few adventures. Another typhoon once cancelled a campout. The only phones we had were field radios, so as Girl Scouts we had to learn Marine terminology like "over" anytime we wanted to call a fellow scout. "Nine" would never again be just "nine" in our family, it was now "niner." Dotes's odd nicknames suddenly made more sense to us all.

We regularly had to go to air raid shelters. We lived with a suitcase packed at all times in case an invasion happened. Naval aviators practiced bombing runs near us where they would drop sacks of flour on marked targets. One even hit our housing area.

NANCY

One of our dad's jobs on base was that he led the Marine Corps band during parades. He marched in front with a baton, like our own "Music Man." A lot of the Corps' pomp and circumstance was just a breath away from show business, to be honest.

Our mom was a bit of an amateur filmmaker, and she used her Super-8 camera to shoot Dotes marching in countless parades. She also filmed our birthday parties and scout picnics. She taught us to operate the camera, and at a very young age we were all amateur filmmakers. We made short five-minute reels that were inspired by the Keystone Kops and Charlie Chaplin, whom our mother adored. Sometimes we used subtitles because the Super-8 didn't record sound. Those films were our first taste of performing. That camera was part of the fertilizer that fed the seed of life on the stage for us. We all became total hams, but no one more than Ann. I was shy in the early home movies, but Ann was shoving people out of the way.

When friends or family would come over, we'd pull out the projector and force them to watch our home movies. We'd invite someone over for dinner and as soon as the plates were cleared, we'd pull out the films. Our guests might say, "I've got to get up early," but we held them hostage.

We'd watch the same clips again and again, and everyone in "The Big Five" found amusement in their repeated viewing, even if the neighbors didn't.

After three years in Taiwan, our dad was transferred back to Camp Pendleton. Whenever transfer orders came, a squad of enlisted men would show up at our house, and everything we owned would be loaded into cardboard barrels and put on a troop transport. We never owned a single houseplant because we never knew when we would have to move.

Wherever we'd move, we'd make friends with the neighbor children, but we always lived with the knowledge that, with only a day's notice, we might leave for a different post, a different base, or a different continent. Usually we went to school on base, and our classmates were just as apt to move around as we were. It was hard to make real, lasting friendships. We learned at a very young age not to make deep roots.

As a result, the relationships inside our family took on more significance, and we were much closer than siblings generally are. Many times the only entertainment we had was inside "The Big Five," so we became a self-contained vaudeville show, with our sing-a-longs, and Super-8 films.

Once we arrived to a new post, our dad was off being a major, so the task of unpacking and arranging furniture fell to our mother. It was not the life Mama had imagined when she was studying home economics in college, but she made the best of it. We had very little, because pay for a major was not much, but she did what she could to make every house a home.

She tried hard to make our humble life appear elegant. We sat at the dinner table together each night, and we ate by candlelight. We had inherited one set of china and a set of silver, and we used those with linen napkins for every single meal. Mama never served food from a carton. It was always put into another bowl, which meant more dishes, but "The Big Five" pulled together to wash them.

One time Ann and I ate dinner at a friend's house, and it was served on Corelware with steel utensils. When we returned home, Ann asked mom why we used the silver all the time. "There is no one more important than my family," Mama said. "There is no guest more deserving than you."

We were expected always to have proper manners and to be ladylike at the table. "I want you to grow up so that if you are invited to dinner with the president, you'll know how to behave yourself," she said. She told us this so many times, we grew up thinking our White House dinner was already scheduled for the future.

Still, when orders came to move yet again, our mom was always a little downhearted, if only briefly. I knew it was exhausting, but I never heard her publicly complain.

Instead, she came up with elaborate rituals to help us deal with all the transitions. One was that on the day we left a house for good, she would have us stand outside the threshold and tap our feet together to "dust off your shoes" because that would give us good luck on our next journey.

When we left Taiwan, we knocked our shoes together and climbed back on a troop transport for the long journey across the Pacific Ocean. We briefly moved back to Camp Pendleton and started all over again. Almost as soon as we'd unpacked the cardboard barrels, our dad was transferred again, back to the South Pacific to Okinawa.

It was an eighteen-month posting and my mom had just taken her three Girl Scouts on a nearly month-long crossing of the Pacific Ocean on a rusty World War II troop transport. She decided we would stay on in Camp Pendleton without him, and await his return.

ANN

The next year at Camp Pendleton was relatively uneventful, as we waited for word from our dad. The U.S. presence in Vietnam hadn't started in earnest yet, so it wasn't as tense as his previous tours, but we also knew he might be sent there. I started fourth grade at the elementary school on the base, and Nancy began kindergarten.

When our dad returned, we had just a few weeks of "The Big Five" living together on Camp Pendleton before he was transferred again, this time to the Northwest. This transfer was one we looked forward to, however, because it would take us back to an area we loved, and it was near our extended families. Our dad had received a position as a recruiter covering Washington, Oregon, and Idaho, and though he would have to travel a lot, we didn't have to live on base. We packed up the cardboard barrels, dusted off our shoes, and headed north.

Our parents decided we would settle in Bellevue, Washington, in a neighborhood called Lake Hills. They rented a blue two-story colonial. It had a front and back yard, and it was the first real home we had lived in for years. During most of my childhood my sisters and I shared a room, but in the new house Lynn got her own room and Nancy and I shared another. Lynn was fourteen and starting high school that fall. She was social and made friends easier than I did, and her life began to shift away slightly from our family cocoon. That subtle change ended up making Nancy and me closer, and we became inseparable. We'd listen to the radio in our room, waiting for the new rock 'n' roll hits, as DJs Pat O'Day and Lan Roberts counted down the hits.

I began fifth grade that fall, and Nancy started first grade. For me this was the beginning of a difficult socialization. I was heavier than my classmates, and other girls started to notice and make comments. My mother bought my clothes from a line named "Chubette." I was a shy and sensitive girl to start with, and I didn't want anything about me to stand out, but it seemed as if I always did. No one ever came up to me in school to say, "I love your dress, it's a 'Chubette,' isn't it?" but I lived in fear that the label would show.

I couldn't wait for school to be over each day, and when it was, Nancy and I roamed the neighborhood on our bikes. Though we were girls, at that age we did mostly "boy" things. We lived in a new subdivision, at the edge of the trees, and there were many wooded lots nearby that we explored. The annual hydroplane races in Seattle were always fun to watch, and we made our own model hydros and dragged them behind our bikes. This was an era when children ran free without any parental supervision. We came home only when our mom yelled that supper was ready.

Our mother continued to be the on-deck parent. Dotes's new job required that he be on the road a lot, and when he was home he would retire to his study and have a few beers. I know he drank to deal with his memories of war, and as time went on he drank more.

When he was on the road, our mother's moods would often become explosive because the pressure of running the family would become too much for her. She and the teenaged Lynn would often get into arguments, yelling at each other and throwing things. Lynn took it on the face a few times, as did I, and it was really terrifying.

I was not a "Type A" personality. I was a kid who would go hide under the table like a rabbit if she got scared. But Lynn would fight back and say, "Fuck you." Because Nancy was four years younger, she never really got into it with our parents. She learned, from watching Lynn and me, how to escape our mom's wrath. But Lynn just crashed into it headfirst.

I'm not sure I truly understood it at the time, but all the traveling and the constant transfers had exhausted our mom. She loved our dad, but she was done with being a Marine wife. She was married to the Marine Corps as much as she was married to Dotes, and all those marching orders had worn her out.

Mom was a very competent homemaker who could clean, cook, and sew with the best of them. For decades she had made lemonade out of lemons. But there was so much pressure on military wives to hold everything together, it caused an incredible turmoil inside her. Sometimes the stress would have to come out, and she'd just blow. She'd yell, get in the car, which she called "Blue Bird," and careen away. She'd come back a few hours later, calm, once again in control. She never had more than a drink or two, so she wasn't in a bar, but I never knew where she went.

Our mom couldn't do anything about the invisibility of being a Marine wife. The Marine Corps was just too big, and too powerful. She had no choice in how her life went. She had to take their orders, just as if she had enlisted herself. But she hated it.

One time when Mama stormed off in a fit in Blue Bird, she nearly came to her end. She ran into a traffic jam in the middle of Bellevue. Perhaps she was so steamed she didn't notice, or maybe it was just bad luck, but she ended up over railroad tracks just as a train was coming. The train hit the back of Blue Bird, mangling the car terribly. Our mom survived uninjured, and Blue Bird was eventually repaired at the body shop. But it gave us one more odd battle scar in our family: We could honestly say that Mama got hit by a train.

3

DUST OFF YOUR SHOES

Ann discovers Marlon Brando's eyes and searches for an Officer and a Gentleman. A Cotillion experienced "Alone," and the isolation in the middle of a gymnasium. . . .

ANN WILSON

After spending much of my childhood in hot dry climates, I learned to love the Northwest more than any other place. I would wake up to the soft gray skies and ride my bike through the canopy of Douglas firs. I cherished the constant fresh drizzle, and the smell of wood smoke from our fireplace. My favorite seasons were fall with frosty Halloween nights and the mild summers when we'd have backyard barbeques.

By the time I started seventh grade in the fall of 1962, a loud musical dialogue had begun in my head. It was a many-layered sound collage of the voices I'd heard all my life: the sweet bluesy songs my mother had sung to me when I was a baby, crazy Spike Jones stuff, and the Hit Parade of the fifties my parents played at cocktail parties. I'd also begun to explore the artists of my own generation: the Shirelles, the Supremes, Little Richard, Brenda Lee, but I also liked the song "Purple People Eater."

That year I started to play the flute and joined the school band. Bellevue schools were very supportive of the arts, and my band teacher was first rate.

For each instrument there was a chair ranking, and to move up a notch you had to challenge the person ahead of you to a playoff. I started as seventh chair, but after two successful playoffs, I moved to fourth chair, where I held steady. Anything above third chair was nearly impossible to obtain, and would have been held by girls who got straight A's, and were super committed, which I was not. Still, being good at the flute was one of the few areas in my life where I felt I was on solid ground.

In my social interactions outside class, I felt increasingly shunned because of the way I looked. I wasn't the heaviest girl, but I felt that every pound I gained was noticed, and noted.

If that wasn't hard enough, I began to stutter. It didn't always grab me, but if I was nervous or trying to talk to a popular kid, it seemed to clutch me. The teacher would call on me, and the moment I heard my name, something grabbed my vocal chords and shut them. In my head, I could hear myself talking clearly, but what came out were small, clipped syllables. Once I felt the fear, I was lost. I'd stuttered a small amount in elementary school, but it wasn't until junior high that it defined me. I became "the girl with the stammer."

I started speech classes. At a certain point each day, my teacher would announce, "Ann Wilson, time for speech class." Everyone watched me head off. I was mortified. The speech class was a series of recitations, with the concept that if I practiced difficult phrases, the stutter would go away. The effect only lasted during speech class. The moment I was back in homeroom, and the teacher called on me, the vicious cycle started all over again.

In junior high, we were often asked to read aloud in class, and this was one of my biggest challenges. I had managed to make a few friends who helped me with a ploy to make my stutter less obvious. The teacher would have the class take turns reading and we'd cycle around the room. When it was my turn, the boy next to me would finish, and the girl who sat one over from me would immediately start reading, and many times the teacher failed to notice that I had been silent.

▪ ▪ ▪

In November 1962, *Mutiny on the Bounty* came to the John Danz Theatre in our town, and it moved me like nothing had in my life. Every move, every plane of Marlon Brando's face, the way he simmered with complexity, floored me. He was refined, combustible, and elemental. His interpretation of the foppish, highbred Fletcher Christian to me was the stuff of rock stars. I look back now at some of the English navy-inspired tunics I wore onstage in Heart's eighties videos, and I see only *Mutiny*. It was for me what *Gone with the Wind* must have been for my mother: an escape to a romantic otherworld.

Playtime now meant exclusively recreating scenes from *Mutiny*. I was always Fletcher, and Nancy was Seaman Mills. Neither of us wanted to take the role of the king's daughter. The previous year, *West Side Story* had also become part of our play, and with that, both Nancy and I were also drawn to the male characters. Maria didn't do it for either of us: We wanted to be Sharks and Jets with switchblades, or British naval officers.

It's no coincidence that a handsome, erudite gentleman in a tailored dress uniform resonated with me. I looked at Fletcher Christian and was intoxicated by something that had hovered in the air in my house since the day I was born: my mother's myth of my father's knighthood. It was the same myth that had disappointed and stifled my mother, too, even as it fueled her desires.

One time I chipped my front tooth, and was crying, believing more than ever that I was truly and forever ugly, and my father came to comfort me. He was wearing his dress blues, and he hugged me. He wasn't usually physically demonstrative, but that day he held me against his blue uniform with the brass buttons. It meant so much to be near that chest.

Our parents had always owned soundtrack albums, and we loved *A Star Is Born*, and *West Side Story*. But when the score to *Mutiny* was released, it became one of the first records I ever bought. I listened to that album again, and again, and every time it took me away from my stuttering, and into a majestic world of imagination.

■ ■ ■

During the summer of 1963, I officially became a teenager, turning thirteen a few days after I finished seventh grade. That month our parents announced we were moving again. We were headed back to California and Camp Pendleton. We had lived in Bellevue for almost three years, and it had been our longest time in one place. "Get ready to dust off your shoes again," Mama announced. There was no time for protest.

Our sister Lynn did protest loudly, however. Lynn was seventeen and was to start her senior year of high school that fall. She was popular—more popular than Nancy or I would ever be—plus she had a steady boyfriend. "You're going to ruin my life," she wailed.

Because of our later career choices, many assume Nancy and I were the rebels of the Wilson family. We were not. Lynn and Mama would get in more battles over the course of one weekend than Nancy and Mama would get into over a year. Nancy and I just stood to the side and watched the show.

Lynn's rebelliousness, and her battling with our parents, did have unintended effects on us, though. By the time we were going through our own defiance, our parents didn't seem to have much fight left. Our sister wore them out. The result was that our decision to be in a band, which in many ways was less conventional and should have been more troubling than anything Lynn ever did, just sort of slid under the radar.

The year I was thirteen, no Wilson daughter had any sway with a Marine order. We were all moving to Camp Pendleton, and it was non-negotiable, which made the very fact that Lynn put up a fuss all the more extraordinary. She cried for what seemed like two days, but eventually, she was cried out.

In the end, we packed up the station wagon two weeks later. Even Lynn, still tearful from her good-bye with her boyfriend, dutifully carried her suitcase to the car.

"Dust off your shoes, girls," Mama said. I did as she commanded, and so did Nancy. Lynn sat there in the backseat, refusing to make eye contact with anyone, even her two sisters. Then, in a sign of surrender, she tapped her feet together. With that, we were off.

Our move to Camp Pendleton was like coming home in some ways, since we had lived there before. This stint we moved into officer's quarters in the "Seventeen Area." Our house was on the edge of the vast, arid Southern California bush. It was not a hospitable place. There were war games going on constantly, and the muffled sound of artillery could be heard from our front porch at all hours. Our backyard was 125,000 acres full of rattlesnakes, jackrabbits, coyotes, tarantulas, red ants, and unexploded shells. As a younger kid, I had played out there, digging for diamonds and gold. I never found riches, but I often found sparkling quartz, which was just as beautiful in the hard daylight.

For this stint I was a teenager, and digging in the dirt no longer held much appeal. The harsh elements of Camp Pendleton were perfect for young, hard men training to be "The Few, the Proud." But it was no country for white-skinned, complicated young girls.

I began school at James E. Potter Junior High in nearby Fallbrook, since there was no junior high on the base. The trip took forty-five minutes each way with my mom driving. It required travel through the Naval Weapon's Station, basically a bombing range. It was extremely high security, so we had to stop at a guard gate, give our names, and they would hand us a clipboard. When we got to the other side of the naval base, we turned our clipboard in. If we delayed, we would have been arrested. It was a stressful way to go to school.

School was much more difficult that year. The first day, my stutter was incredibly bad, and the other children laughed. The teacher took me aside after that first day. "You have to keep your powder dry, where this reading aloud thing is concerned," she said. I looked at her aghast, unable to explain myself, because to speak would be to stutter. It was as if she felt I was stuttering to get attention, as if it were a choice. She seemed to think I stuttered on purpose to give the other kids entertainment.

Though school was where my stammer was worst, I stuttered at home as well. It might occur at the dinner table, but it was guaranteed to happen if I tried to answer the phone. Mama had taught us to answer in a "lady-like manner," with a script she had composed. "Wilson residence, Ann Wilson speaking," was my line. I began to dread the sound of the telephone ringing, particularly if it rang when I was the only one in the house. This was an era with no message machines. When the phone rang, it might be an important message for our father, so I had to answer. I didn't need to say my name after a while: Everyone who called knew that if someone was stuttering, it was Ann.

But in our house, my stutter became part of the landscape. Like the many wounds we were all hiding—particularly the real and metaphoric scars my father carried—my stutter was just one more Wilson pain we lived with, we coped with, we carried.

We had always been an army unto ourselves. With my socially unacceptable stutter, I spent more time than ever with my sisters, inside the family cocoon, oftentimes singing. Music and singing with my sisters became a huge part of my life.

The only time I didn't stutter was when I sang. No one could understand why back then. But now, decades later, I think I can I explain it. I believe that because of the uninterrupted airflow that happened during singing, my brain no longer controlled my voice, and my body took over. Singing used a different part of the brain from talking, a part that wasn't encased in fear. Singing meant an escape from stuttering, and it became one of the few places where I was free.

I sang more and more. It was my solace, my escape, my sanctuary.

It became the only place I could be me.

▪ ▪ ▪

If my stutter was nearly impossible to live with, at least if I was silent, no one knew. But my weight was always obvious. Even in that era in California, girls were tan, blonde, and all had bare legs. They looked at me like they were standing in the sunshine peering into a darkened room.

There were two days I dreaded most during the school year: Health Assessment Day and Valentine's Day. Health Assessment was when the entire school was weighed and measured. It became so painful for me that every year I vowed I would skip school the next time it came around. At Fallbrook, they sprang it without warning. With a bombing range between school and home, I was stuck.

Today, a health evaluation would be done in private, at the nurse's office, or at least behind a curtain. In Fallbrook, they simply marched us all to the gym. Each student was called by name to a scale in the center of the room. One teacher with a clipboard wrote down results, while another teacher measured your height, and another moved the counterbalance along the scale and announced your weight as if it were a breakfast order at a diner. The entire eighth grade class watched. I remember to this day the names of the students who preceded and followed me, and the exact numbers announced.

"Linda Whittle, come forward," said the teacher with the clipboard.
"Linda Whittle: 62 inches," announced the teacher with the measuring tape.
"Linda Whittle: 78 pounds," announced the teacher operating the scale.
"Ann Wilson, come forward."
"Ann Wilson: 58 inches."
"Ann Wilson: 116 pounds."
"Joe Winfield, come forward."
"Joe Winfield: 64 inches."
"Joe Winfield: 92 pounds."

My peers let out a “whoa” when my weight was announced. The teachers let this pass. My humiliation was allowed. My weight, my life, had been distilled into a number.

My mother became concerned enough about my weight that she took me to the family doctor on base. There was not a lot of scientific information on weight issues then. He said: “The first thing we need to do with this girl is to have her eat nothing for two weeks, so she can shrink her stomach.” I tried that, and was so starving I eventually ate more calories than I’d saved. Next he wanted me on a strict diet of canned peaches in water. I dropped weight, but it was torture.

We went back to the doctor. He talked about “willpower” and “control.” He gave me a pamphlet that was like those cartoony brochures they’d given us about menstruation. It said things like “Try not to eat big meals every day.” “Avoid fried chicken.”

Valentine’s Day was even worse than the day we were weighed. Nothing seemed unusual in elementary school, but as the years went on, and my weight increased, I noticed I received fewer valentines than anyone else. That seemed odd because we were required to give a valentine to everyone in the class. If there were twenty-five kids in class, I might get twenty-two valentines.

Some of the valentines I received were also different from those received by the girl sitting next to me. The ones I got might have elephants or a rhinoceros on them. One, with a picture of a star-crossed hippopotamus, had the tag line “I’ve got a crush on you.” It showed a hippo sitting on a child.

These were not hand-drawn valentines: They were store bought. I know this probably wasn’t the case, but it felt as if they made sure that Ann Wilson got the card with the elephant.

It was a message that got through to me at an early age. I was different, and I was wrong. I stuttered, and I was overweight, and those things were not allowed.

▪ ▪ ▪

One of the only positive things at Fallbrook was that the music program was so far behind Bellevue, I immediately was first chair flute in the school band. It was so easy I took orchestra as well, and a night class in music conducting. I had nearly perfect grades that year.

When I wasn't in school, I listened to the radio, read teen magazines, and dreamed of boys. Just because I wasn't popular, didn't mean that I didn't imagine being popular.

Back when I was in seventh grade in Bellevue, there was a freckled, crimson-haired boy whom everyone called Red. Red sat next to me in class, and he had been kind enough to help me deceive the teacher during the read-aloud. I considered him a friend.

Red was a right-down-the-middle guy, not super popular, but not an outcast. He would sometimes lean over when the teacher wasn't looking and tell me funny jokes. I'd tell him jokes too, and when I did, I didn't seem to stutter as much, and he'd always laugh.

I started to "like" him, but I didn't dare tell him. I harbored this crush for the entire school year. Then toward the end of the term, I was in the lunchroom with other girls confessing their secret crushes. One girl kept asking me, "Ann, who is your crush?" I didn't answer the first ten times, but finally I confessed.

"I guess it would be Red," I said.

Within minutes this had gotten back to Red. He had been kind to me the entire year, but that afternoon was different. As the teacher had her back to us writing on the blackboard, he turned to me and announced so loudly that the entire class could hear, "I don't like you, you fat thing!" It had been perfectly acceptable for him to be friends with me, as long as that friendship hadn't been something public. But in public, he felt the need to humiliate me.

I didn't cry. I didn't even react.

Everyone in my family always talked about how I was "just like my father." It was a way of saying that I had inherited my father's "big bones" and brunette hair. It was their polite way of explaining my weight: My Marine father had passed "big bones" on to me.

They were probably right about the DNA. But there was another way I was also like my father. Like Dotes, I carried my wounds privately, and I retreated inward. I just disappeared. A part of me, like him, was internal and would rarely come out.

One of the only boys I befriended on Camp Pendleton was a young enlisted man who helped at the base stables. It was just a chaste friendship, and he was several years older, but he talked to me and asked about my life. Then I noticed he was no longer there. I asked where he was, and the guy working there told me he'd been transferred. My mother had seen me talking to him, and it was forbidden for an enlisted soldier to be friendly with an officer's daughter.

The Marine Corps did not make anything easy for me. The base held a cotillion every year, and my mother insisted I attend. She designed a dress for me, and together we sewed it from scratch. It was beautiful. Dotes dropped me off at the camp ballroom, and said, "Knock them dead, girlie."

Girls did not ask boys to dance at a Marine Corps Cotillion in the fall of 1963. And boys, for their part, did not ask Ann Wilson to dance. I sat there the entire night, and not a single boy asked me to dance. As with my earlier disappointments, I never showed emotion. When the dance was over, Dotes picked me up and drove me back home.

But once I was in our house, I just lost it. I wept, I wailed, I screeched at the world. This went on all night long. My mother sat with me, holding my hands as I cried. She didn't know what to do or what to say. All the magic she could muster had failed to find me a knight.

4

MEET THE BEATLES

Four young lads from England start a fire, and Nancy adopts a fake British accent. Meanwhile, Ann finds solace from school in "A Hard Day's Night" and a guitar. . . .

NANCY WILSON

The ninth day of February of 1964, a lightning bolt came out of the heavens and struck us. We had our life before February 9, and we had our life after. Who we were, and more important, who we imagined we could be, shifted forever on that day; we never turned back. From that point forward, we were aimed like arrows.

I was a month short of ten years old that day, and Ann was only thirteen and a half, but in a few short minutes we both grasped a forceful vision of adulthood that would stick and not let go.

The cause of our transformation was an encounter with four young lads: John, Paul, George, and Ringo. They were from exotic Liverpool. We had lived two dozen different places by then, but it felt like we were from nowhere. That Sunday night we were at our Grandmother "Maudie" Wilson's house in La Jolla. This was before La Jolla, California, was a tony address. Maudie was a Marine widow on a pension, with a tiny black-and-white television. It was where we watched *The Ed Sullivan Show* week after week, reveling in the humor of Topo Gigio, or looking forward to the next musical discovery Ed was about to unleash on the world. And the second week of February, the Beatles were scheduled.

"I Want to Hold Your Hand" had become a radio hit the week before, and even in my elementary school, kids were talking about the song. *The Ed Sullivan Show* was anticipated as if it were the lunar landing. We couldn't miss something like that, so we tuned in, along with seventy-three million other Americans, the largest audience for any television program to that point.

We had no idea what was coming. From the first moment we saw them on that tiny screen they became everything to us. Their outfits, their hair, every word they uttered, and every word they sang became imprinted on our brains. The caption under John Lennon read, "Sorry girls, he's married." Ann and I repeated that one line endlessly in fey British accents.

In that first appearance they played four songs: "All My Loving," "Till There Was You," "I Saw Her Standing There," and "I Want to Hold Your Hand." I knew little about adult love at that point, but I could nonetheless see their sexuality bursting at the seams. Though those songs now seem innocent, then they felt culturally defiant, as if the Beatles were pushing hard against the morality of the times. They had hair that went over their ears, and to me, a girl living on a Marine base, that made them seem the most dangerous rebels I had ever seen.

But from that first moment we "met" them through television, the love we had for the Beatles was far more than a schoolgirl crush. We didn't just fall in love with them; we fell in love with Great Britain, rock 'n' roll, and with ourselves in a way. They were the lens through which we imagined a bigger world.

The next day at school, the first topic was "Did you see the Beatles?" All my girl classmates would clutch their books to their sweaters, look to the sky as if they had "X"s and "O"s for eyeballs, and say, "Oh, Paul is so good-looking!" "Oh, that George." "Oh, John is my favorite." "Oh, even Ringo is kind of cute!"

Suddenly, the Beatles became the thing we talked about almost exclusively. They even became the center of our play: Instead of imaginary switchblades, we took up air guitar pretending to be the Beatles. Ann always had dibs on Paul, and I was either John or George (George, the serious, shy guitar player was forever stamped on my nine-year-old brain as a template). We'd sing the songs they did on *The Ed Sullivan Show* in order, recreate their stage patter, and put on a Beatle performance "live for one afternoon only" in Camp Pendleton housing! Only it wasn't just one afternoon: It became every afternoon, particularly after we watched their appearances the next two Sundays when they returned to *The Ed Sullivan Show.*

Similar crushes were happening all over the base, all over America, and all over the world. It was like a virus among teen girls. But there was already a chasm between us and the other girl Beatle fans. It revealed more about our individual characters—*who* we became, and *what* we became—than any facet of our childhood.

I discovered how we were different while playing with neighbor girls that spring. By April of 1964 the Beatles held the top five slots on the *Billboard* charts, so they were a common topic. I asked these other girls to join our pretend Beatles band. Ann took Paul, I was George, and we asked who they wanted to be.

Only they didn't buy into our game. "I want to be John's wife," one girl said.

"I want to be Paul's dreamy, gorgeous girlfriend," announced the other. Ann and I were aghast. If they were going to be Beatle girlfriends, who was going to be the rest of the band?

It was a conflict that would often repeat. The girls we grew up with saw the Beatles, or the Rolling Stones as romantic conquests, their music simply a soundtrack to kissing, hand-holding, to girl-boy love stuff. It's not that Ann and I didn't imagine romance as part of our future, because we did, but music was more important. To us, the Beatles were deadly serious stuff, something we studied like scholars, looking for meaning and wisdom.

We didn't want to be Beatle girlfriends. We wanted to be Beatles. All the other girls gushed about wanting to marry a Beatle, but we felt that lowered the Beatles to something crass and base. We didn't immediately see ourselves as musicians—that would come soon enough—but it was the music, and not Paul's dimples that had hit us.

It is important to note that during this time, although there were tremendous female singers like Ronnie Spector, or Aretha Franklin, there were no female Beatles. The Supremes were a powerful vocal group, but men played behind them at every tour stop, and on every record. The thought that women could play instruments, write their own songs, and sing, the way the Beatles did, would have been ludicrous to anyone, maybe even us back then. But the Beatles gave us a glimmer of a dream.

It was an impossible dream for two teenage girls during that time. But, for reasons I do not understand even today, it became a dream that drove my sister like a fire.

For Ann, it couldn't have come at a more desperate time. Though she was one of the most gorgeous girls you'd ever want to see, she was called "tub o' lard," and "fatso" all the time. It cut into her, and me, too. I was her little shadow of a sister, but I was on her team.

I think the pain she felt at school made Ann move inward, and made our relationship closer than the normal bond between sisters. In our house, everything was safe, imagination was allowed, and everyone was accepted and loved. You could leave all that other crap at the doorstep, and you could pretend to be female Beatles, and no one would tell you that was absurd.

And now, with the Beatles inside our home, coming from the hi-fi, my sister and I were closer than ever.

ANN WILSON

I turned fourteen that June, and finally escaped the eighth grade. Dotes returned that summer, as well, and we all moved once again to the Northwest, back to Bellevue. We packed up our belongings, and said good-bye to our family in Southern California. It was time to dust off our shoes again—we didn't know at the time that it would be the last time we enacted that ritual.

Before we left California, Maudie gave me a present. Our parents tried never to play favorites, but Maudie liked me the best because I reminded her of my dad. She had heard me talk about how I wanted to play guitar, so she handed me fifty dollars for a guitar. It was a tremendous amount of money in that day. Maudie died the next year, but I never forgot her kindness.

Not long after we arrived in Bellevue, I bought a Kent brand acoustic guitar. Armed with my Beatles albums, and a Mel Bay chord booklet, I learned to play all their hits. My parents bought Nancy her own guitar not long after, a cheaper three-quarter sized Lyle because she was small. But she complained that hers was too hard to tune, so my guitar became hers as well.

We both played incessantly, usually Beatles songs, but also folk songs, and other popular hits I loved by Aretha Franklin, or Fontella Bass. We started off playing in our rooms, but soon were all over the house. Lynn had moved out that summer to start college, and so Nancy and I each had our own rooms for the first time in our lives. But the change was only technical because we were always both in my room, usually playing guitar, or singing.

Our parents often had friends over for dinner, and on these occasions we would creep down to the den and put on a little show. We were always well received, but then our mother was also providing dinner. Soon those little den concerts with Nancy and me playing guitar became as common in our house as my mother's meatloaf.

Almost as important as learning the guitar was the premiere of the Beatles' *A Hard Day's Night* at the John Danz Theatre that summer. Our parents dropped us off, and Nancy and I waited in a long line to get in. Once it was over, we needed to see it again immediately, but we had no more money.

So, we lay down on the theater floor when the auditorium emptied between showings. As soon as the lights went out again, we popped back up. We spent all day in that theater.

A Hard Day's Night cemented our idea that being a Beatle girlfriend wasn't what we wanted. The movie showed mobs of silly girls chasing the Beatles, and throwing themselves at them. It was very important to us that we didn't act like that. That would have made us like everyone else, and we thought our fandom went much deeper than any other Beatle fan. And once the Beatles inhabited us, the imprint was so powerful that nothing else could get in: not boys, not clothes, none of the typical things young girls are obsessed with.

To be accepted among other teenage girls, you had to fit into a very defined mold. I couldn't fit into anything so refined, nor could Nancy. We could act, we could pretend, but we never really fit in.

I started ninth grade that fall and found Sammamish High School more difficult than junior high. Social cliques had begun in earnest, and I didn't mesh with the jocks, the nerds, the socialites, or the greasers. You were required to take sides, form little groups, and pick between the Beatles and the Rolling Stones. I liked both, though the Beatles would win any contest, of course.

There had always been a duality in my life, but it increased that year. I had horrid experiences at school, and then I had the imaginative musical world at home with Nancy where we played guitar and sang all day. On the rare times we had friends over the other girls either joined in singing, or sat watching us. Two of Nancy's friends were good singers, so we often added Sydney Osborne and Bonnie Allen to the mix. There were four of us, and four of the Beatles, so we called this combo our first "band," although it was really a four-part harmony vocal group. Our den was our only venue, and our parents and their friends the only audience.

In high school, I was an outcast. I thought that further connected me to the Beatles because they seemed like outcasts, too. They had found a way to be cool, to have this friendship among themselves, to laugh at inside jokes, and to do it all while making amazing music. That's what Nancy and I did with our own band. We decided to call ourselves the Viewpoints.

To me, a girl who struggled with her weight and still stuttered in class, it looked divine to be a Beatle. It looked like a sublime way of survival.

5

BLOOD HARMONY

One warrior lays down arms; another weds. August 25 becomes a day to live in infamy and navy blue suits, and back in school a friend meets a friend. . . .

ANN WILSON

Our return to Bellevue also meant our dad was finally retiring from active duty in the Marine Corps. He could have continued on as a part-time recruiter, but with the Vietnam War ramping up, he announced he just couldn't stomach the military life anymore. He told us Vietnam was a "dirty war," and he was unhappy with how the top brass was running things. But I think the fight had gone out of Dotes a long time before.

For the first time in a hundred years, no one in the Wilson family was an active-duty Marine. Our grandfather and uncle were dead, and our father had retired. We were all a bit relieved. I had lived my whole life with the fear that our dad would be killed in action. Dotes retired with a rank of major, proud of his service, proud of the men he served with, and of the valor of the Marines. But he was also terrified of what was happening to our country in Vietnam as divisiveness increased.

But even in retirement, the war did not end for Dotes. He still slept with a pistol near his bed. He would often wake up screaming from a horrific nightmare, and try to grab that pistol. Our mom would soothe him, comfort him, and try to bring him back to the reality of our little blue colonial house in suburban Bellevue. She repeatedly took the bullets out of the pistol when he wasn't looking. He put them back in.

When we moved back to Bellevue, Dotes started taking classes at the University of Washington to get a teaching certificate. By the fall he was doing substitute teaching at a nearby junior high. He was the same Dotes, but as a teacher his whistle had a higher and more joyful pitch than it did when he was a Marine.

But even while teaching English, something he adored, there was a part of Dotes that had been left on the battlefield. When school was done for the day, he drank. Our family code for this was that "Dotes is in his cups again." He wasn't a mean drunk, and he still whistled, but you could tell he wasn't all right. He'd sit and listen to music with these big conical headphones on, protecting himself from the outside world, and trying to find peace inside of himself. The whole family evolved and adapted around his isolation. He was there, but in a way, he wasn't.

He talked about the wars so rarely that on the few occasions he did, it seemed truly remarkable. Once on Christmas Eve, he told Nancy about that horrible night in Korea he had survived underneath his dead comrade. He said he fell asleep on the battlefield and dreamed of a time he spanked Lynn. He told Nancy that when he awoke from that nightmare, he swore he would never hit any of us again. And he never did.

There was only one time in my entire life when Dotes talked to me about the war. He was deep in his cups that day, and he and I were alone in the house. He told a story of being stuck in a valley in Korea with enemy on both sides. He ordered an airstrike. After the bombs had struck, he marched his men through the valley and witnessed the carnage. Everywhere lay burned flesh that looked like overdone roast beef. More disturbing to him, as father of three daughters, was when he realized some of the dead were women who had been nurses. He went to Korea to fight for his country and for his fellow Marines, but he hadn't imagined he would kill women in the process.

Dotes had been born into a Marine family. He didn't choose to be a soldier—it was chosen for him, and, in a way, he was enslaved by it. It was fate that had made him a Marine, and fate that sent him to Guam and Korea. And it was fate that never let him leave.

NANCY WILSON

Our Dad's retirement from active duty also set our mom free. It meant that we'd be a two-parent household permanently, and that we could make roots in a community. We had lived in twenty different cities, in thirty different houses, but once we moved to the Lake Hills neighborhood of Bellevue the second time, we stayed until we left home as adults. It was the first house that felt like ours. When our dad poured cement for a back patio, we put our handprints in the concrete, and we bought houseplants.

Our mom began to immerse herself into the world around her. She became a volunteer at our schools. She befriended her neighbors. And she decided we would find a church.

The Wilson side of the family was Catholic, though neither of our parents was very religious. Our mom had always been a seeker, though, and read many spiritual books. She felt a church should be less about scripture, and more about taking faith into action. She investigated several Bellevue churches and settled on First Congregational Church. Our mom's choice would shape our lives in profound ways.

First Congregational was located in the center of Bellevue, and the bell tower was one of the tallest structures on the east side. It had 1,400 members the year we joined, including the mega-developer Kemper Freeman, the owner of Bellevue Square. A charismatic minister named Lincoln Reed led the church. He would preach from the Bible, but his sermons mostly focused on social justice, with little fire and brimstone. His favorite phrase was, "This is the day the Lord has made. Let us rejoice, and be glad in it." He became a close friend to both our parents and was often a guest in our home.

We didn't attend every single Sunday, but when we did, we always sat in the third row. Our dad often didn't cooperate, though. When Reed might say, "Please turn to page sixty-four and recite the passage," Dotes would say, "gobby, gobby, gobby," over and over again. He'd also "gobby, gobby, gobby" his way through a hymn. It was just one of his many eccentricities.

The biggest influence the church had on our lives was social and political. The church was heavily involved in causes, protests, and petitions. It was a happening church, turning conservative Bellevue on its ear. I always thought that our church was revolutionizing religion, as the Beatles had music. We attended the church youth group every week, and that basement meeting room was the most exciting place in Bellevue during that decade. There were parents involved, but they were hip parents. We'd sit around and talk about pushing against the old ways, and making something relevant. Kids were allowed to smoke in youth group if they had their parents' permission. It was a place where we were allowed to rebel against the very church we sat in. Both Ann and I came out of those meetings with a sense of great purpose. We had the bit in our mouths after that.

In the spring of 1966, the Congregational Church was also the setting for our sister Lynn's wedding. Lynn was wilder than Ann or I would ever be, and I think our mom was just happy Lynn was doing one traditional thing. Lynn wasn't even pregnant, though she would have her first son Tohn the following year.

Lynn's wedding was a huge deal to our mom. Even though Lynn was the family rebel, our mom latched on to an idea about the perfection of this wedding. She planned every detail for months and sewed all the clothes. She made Lynn a white linen wedding dress with open work Venetian lace sleeves and a flounce hem. Ann was the maid of honor and wore a gold linen dress. I had just turned twelve, and I was a bridesmaid. My mom made me a dress of yellow linen in a flower pattern. And my mother made her own outfit as well: a blue velvet long-skirted theater suit with a matching blue satin jacket with wide-notched collar and cuffs. We all looked like something out of a fashion magazine. My mother's own wedding had been very simple, so maybe planning Lynn's wedding was Mama's way of creating the wedding she had wanted.

It was a candlelight ceremony, officiated by Lincoln Reed. My only real job was to walk up the aisle and stand on the side of the altar waiting for my sisters. But it still felt like a lot of pressure on me at the time, as if my bridesmaid duty was the most important thing I'd ever done.

When Lynn walked up the aisle of the church to where Dotes stood waiting to give her away, I could not stop weeping. I just went to pieces. I don't think I understood in my youth that getting married didn't mean leaving the family for good. I still don't know if my tears that day were joy for my older sister or sadness because I thought "The Big Five" was no more.

ANN

During the summer of 1966 it was announced on the radio that the Beatles would play at the Seattle Center Coliseum in August. I ordered four tickets in the mail for our band the Viewpoints: Nancy, Bonnie, Sydney, and me. It seemed to me that if we were a band, we should go together. Tickets were six dollars. They arrived a few weeks later.

The *Seattle Post-Intelligencer* newspaper ran a contest for teenagers to write an essay on "Why I like the Beatles." Thousands wrote in. My essay won. My picture appeared in the newspaper, alongside the essay, and I won a Revere "Magic Eye" movie camera. It was the first time my name or photo was in print. The essay read in part:

"They have led us to a new way of looking, acting, thinking and moving; to a new and sensitive way of expressing ourselves in music; to freedom in conformity."

▪ ▪ ▪

It wasn't the first thing I had ever written about the Beatles, but it was the first thing ever published. Starting the previous year, I had started writing long novels that were loosely based on the Beatles. One was titled "April Come She Will." The lead character was a dashing young Brit named Dusty Kellar who looked like a mix between Keith Richards and Paul McCartney. The female character, based on Patti Boyd or Jane Asher, was called Megan Eastman (Linda McCartney's maiden name). The male characters would pop into a teashop and say, "Hi Bird." Another would say, "Right smashing, Dolly Birds." I drew illustrations for the novels as well. All the girls were gorgeous and fashionable and thin. I showed the novels to Nancy, but no one else.

The day of the Beatles concert, our mom drove us to the show and dropped us off underneath the Seattle Space Needle. She also made us matching outfits so the Viewpoints would look proper that day. Our mom had scoured the paper to see what the Beatles had been wearing at each concert of their American tour. She had seen two different sets of outfits, so that's what she made for us. One was a military-style tunic, and the other was a navy blue, double-breasted English waistcoat. We had no idea which one they would wear at the show we had tickets for, so we took our chances and went with the English waistcoats. But the Beatles had a third outfit our mom had missed—pink and gray striped suits—and that's what they had on at our show. If anyone at the concert had asked me why we were dressed so strange, I would have announced that our purpose wasn't to go dressed as the Beatles, but instead to look like a unified band.

The concert itself was both an ultimate high and an annoyance. We were trying to study everything the Beatles were doing musically, to pick up pointers, but because of the constant screaming and flashbulbs, it was hard to concentrate. The sound was wretched.

But the real-life Beatles onstage before us were still magical. We were in the room with what Timothy Leary had called "Divine Avatars." Everything they did had a special aura, even if what they were doing was ordinary. When George Harrison broke a string, that simple act somehow helped us to feel that we were real musicians, because we had broken strings ourselves. John Lennon chewed gum, but he chewed it in such a John Lennon–like manner, that it seemed illicit. "It should be illegal to chew gum like that," Nancy whispered in my ear.

They played only eleven songs, starting with Chuck Berry's "Rock and Roll Music," and ending with Little Richard's "Long Tall Sally." The entire concert lasted less than thirty-five minutes. But August 25 forever became "B-Day," for "Beatles Day," to us, the most important anniversary of our childhood.

Not a year has ever gone by without us acknowledging it to each other.

There was one other reason that the Beatles concert ended up being such an important date: It marked the start of our friendship with Sue Ennis, the dearest friend Nancy or I have ever had. She attended the same concert and had seen the article in the newspaper with my picture. Here's how Sue recalls our meeting:

SUE ENNIS

When my family moved to Bellevue in 1966, the Beatles were the only thing that mattered to me. In the paper, I saw a photo of a girl from my school who had won the Beatles essay contest. I knew I had to go get her. Turns out, she was taking German, as I was, because the Beatles had recorded "Sie Liebt Dich," and "Komm, Gib Mir Deine Hand." That afternoon I slipped into the desk behind her in class.

Revolver had just been released, and I knew if Ann were a true Beatle fan like me, she'd know every track, and not just the single "Good Day

Sunshine." I hummed the sitar riff from George Harrison's obscure album track, "Love You To." She took the bait instantly, whipping her head around. "Is George your favorite?" Our lifelong friendship began at that moment. I asked if she'd gone to their show.

"Yes, I saw them with my group," she said.

"You have a group?" I asked.

"We're called the Viewpoints and we're about harmonies. There are four of us, including my sister. She's twelve."

A week later she invited me to their house to watch them rehearse. I was shocked at how professional they were, even her little kid sister. They played a few Beatles songs, but also other songs rich with harmonies: "Cherish" by the Association; "The Cruel War" by Peter, Paul and Mary; and "Walk Away Renée" by the Left Banke.

The other two girls were good singers, but the Wilson sister harmonies freaked me out. They were pitch perfect, matching the original songs note for note. They had an intuitive way of knowing exactly when to start and stop, when to turn it on, when to lighten up. I don't think they ever had the discussion about how they would sing a song—they just fell into it. It was blood harmony. Like the Carter Family, the Everly Brothers, the Bee Gees, or countless other family singing groups, their DNA—their common blood—supplied one voice where there had been two. They were insular, but once they sang, they were like twins.

Ann took the group very seriously. She had formal business cards printed up that read: "The Viewpoints. For bookings call Ann Wilson. Sherwood 6-2710." She sang with fury, and die-hard commitment. I was beside myself with joy to have found her, privy to an amazing secret: that my new friend, the withdrawn girl from my school, was a hurricane.

In 1966, most schoolgirls in Bellevue accepted or even welcomed the fact that they were heading for a little college, perhaps, marriage, then mommy-hood, and finally whatever was required to support her husband's dreams. Ann seemed on an entirely different arc, and I couldn't understand where she got the confidence to claim that she was going to be "a professional musician." I secretly thought she was naive, but I was in awe of her clueless, unquestioning drive toward a single goal. She offered me a new model of freedom. After that, I never wanted to be apart from the Wilsons.

6

CRYIN' IN THE CHAPEL

Ann dials up an LSD festival and asks for a gig, and two soon-to-be famous television personalities walk by the serenading Wilsons, as the beat goes on. . . .

NANCY WILSON

The Viewpoints' first public show was a folk festival on Vashon Island in 1967. We rode the ferry over in our stage costumes, which at that point consisted of granny dresses. We did four songs: "Jesus Met the Woman at the Well," "Cherish," "The Cruel War," and "Walk Away Renée." We didn't get paid, but because there were people sitting in folding chairs, we considered it a professional gig.

That same fall, we played at the Sunset Drive-In Theater near our house. There was a mic and a wooden fruit box down in front of the screen, and we were the pre-movie entertainment. We did a handful of other shows at outdoor festivals and schools. We even played the Seattle Auto Show, standing near that year's model cars as we strummed our acoustic guitars. At the car just over from us, the entertainment was the typical girl in a bikini.

That spring, Ann and I also made our public debut as a duo. It happened on the altar of the First Congregational Church on Mother's Day, and it was a show that no one present would forget.

Like the nation, our church was torn apart by the Vietnam War. Lincoln Reed often preached about righteousness, but there were conservative members who felt the church should support the war. There were frequent antiwar demonstrations on the streets of Seattle, and even some in Bellevue. Ann and I marched in a few, sometimes alongside our parents. To see Dotes, a lifelong Marine, protesting the war was something else. It might have killed his parents had they been alive, but instead it delighted his high school students.

Once a year our church had what they called "Youth Sunday," when they turned the preaching over to Youth Group. We were slated to play three songs on the altar, and with five hundred members packed into the church, it was the biggest audience we'd ever faced.

We started with "The Great Mandala (The Wheel of Life)," by Peter, Paul and Mary. The song is one of the most devastating antiwar songs ever written, but it wasn't so much the political message as it was one word in the seventh line of the song that went through the church like an electric shock. "What the *hell* does he think he's doing," Ann and I sang. We thought we had really nailed the powerful harmonies, but we had failed to consider what singing the word "hell" in church might mean to some of the members. Several walked out.

Our next number didn't help us, either. We thought it would be funny if we did a cover of Elvis Presley's "Crying in the Chapel," as a sort of spoof. We thought wrong. By the time we were finished, a third of the congregation was gone.

We continued on with our last song, which was our most misguided idea. The Doors' "When the Music's Over" had just come out, and we imagined it would perfectly end our brilliantly conceived set, as the music would "be over" when we were done. As we sang, the audience kept streaming out, at a fast clip. And when we sang the line "cancel my subscription to the Resurrection," it was worse than if we'd said "hell" in church. By the finale of our first show as a duo, 60 percent of the audience was gone. Our parents were some of the only adults left.

I felt equal parts guilt and pride. I felt sorry for the people we had offended, but one of the things we had learned from Reed, who I was proud to see was still there, was that Jesus meant his teachings to change the world. Looking at that half-empty auditorium, I wanted to change things even more.

Many in the church thought the performance by the Wilson girls was a disgrace. But it lit a bonfire under us because we saw for the first time that what we did on stage could have an impact on an audience, even if it was a negative impact. Before that point, we had sung for ourselves or small groups of friends.

It was a turning point. We started to play out more often after that. We started to *want* it in a way we never wanted it before.

Over the next year, the church's membership collapsed, when half the members left following development tycoon Kemper Freeman. A few people thought the Wilson sisters had something to do with it, but the Black Panthers, whom Reed invited to speak one Sunday, probably drove more members away than two long-haired girls with guitars.

The First Congregational Church would also serve as the place where I met one of my dearest friends, Kelly Curtis, who years later would go on to be Pearl Jam's manager. My mom knew Kelly's mom, Dot, from the church newsletter. Dot said she was looking for guitar lessons for her son. My mom offered up Ann. Here is how Kelly remembered it:

KELLY CURTIS

My mom arranged for me to take guitar lessons from Ann. Ann was about sixteen at the time, and I was ten. I went over there a few times, and she showed me some chords, but Ann never seemed that into teaching. Nancy was always there, and she was closer to my age, and she and I just really connected. She slowly took over my lessons.

My mom would pay Nancy ten dollars a lesson. As Nancy and I got to know each other better, sometimes we'd just listen to records. When the Beatles' *Sgt. Pepper's* came out, we spent that entire lesson just listening.

Sometimes, Nancy would take the ten dollars to a neighbor to buy pot, and we'd smoke that. Then she'd show me a chord or two so I could prove to my mom that I had learned something.

Every time I was there, Nancy and Ann would be playing something. I had never seen people actually performing music live before, so to be in the same room with them, to watch them play a Beatles' song, was mindboggling. I just fell in love with them, and I fell in love with music through them. It was life changing.

NANCY

In junior high, singing with Ann and playing the guitar became my life. I didn't date, and other than music I had few outside interests. I took a handful of classical guitar lessons, but I didn't stick with it. I did learn a few classical tricks, though, that I later used in Heart songs.

My mother played piano. She had Ann and me take lessons, though neither of us stuck with that, either. Ann was more interested in bass, and she bought a Höfner that year (Paul McCartney used one) and learned to play. We also were both in choir and had an excellent choir teacher. The fact that our schools promoted the arts had so much to do with making us feel encouraged.

Between church, school, and home, we were completely ensconced in the dream of music. It became what defined us as people more than anything else. And although we both played guitar, and both sang, our roles were starting to shift, at least as our peers perceived it.

Ann was the girl who sang.

I was the girl with the guitar.

ANN WILSON

By the time I was a junior at Sammamish High School, Dotes had gotten a job teaching English there. His students loved him, and having him at my school made a difficult environment feel more secure to me. I'd see him in the hall every day.

"How you doing, Ann?" he'd say. And then he'd whistle to his next classroom.

He loved teaching, and it made our home life easier. My mother was happy to finally be free of being a Marine wife. They had more friends over, and a kind of informal salon of thinkers, players, and talkers started to make our dinner table a very interesting place for conversation.

Mama would still occasionally go off and leave the house in a huff, but that was less common. Our parents never had a relationship where you saw them holding hands, but it was romantic. In our Lake Hills house, the walls were thin and I could hear them loudly making love at night in their bedroom. Divorce was becoming commonplace around us, but there was rarely a time Nancy or I lived with the fear that our parents wouldn't be together.

The one moment the idea they'd divorce crossed our minds turned into a comical and odd incident. It played out because by my junior year of high school, Nancy and I were regularly smoking pot. Our mom knew enough to figure that out from the smell (we also grabbed the occasional cigarette when we could). Mom asked if I had smoked pot, and I admitted I had.

A few weeks after that, our mom came up to my bedroom and asked Nancy and me to come to the dining table for "a serious family discussion." We never had a problem with communication in our family, so we nervously went down the stairs.

"What do you think it is?" Nancy asked me. "Do you think they are getting a divorce?"

Our dad was sitting at the table waiting for us. Our mom sat down and folded her hands on her lap.

"Girls," she said, "your father and I have an announcement to make." She paused for effect. "We've decided that since we know you girls are smoking marijuana, we would try it, too. We tried it last week. So if you need to talk to us about what it's like, we understand."

Nancy has never been good at hiding her emotions, but if she'd been drinking a soda at the time she would have spit it across the room. Instead, her eyebrows jumped. We had no idea what to say, but eventually I meekly uttered "okay" and we retreated to our rooms. Well, they weren't getting a divorce.

Matters became more complicated a couple of weeks later when after dinner one night, our parents suggested we smoke pot together. We couldn't exactly refuse, so we sat very uncomfortably, while Dotes lit up a joint, and it was passed around. It wasn't the best pot, but I wasn't about to share my connection with our parents!

They only smoked one other time around us, and my sense was it had just been part of a phase when they were exploring counterculture. My mother was fascinated by Alan Watts and read many books about expanding consciousness. And for Dotes, who was into his cups most nights, it was just another way to escape. But the whole thing was totally embarrassing to us. Marijuana was supposed to be the province of teens. They were edging into our turf.

In that era, few things went on in our house that Sue Ennis didn't immediately know about. She and I would talk for hours at school, she'd come over after classes for a few hours, and then later that same night when she went home we'd talk for hours on the telephone. Much of our conversation was about the Beatles, or the other groups we had started to love by then, the Moody Blues or the Rolling Stones. Sue's parents were Republicans, and they were always a bit suspicious of anything in our home to start with, but I couldn't imagine what they would think if they knew my parents smoked pot. Even Sue had a hard time understanding when I phoned her.

"They did WHAT?" Sue said.

She never mentioned it to her parents, of course.

Having Sue in my life made so many things easier for me. She became such a dear friend to us we decided we needed a name for our trio of friends. One night when we'd smoked too much pot, we started calling each other

"Connie." We'd seen an ad in the paper for a music act named "Connie Ted Slats," and we thought the androgyny of that sounded hilarious, plus Connie was such an average high school girl name, and we were not average high school girls by any means. From that day forth, the three of us were "Connies." I'd call Sue and say, "Hey, Connie, want to come over?" And she'd reply, "Sure, Connie. Tell the other Connie to get her guitar tuned."

Having a friend at school was great. If someone teased me, it simply became more fodder to talk about with Sue. But in my last two years of high school, I went though internal transitions, too. I didn't care as much if I wasn't popular, because I could see a world beyond high school. Additionally, the concerts I was playing gave me self-confidence that I was good at something.

By my junior year, my stutter was less pronounced. I never knew why it came in the first place, so I didn't know why it went away, but the shift made me less ostracized.

And though I would battle with weight in coming years, as I turned seventeen my metabolism shifted, and suddenly weight began to drop off me. I lost fifty pounds in a year. I didn't feel slim, but by most standards I was average. And average didn't stand out.

If losing weight made me feel normal for once, my first encounter with a real female rock star in 1967 made me realize that there was a skewed standard toward women in the entertainment industry. Even decades later, I could recall her hair, her shimmering beauty, and her fragileness, but mostly I could remember how skinny she was. For one brief moment, I was her opening act, sort of, something quite different from watching the Beatles from the audience.

It was the summer of 1967, and the radio had announced that the Trips Lansing Festival would occur at the Greenlake Aqua Theater. Nancy and I had changed the name of our band to Rapunzel and had decided to make our style more psychedelic. We were trying to do contemporary songs that you might hear on the radio, and we had lost the granny dresses. I thought we'd be ideal for the Trips Festival, so I called up the promoter.

I started in on a long explanation of how we'd played drive-ins, high school assemblies, and arts and crafts shows, but the guy cut me off. "Sure," he said. "Come on down for a few songs." It says much about how casual this festival was that we were approved on the basis of a phone call, and not an audition tape, or any references.

The headliner at the festival was Sonny and Cher. This was the 1967-model of Sonny and Cher, different from the one America would discover when their network television show debuted four years later. In 1967, Sonny and Cher still had a hippie vibe to them, with their macramé vests, go-go boots, and Sonny's trippy solo album *Inner Views*. There were a dozen other bands on the bill, including Vanilla Fudge, and our fellow local Merrilee Rush, who would record her chart-topping hit "Angel of the Morning" just four months later. And, most important, there was Rapunzel. My band's name did not appear on any advertisement or handbill. All our friends had to take our word that we were even on the bill, and so did the promoters when we arrived—they had forgotten we had asked to play.

I had to press them to allow us to perform. I guess my brief twenty-second phone call had not been memorable. Eventually, we were directed to a small cement pallet that was actually *outside* the venue. It was near the performer's entrance, so we played to an audience of arriving bands, on the way to the main stage to play their shows.

We played "The Cruel War," and Janis Ian's "Society's Child," which Nancy sang. A few people clapped when we finished. Somehow it still felt like a huge victory that we had participated. We didn't so much leave "the stage" as we simply walked off our cement pallet and moved back into the crowd.

But the odd positioning of our "stage" turned into a stroke of fortune. We were hanging out near our cement pad later, and that was how we came to spot Sonny and Cher as they were leaving. As they walked toward their limo, they were right next to us for a brief moment. Sonny was wearing a saffron-colored pants suit with matching Beatle boots.

And then Cher was right next to me. She looked at me for a moment, as if to say something, though she didn't speak, and neither did I. We had . . . a moment, or at least I had a moment. Her hair was like shining black satin. She was breathtaking: her makeup, her hair, and her short dress that matched Sonny's suit. She seemed the perfect sixties Kabuki doll, complete with a pale, otherworldly expression. She was impossibly thin, gamine even. She was the most perfectly beautiful thing I'd ever seen in person. She was everything I felt I was not.

Seeing Cher Bono standing there next to me was a turning point in my youth. It was an epiphany for me. Here, in front of me, was the perfect fantasy girl of my imagination, who looked much like the drawings—fashioned after Jane Asher or Pattie Boyd—in my Beatles novels. Cher was present, but distant. She was beautiful and yet broken, I felt. It is an image that will never leave my memory. She wasn't an image on a television screen, or a picture in a magazine—she was a human being. And it was obvious even to my youthful self that she was a human trapped in the consequence of her fame, trapped inside a bubble.

Cher and her hippie prince climbed into their black stretch limo. The window went up, and she was in a capsule, on the other side of the mirror. Safe, protected, a far cry from the happy, tripped-out hippie mythology of Monterey.

I stared at that limo for a long, long while. Eventually, the traffic around it cleared, and they pulled away.

What I did not know at the time was that the distorted reflection in that limo window—the woman behind the mirror, fresh from the stage, all dolled up—would one day be me. Our adventure at the Trips Festival ended, like most of our shows in those days, with us at a payphone, using the change Dotes had given us to call for a ride back home.

And then, magically, a half hour after we called, there was Dotes tooling along in the car. He drove up to the Trips Festival as if he were picking us up from a high school football game. He never doubted us, never wondered whether we got in trouble, never for a second seemed to think we weren't capable of handling anything we ran into, even a Trips Festival.

He seemed to innately know how important it was for us to play music, and he and my mom supported that. It wasn't because they thought we'd be famous one day—that dream didn't exist in a suburban home in 1967, even a supportive one. They did it simply because they wanted us to be happy. Their belief in us was absolute. That gift had an even stronger effect on my life than Cher's saffron-colored mini-dress.

On our trip back from the Trips Festival, my dad whistled all the way home.

7

A BOY AND HIS DOG

A visit to Hamburg's notorious Red Light District. Nude photos get Nancy in trouble. And Ann auditions for her first big-time band. . . .

ANN WILSON

In my junior and senior years in school, choir became a huge part of my life. I was a second alto. The hundred-member choir was filled with cliques like the rest of school, but our instructor, Allen Lund, changed my life and was the best teacher I ever had. He taught me how to breathe while singing. He said to imagine my body as an empty pitcher, with my breath being water going into the vessel, and to breathe from the part of the pitcher where the water hit first. Once I learned that, my voice soared.

But the most exciting part of choir came senior year, when we traveled to Europe for a series of performances. Our mother organized fundraising for the journey and signed on to be a chaperone, and consequently fourteen-year-old Nancy got to tag along. We went to Norway, Sweden, Holland, and Germany and sang in cathedrals and opera houses.

In Amsterdam, Nancy and I slipped away from the group and went to one of the city's infamous coffeehouses. In the Bulldog Coffeehouse, wearing our little red blazers with logos that said "Sammamish High School," we smoked hash.

We were even more brazen in Hamburg. To a Beatles fan, it was a legendary city, and we weren't about to miss the sights just because they were off-limits to anyone with a red blazer. "Can we go get a soda?" we asked our mother. I had been studying German in high school because the Beatles spoke a few lines in "A Hard Day's Night," so when we left I found a city bus downtown. My tiny blonde sister and I strolled through the notorious Reeperbahn, with its drug dealers, pornography shops, and prostitutes on every street corner, to visit the Star Club, where the Beatles had honed their live act. We had now walked where the Beatles had walked.

That year my life took another unexpected turn when I began dating a boy. He was a senior named Don Smith, and he took me to my junior prom. My mom made the dress, of course. For the first time in my life, I got to dance at a dance.

Many of my dates with Don were centered on music, and that year we saw the Association and John Mayall. But sometimes we'd just get together to do drugs. I had started dropping LSD occasionally, and Don and I would trip together in Seattle's Volunteer Park or go to the movies while high. Once we made the very bad decision to take acid and watch *Rosemary's Baby* at the drive-in. It was instantly a bad trip. I sat on some chocolate, it got everywhere, and we both thought it was blood that had spilled in from the movie. Don freaked out and couldn't drive us home until he came down. I was also on acid with Don the very first time I heard Led Zeppelin at a party, where everyone else was high on speed, and it was a revelation.

Acid, cars, and teenage hormones added up to some of the first make-out sessions of my life, and plenty of heavy petting, but somehow it never fully consumed me. I didn't sleep with Don. The world of the Connies always seemed to trump everything else. None of the guys I met were able to provide the emotional partnership I needed to be in love, and none of them stacked up against the dreamy, perfect English boys of my novels. I was sophisticated enough to take LSD, but also quite old-fashioned.

I left Sammamish High School in June of 1968, as I began: like a virgin.

NANCY WILSON

In the fall of 1968, I started high school just after Ann finished. She was now attending Cornish Institute in Seattle, studying fashion and art. Sue moved to Salem, Oregon, to start college there. And though that seemed sad at first, it simply gave Ann and me an excuse to travel there for frequent Connie reunions.

Lynn had moved back to Bellevue, and I got to see her often. She and her husband started a commune not far from my parents' house. I was often over there listening to music, or playing my guitar for whatever hippies were hanging out.

At a young age I had already discovered that older men were often sexually inappropriate with young girls. The year before, one of my medical professionals had tried to kiss me, and though the police weren't called in that era for such actions, my parents got involved, and we switched providers. The year I started high school, Lynn's husband asked if he could shoot a nude photo of me. In the commune where my sister and her family lived they had a nude portrait of their whole group on the wall, with the caption "The Hoopers," a take-off on the word "hippies." I said, "Sure, I'm a flower child." I sat nude by a window in a patch of sunlight, and he photographed me. It was an artistic picture, but my mom got wind of it and blew up with a fury I had never seen before. She slapped me in the face. She ordered me never to go to Lynn's house again. She told me never to take my clothes off in front of a photographer, or a camera, ever again.

Mama was always afraid Ann or I would become pregnant and turn into what she called "a fallen woman." She repeatedly cited Judy Garland as her example of someone who had been destroyed by the entertainment industry. "She takes pills," my pot-smoking mother said. And when Judy died the following year, Mama's view was cemented. Show business, she was convinced, was a dangerous place for a woman. Maybe she was right.

But my mother's prejudice didn't stop us, and that year I began to write songs. Both Ann and I were shifting away from the idea that we would be interpreters, and toward the concept that we had something to say. My first original was titled "Rain Song." I was channeling Paul Simon and celebrating our return to Seattle after the time we'd spent in the California desert. Though the Beatles would always be the big shadow in the room—and *Abbey Road* was a revelation—Paul Simon, and soon Joni Mitchell, would rival them. And when Elton John's first album was available in the United States in 1970, the year I turned sixteen, it floored me. By that point, I listened to music to hear the songwriting, and you couldn't beat Bernie Taupin for lyrics or songcraft.

During my first year of high school, at a choir competition, I became friends with a brainy girl named Jan Drew. We developed a deep friendship based on our mutual quest to become intellectuals reading great books, and, as the years went by, we tried to do that while being incredibly stoned on pot.

We were a long way from Judy Garland, but if my mother had known the half of it, she would have freaked.

ANN

In my last year of high school I met a classmate who was a drummer, Chris Blaine. He became my best musical friend, outside the Connies, over the next few years. Chris was playing with a few guys, and he asked if I wanted to sing. I went to a rehearsal at Chris's parents' house, and that day I joined my first "real" band. We decided to call ourselves "White Sail."

We got a gig at a local club, but as we arrived at the gig, I saw they misspelled our name on the marquee as "White Sale." It would have been comical later in my career, but not when I was so vulnerable and raw. In that band, we played only covers, and only big radio hits.

The next month we changed our name to "Daybreak." We got a regular gig playing the enlisted men's club at the Fort Lawton Army Reserve Base in Seattle. Nancy would often come to our shows, and sometimes she would sing background vocals.

Chris had a separate gig with a country songwriter who needed a band to play on his songwriting demos, and Daybreak got the gig. Chris thought there might be a bit of extra time at the end of the session, and he asked if Nancy and I had any songs we might want to record.

I had never been in a recording studio before, and even though Audio Recording was a tiny place, it might as well have been Abbey Road. It was where the Fabulous Wailers, the Sonics, and the Frantics had made records. We played on three country songs, including "Drank My Hurt Away." There was just enough time left over for us to record one Nancy and I had written called "Through Eyes and Glass." I even played flute on that one.

Kearney Barton ran Audio Recording, and he had his own record label called Topaz. He liked our songs enough that he offered to make up five hundred copies of the two singles made from the demos if we paid him a few bucks. So on the B-side of one of the country tracks, titled "I'm Gonna Drink My Hurt Away," our song appeared. The track was credited to "Ann Wilson and the Daybreaks," not the name of our band, plus I was listed as the sole songwriter, leaving out my sister.

When we got the forty-five back from the plant, Dotes spun it again and again on our hi-fi, while our voices came out of the speakers. For so long Nancy and I had a dream that we would be real musicians, but here was actual physical proof we'd done it. It felt like major progress. I could honestly tell people, "I've got a record out, Topaz T-1312." I was a Topaz recording artist.

The record was sent Seattle radio stations. We listened and listened, and though Kearney said it had been played, we never heard it. We tried to keep track of sales, and airplay, but the single never became another local sensation like "Louie, Louie" had.

In the end, Kearney sent 250 unsold copies to me in a giant box. Even that felt like a victory of sorts: Somewhere, somehow, a few people had bought or shoplifted my single. Topaz T-1312 might not have topped the charts, but it was a start.

We then changed our band name again to "A Boy and His Dog," a salute to a popular sci-fi novel. This line-up featured Chris Blaine on drums, Mick Etchoe on guitar, various bass players who came and went, and both me and Gary Humphries on vocals. It was an era where most bands in the Northwest had two, or sometimes three, different singers, switching off songs or sets.

A Boy and His Dog landed a regular gig at the Hatchcover Tavern in Bellevue every Sunday, Monday, and Tuesday. These were the deadest nights at any club, but we still drew good crowds. We were doing only covers, but I started to have a fan base. "Every time you do 'By the Time I Get to Phoenix,'" one guy told me, "it about makes me cry." The band was making a small amount of money, and I received as much as two hundred dollars a month. It was enough to get my first apartment, a few miles from my parents' house. The move was only temporary. The lure of my bond with Nancy was strong enough that I was still often back in Lake Hills, or Nancy was at my place. Eventually, A Boy and His Dog broke up, and I moved back in with my parents.

I also started thinking about getting a job. Other than guitar lessons, and babysitting, I'd never had a job, and I had few marketable skills. But I was hired at the Kentucky Fried Chicken in downtown Bellevue. I worked there a total of two days, and at the end of my second day I was fired for having "a bad attitude." It was the last job I ever had, outside music.

Chris Blaine and I stayed in touch, and that year he alerted me to an advertisement in the *Seattle Post-Intelligencer* for a band seeking a drummer and a singer, a perfect combination for us. Chris talked to the guys who placed the ad, a bass player named Steve Fossen and a lead guitar player named Roger Fisher. They were both well known on the local scene and had been in a half dozen bands by that point. For a time Steve and Roger had been known as the Army, but they had to change that since it stopped them from getting gigs on Navy bases. They had been called White Heart, after another sci-fi novel, and then later just Heart. I'd heard the name Heart on the radio when they were playing at local radio station KJR's Battle of the Bands. They now wanted to call their new band Hocus Pocus, and they asked if Chris and I wanted to try out with them. We asked Gary Humphries to come, too, and arranged an audition at Chris's house. They knew Mick Etchoe, so he came to the audition as well.

I borrowed my parents' car. Because these guys had been in some well-known local bands that I had heard about on the radio, I felt like I was going to play with the Beatles. I think Steve and Roger were reticent when they saw me. I overheard Steve ask, "Do you think she is the kind of girl who can do this?" Mick Etchoe, our old bandmate, said, "Just listen to her sing."

We started with "Son of a Preacherman," and from that first song it was magic. I then tackled the Beatles' "A Long and Winding Road," and by then I had won over the doubters. Roger was beside himself, and I was happy to play with an electric guitar player as good as he was. It went so smoothly that an hour later we were a band.

It was only later I learned that although Roger and Steve had big dreams, they were penniless. They had been living in a local campground. They were hippies with long hair and ideas about love, sex, and freedom that seemed straight out of *Easy Rider*, which had been released that year. But it was obvious from that first rehearsal that they were great musicians, and by playing with them I was upping my game.

Roger and I planned to get together separately that next week to see if we could work out some material between my flute and his guitar. I gave him my address, but he said his car wasn't working. He asked if I could pick him up. He said he'd be on the corner of the highway, near a turnabout, at a certain time, and I was to find him up there. I had to get Mama to drive me. We drove to the turnabout, and there was Roger waiting with his guitar in hand, jumping up and down to get our attention. He jumped in the backseat of the car, and I moved back there with him as we began to discuss what we might do in rehearsal. To anyone witnessing the sight, it would have seemed that my mother, wearing her white driving gloves, was chauffeuring my new guitarist and me all the way home.

8

SHE'S HERE TO SING

Ann sees a nude Fisher brother for the first time. The Delfonics try to seduce a young Wilson. And an eye-lock leads to a bed made out of driftwood, and a new chapter. . . .

ANN WILSON

The first nude man I ever saw was our guitar player Roger Fisher. I'd seen pictures in *National Geographic* of naked tribesmen, but Roger was my first in the flesh "full monty," and it was unforgettable. I had been sheltered from displays of male anatomy growing up because our father was incredibly modest. But as Hocus Pocus began to tour in the early seventies, I was the only female on the road with five uninhibited young men. It was quite an education.

I saw Roger's penis five minutes after we'd checked into a motel for our first out of town show. We were booked for a two-week gig at the Town Crier in Richland, Washington. Once in our room, Roger was naked almost immediately, an unleashed stallion walking around. He had no shame about it. Nudity wasn't sexual with Roger, usually, just an extension of his hippie spirit. He had a great body, which stayed toned and fit not through exercise, but by being in a perpetual state of motion. Clothing just seemed to fall off Roger, and even onstage it was rare to see him with a full shirt on. The clothes he did wear were usually skimpy, or suggestive. He was fond of a pair of jeans on which a girlfriend had embroidered DIG IT across the ass.

Roger's onstage demeanor and his guitar prowess played a big part in the success of Hocus Pocus. He never played with the touch of a scientist. Instead he had a wide open flame, and many times it would explode onstage, pulling the entire audience in. He was a huge fan of Led Zeppelin's Jimmy Page and Deep Purple's Richie Blackmore, and he could play anything he heard by ear. He was a feel player and a bit of a dervish onstage, constantly twirling around. I had to be careful not to get bonked.

I was still finding my sea legs onstage. I shared vocal duties with Gary Humphries, Steve Fossen, and sometimes with Don Wilhelm, who occasionally sang with us then. I usually did the ballads or the bluesy numbers. We felt having a few singers in the band gave us the ability to cover any popular hit of the day. I'd sing one or two songs and then take a break, while someone else took over. I didn't have the lung stamina to sing for the five hours we were onstage. I was smoking cigarettes and still learning how not to get hoarse while performing.

We toured throughout the Northwest that next year, all the way east to Montana, and south to Portland. When we'd get a motel room, usually we had one room with two beds. Though most of my bandmates, particularly Roger, were quick to flirt with any passing female, they were protective of me. "She's here to sing, buddy," was a line that was uttered so many times by the band to my unwanted suitors, we could have had it put on T-shirts.

I was still very naive about the ways of sex. At one show in Great Falls, Montana, the soul band the Delfonics were in our club, and they bought me drinks. I was flattered beyond belief because they were one of my favorite bands, and when they asked to come back to my room to discuss music, I said sure. My Hocus Pocus bandmates showed up just as the situation grew tense, and relieved me of my two overly friendly Romeos. Another time at a Portland motel, I opened the door to my room thinking it was a bandmate, and a drunken man tried to storm in. I managed to push the door closed, but it frightened me terribly.

We played almost exclusively in taverns to audiences of drunk or high music fans, and it was a war zone for a twenty-year-old female. The catcalls, hoots, pinches, and sexual slurs were practically a daily ritual. In 1970, the only women who had been onstage in many of the taverns we played were barmaids bringing drinks to male performers. Rock had been entirely a male invention, and from Elvis's hips to Robert Plant's pants, rock music was charged with male sexuality. I was something entirely different onstage, and both the audience and I had to figure out what that was. If my onstage persona was too aggressive, I looked like a dominatrix. If I was soft and demure, I'd come off like a pushover sex kitten, and a song might overwhelm me.

We played popular radio hits, and I was still discovering what songs I could own. I felt it wasn't honest to flip the gender of lyrics, but if I sang "My Girl," there might be raised eyebrows in the audience. I also learned that songs a man could tackle might be problematic for me. That lesson came after I launched into the Who's "See Me, Feel Me," only to find the audience on their chairs swinging their jackets around like they were at a rodeo. At one show a drunk suggested I hike up my bra straps, followed by other lewdness. Sometimes the owners of the clubs were worse than the audiences, offering up "just listen to me" harangues on how I'd do better if I adopted a certain style of dress, one that emphasized sexuality over substance.

Everyone in Hocus Pocus was committed to the socialistic idea of the band as family, and the challenges bonded us. We were making good money for a bar band, but between gas, gear, and instruments, there was never enough. Roger and Steve were resourceful cooks, making meals of rice, garlic, cheese, and vegetables on a camp stove in our hotel room. Roger talked incessantly about his brother Michael, who had dodged the draft by escaping into Canada, and he said the recipe was his. "You've got to meet Michael," Roger said. "He's got great ideas about the band."

▪ ▪ ▪

I turned twenty-one in June 1971, and Hocus Pocus had become my life. I was still living at home, but the band was on the road constantly. One of our gigs that summer was at the Iron Bull in Bellingham, Washington. We had played the club a few times, and always drew a diverse crowd of college students, plus the occasional Canadian tourist because the border was only twenty miles away.

We arrived at the club in the afternoon to rehearse new material. We were learning the Janis Joplin song "Move Over," which I sang. I was sitting on the floor cross-legged with the lyrics on a sheet of paper in front of me when Roger's brother Michael walked in. Michael had snuck through the border to check out his brother's new band. He was tall, handsome, and had piercing eyes.

We locked eyes. It was one of those eye-locks that happen once in a lifetime. It was long, unafraid, and neither of us looked away for what seemed like minutes. No words were exchanged. It was just eye on eye.

"Ann, meet my big brother," Roger said.

Yes, indeed, meet him. Meet Michael Fisher.

I was never the same again.

We talked for hours that night after the show. Michael had escaped to Canada two years before to avoid the draft. He felt his local draft board was corrupt, and later found out his lawyer's office was bugged. With the Vietnam War, and Nixon's dirty politics, 1970 was an incendiary time in America. It was dangerous for Michael to be in the States since he was a wanted man, and he looked around a room before he entered, and always had his eye on an exit. When we talked, though, I seemed to have all his attention. He was smart, deep, and spiritual. Though he was only two years older than me, he was more self-assured than anyone I had met.

He went back to Canada that night, and we returned to Bellevue, but we began to talk on the phone. I wasn't completely sure if Michael was even single—that topic never came up. Long distance calls were expensive, but during set breaks at our shows, I'd sneak into the manager's office and call Michael.

He snuck down again to catch another show we had near Portland. Michael's excuse was that he was coming to help run our sound, but he knew, and I knew, he was coming for me. Normally when I was onstage, I didn't want to get off, but I found myself that night anticipating when someone else would sing. During the set breaks, I completely ignored the band and spent all my time talking to Michael.

After the show, we went back to our motel, which had little individual cottage-type rooms. Michael offered to walk me from the van to my room, which was all of fifteen feet away. This was not the kind of chivalry the members of Hocus Pocus were used to, and one made a gagging gesture when they overheard it.

But Michael did walk me. By the doorway, we talked and talked. And there, in front of a crappy little Portland motel at three in the morning, he kissed me for the first time. I went in my room, by myself, and Michael went back to Canada the next day, but I knew then I *had* to be with him.

It completely took me over. There had never been anything in my life that had consumed me the way Michael Fisher consumed me.

Here's how Michael remembered those days:

MICHAEL FISHER

That first day I met her, I just dove into her eyes in a deep way and connected with her instantly. I don't know how that works. I've felt that a few times, but never quite like that. I knew there was this bond there, and I had to explore it. The more I got to know her, the more perfect it was, and the better it got.

She was stunningly beautiful. The most beautiful part, though, was who she was. She was open. . . . She was like a book ready to be read.

I had a girlfriend at the time, and I didn't consider myself available because I was in a relationship, though maybe a troubled relationship, in a way. But my paths with that woman were separating. When I met Ann, she couldn't have been more different from the other person I was with.

Ann was like home.

ANN

So much of my life had been dominated by my connection with Nancy, or Sue, or the Beatles, or a desire to be a musician. But when it came to Michael, I had tunnel vision. I told him on the phone I missed him. "We're going to have to do something about that," he said. To me, that meant, "Come to me." I couldn't think of spending one more day without him. It was the one time in my life I didn't think of my band first.

I called a band meeting to announce I was quitting Hocus Pocus. I simply said, "I'm sorry." Only later did I realize it was a pretty destructive move. We were starting to get good bookings, and everyone had bills for new gear to pay. It was the only time I ever quit a band for someone. It was the most reckless thing I ever did.

I called Michael and said I was heading up. I told my parents, and my mother was concerned, but she was also probably secretly pleased that I had met someone who moved me. I packed a little backpack, and I carried my guitar.

I took a Greyhound bus to Vancouver. When I arrived, I discovered that West Vancouver, where Michael lived, was twelve miles away. I didn't have enough money for a cab, there was no direct city bus, and he hadn't offered to pick me up. I hitchhiked and got a ride that took me a mile away. I walked the rest of the way, up a hill.

I was wearing a gray pinstripe mid-calf pencil skirt, a matching jacket, and boots. I had made this outfit because I wanted to look mod, lady-like, and sexy. I made all this effort to look put-together, but a light drizzle began, and by the time I arrived at Michael's, the rain had ruined my hair and clothes. I looked completely bedraggled.

Michael lived in a little round house, a cottage really, that was stuck in the woods behind a rooming-house mansion. I walked on the little path around the bigger house and arrived at the cottage. His house was built on beams so it hung out over Lassen Creek, a roaring stream. It was Tolkien-esque.

Holding my guitar in one hand, and with my backpack on, I paused at the door, a young hippie girl on the threshold. I wondered if he'd be in there with another girl. I was frozen, afraid to leave my old life behind, unable to go back to the old Ann Wilson, but also terrified that the powerful feelings would completely consume me. Finally, I knocked.

Michael opened the door. He looked surprised to see me. A smile widened on his face, and he ushered me in.

"I'm so glad you're here," he said.

That period, starting from that night, was the most romantic time I ever lived through. Michael had built his bed from driftwood logs, and it was so high off the ground you had to jump to get on it. It became more than a bed: It became the place where I learned everything about sexuality and sensuality. The bed became a nest, and a retreat from the rest of the world, but then so was everything about Michael.

He was very opinionated, and he set about modeling me into the woman he thought I should become. Some of that advice was wise—and his insistence I stop smoking did wonders for my singing voice—but he was also controlling. I didn't know how to cook, so he taught me basic skills to make what he liked, which was mostly rice and vegetables. When he didn't like my unruly eyebrows, he took candle wax to train them a certain way. I put up with his schooling because I so wanted to be touched by him. I was putty in his hands.

His house was very Zen-like. He had Herman Hesse books, and candles, and he spoke a lot about eastern spirituality. Michael was studying architecture at a local college, and he was interested in building things. In a way, he was building me. It was like a school, an old-fashioned women's school, and he was the instructor.

When it came to music, he wasn't a real rock guy. He had a penchant for jazz-fusion, and Chick Corea records, but he also liked Joni Mitchell and the spiritual Led Zeppelin tracks. That's where I helped shape him, by exposing him to music he didn't know about. I was writing a lot of poetry, and I imagined he'd be a scientist, and I'd be an artist.

For the better part of a year I was completely lost in the world of Michael Fisher. My whole life was in that round house, other than one short trip I made back home to get more stuff. Sue and Nancy did come to visit me, perhaps worried that I had completely gone off the deep end, which I had. The big house in front of the cottage was full of hippies, and when Sue and Nancy arrived, they were all naked in the backyard. When Nancy saw these naked hippies, and me living in this tiny round house over a creek, she was alarmed. But nothing was going to pull me away from Michael Fisher.

My mother became increasingly concerned that her daughter was, literally and metaphorically, in another country, and she'd call to ask me to move back home. I kept telling her how wonderful Michael was, and how true our love. But Mama wouldn't have any of it.

In my notebooks, I began to craft a poem about those phone calls with my mother that would eventually transform into a song. The lyrics went, in part: "'Come on home girl,' Mama cried on the phone / 'Too soon to lose my baby yet, my girl should be at home' / But try to understand, try to understand / Try, try, try to understand / He's a magic man, Mama."

The words were straight from my life.

9

THE WHISPER THAT CALLS

Nancy locks lips in a bell tower. Ann issues an order to Nancy's boyfriend. Nancy searches for her idol in Canada. And Ann starts a new band. . . .

NANCY WILSON

I turned seventeen in 1971, and with Ann in Canada, my life shifted considerably. I was a senior in high school that fall, and began to apply to colleges. I also looked for a part-time job. I had given the occasional guitar lesson, but I sought something more lucrative.

My first thought was to become an auto mechanic. I applied at a garage and was told they weren't accepting applications from women. Next, I walked to the Jade East Restaurant and applied to be a bus person. They told me it wasn't a "girl's job." I said I'd work in the kitchen, but I was told that job also wasn't fit for a woman. I said I could be a hostess, something I knew women did, but they said I didn't fit that either. I persisted. "I can play guitar," I said. The restaurant had music at night. That got me in the door, and I auditioned and got the gig. I only played a few times at the Jade East, but it was a taste of independence.

Once Ann began to tour seriously with Hocus Pocus, I began to look for other musicians. One of the first I discovered was a talented guitar player at my school named Geoff Foubert. We played together at a few parties, at church youth group, and at the Bellevue Community College student center. We did songs by Seals and Croft; James Taylor; the Beatles; Peter, Paul and Mary; and Yes. We didn't make any money, but the experience allowed me to see myself as a folksinger. I would have a "small but appreciative audience," I told myself.

A romance ensued between Geoff and me. I had been thinking about kissing him for some time, but needed the right setting. One night, we went to the Congregational Church, and I made him climb the seven flights to the top of the church bell tower. It was one of the tallest structures in Bellevue, and you could see for miles. Geoff meekly followed me. There, under the church bell, I kissed a boy for the first time.

Here's how Geoff recalled those times:

GEOFF FOUBERT

We'd usually rehearse at her house, and her parents didn't have a problem with me being in her room. When it became obvious we had affection for each other, Nancy said, "My mom's really happy because she's finally convinced I'm not gay." It was only then I realized I was the first guy she ever went out with. Boys were not on the top of her list. She loved guitar, and she loved to create music, and those things fulfilled her.

One rare night when Ann was home, Nancy went to the bathroom, and I was walking through the hall. Ann passed by, grabbed my shoulders, threw me against the wall, pulled me close, and said, "When are you going to fuck my sister?" It was as if she was giving me this order, this insistence that I take care of business for her sister. It intimidated the hell out of me. I thought to myself, "Girls don't talk like that."

We named our band "Geoff and Nancy," though we often played with a third guitarist named Art Crowder, and a drummer named Glen. I had managed to get myself under contract with a shady manager, and he booked us into the Keg-n-Cue, in North Bend, Washington. It was logger country, and we played to a redneck crowd. Art and I had to wear short hair wigs because we were longhairs. Nancy was still underage, so we had to get an exemption from the liquor board for her to play there. The manager's wife sewed outfits for us, and Nancy had to wear a Grand Ole Opry–type dress.

NANCY

Although I was most interested in folk music, at the Keg-n-Cue we played primarily country and western songs. We'd sneak in songs by Poco, Neil Young, Simon and Garfunkel, Joni Mitchell, Elton John, and Crosby, Stills and Nash every so often. But mostly we played songs like "Okie from Muskogee," "Snowbird," "Break My Mind," and "Stand by Your Man." Ann was home once when I was playing at the Keg-n-Cue, and she sat in with us. She did two songs by the Bee Gees, "Words" and "Love Somebody," and the crowd went crazy cheering. Geoff and I always got a good response, but I felt a little deflated seeing the reaction to her. Geoff's manager tried to get Ann to sign a contract with him. She immediately tossed it away.

Geoff's manager booked us for New Year's Eve at the Snoqualmie Logger's Union Hall, and that's where I welcomed 1972. One of the loggers paid us twenty dollars to keep playing "Please Release Me" over and over. Our biggest gig ever was in Salem, Oregon, where we opened up for Roy Drusky, a pure Nashville act. There were 3,500 people in the crowd, and they probably all knew that, despite my little gingham dress, I wasn't a country singer. But they were polite, and it felt like a huge victory. For one night only, I loved that my "small but appreciative audience" wasn't so small.

I graduated from high school in June 1972. I was set to start Pacific University in Oregon in the fall, but before that I decided to travel north to Vancouver to visit Ann. I had gone up to see her a few times during her first year with Michael Fisher. It initially seemed like I had lost her to that relationship. She even started to sound different on the phone, speaking with a Canadian accent, and with a more serious demeanor than she'd had before.

When I traveled up that summer, Ann was forming a new band, and that seemed to bring out her old self again. She and Michael had moved out of the cottage and into the bigger hippie house in front of it, and I stayed with her for a few days.

But I had other reasons for heading to Vancouver. I was meeting my friend Jan Drew to travel to Sechelt Island, off the British Columbia coast. We were going to find Joni Mitchell. We read in a magazine that Joni owned an eighty-acre farm there, and we had the romantic notion to go to her. We never discussed what we might do when we arrived at Joni's, and in the haze of youth, I never considered failure a possibility. Neither Jan nor I had a car, so we hitchhiked. We got a ride from a hippie, who drove us up the coast to a ferry that went to Sechelt.

When we arrived on Sechelt, we found a fifteen-square-mile island with several thousand residents. It lacked a single sign directing tourists to Joni Mitchell's house. We flipped a coin, and when it came up heads, we decided to hitchhike south.

A middle-aged man in a Ford truck pulled over, and we climbed in the front with him.

"Where you gals headed?" he asked.

"We're going to see Joni Mitchell," I said. I sounded bubbly. "Can you take us to her house?"

The first sign something was wrong came when our driver didn't know who Joni Mitchell was. The second was when he turned north, when we asked him to go south. The third was when we asked get out, and he ignored us and drove into the woods.

In the late sixties, hitchhiking had been an entirely acceptable method of transportation for any enlightened person. If you saw a driver with long hair, you were part of the same community. It was all very honor system, and it worked really well, for a few short years.

Our problem was those weren't our years. Jan and I both had older sisters, and we were attempting to recreate their lives, their summer of love, when we missed that period. The seventies never quite reverted to the sixties, no matter how much I wished it. And as the seventies began, I was heading into the woods with a rapist at best, and possibly a killer.

Time seemed to stop, and I did the only thing I knew how to do when times got rough. It was the thing Mama and Dotes taught me to do, which was to "pull rank." I started talking crazy talk, crazy Marine-talk.

"My father is Major General John Bushrod Wilson of the United States Marine Corps, and he's expecting us to embark, and if we don't arrive by oh-nine-hundred hours, he'll be sending out a bivouac party, a recon squad, to track us down," I said. I pronounced this with the measured cadence of a drill sergeant, thinking that enunciating every syllable might hide my panic. "If we don't arrive soon, a search party of enlisted soldiers from the Marine Expeditionary Units will begin combing this island with Marine canine units, raiders and dogs, just like the Corps did at Iwo Jima. The few, the proud, the Marines. No woman left behind." None of what I said made any sense. The Marines were not going to make an amphibious landing to save us on a remote Canadian island.

But I guess my words had either enough truth to create worry, or enough craziness to make him afraid of us. He stopped the truck and ordered us out. As we watched his taillights disappear, I swore I'd never hitchhike again.

We still had the pressing matter of how we were going to get from the middle of a British Columbia forest to Joni's garden. We hiked out, found a road, and after hours, came to a general store.

"Can you tell us where Joni Mitchell lives?" we asked the elderly female clerk. She helpfully pointed down the road. We headed in that direction, but after searching for hours, we realized the lady at the store had probably intentionally sent us the wrong way. She was doing what islanders everywhere do: protect their Eden-esque garden from outsiders, and particularly from Joni Mitchell–stalkers. We caught the last ferry back to the mainland that evening.

When we arrived on the other side, we were still thirty miles from Ann and Michael's house. We had no car, and we had spent the last of our money on the ferry. We didn't even have a dime to call Ann. Six hours after vowing to never hitchhike again, I was sticking my thumb out, hoping against hope that some kindly hippie would drive by in a Volkswagen bus.

We swore we'd go back for Joni, but we never did. The closest I would get to Joni Mitchell that summer would be the sound of her voice coming out of a radio.

ANN WILSON

Though my romance with Michael Fisher had initially drawn me away from music, I wasn't gone long. My poetry morphed into songwriting, even if many of the songs I wrote were about Michael Fisher. Two of the first were "Here Song," and "How Deep It Goes." I wrote the latter to express my loneliness when Michael and I had a minor fight: "I don't know what I believe anymore / or whether to leave / or whether to stay / or what I can say / to make you know how deep it goes." Like many of my lyrics, they were melancholy.

Our initial mad passion couldn't be sustained without bumps in the road, of course. While Michael was always supportive of my creativity, he watched everything I ate, and counted every beer I drank. I starved myself to be thin for him. It worked for a time, but I was conflicted. I loved him entirely and deeply, yet I was too young to be that devoted. That first year, I was lost in love, but eventually my real self returned, and I saw parts of Michael that were a bit too Henry Higgins–like for me, straight out of *My Fair Lady*. Our relationship sometimes felt like a tight-fitting garment.

Still, I remained undeniably crazy about Michael Fisher. I began to write a song that year that summed up what being in love had done to me. The words were straight out of the scenes of the wild sexuality that went on in our cottage, but they were also about how love had opened up parts of *me* heretofore unknown, my own liberation: "My love is the evening breeze touching your skin / the gentle, sweet singing of leaves in the wind / the whisper that calls after you in the night / and kisses your ear in the early moonlight / Let me go crazy on you." When I wrote about "the whisper that calls," it wasn't just the literal whisper in Michael's ear, or mine, pulling us to that dreamy driftwood bed. The "whisper" was also a voice calling me toward my muse, my empowered womanhood, my fate. At times it didn't feel like a whisper, but a shout. The whisper of that muse terrified Michael because it was one of the few parts of me he had no sway over.

Michael's alpha-male personality, though, played an essential part in my career. While moving to Canada seemed like I was leaving the band behind, it was only a temporarily relocation: The band eventually came to me. Michael had always wanted to manage his younger brother's band, so Roger Fisher, Steve Fossen, plus a drummer and keyboard player who would later depart, moved to Vancouver. They, and their wives, moved in with Michael and me in our tiny cottage.

We lived for a time, more like a commune of hippies than a band, with all of us sharing pots of brown rice, and Roger Fisher running around with very few clothes on. Roger almost immediately began to damn up Lassen Creek with the idea of making a swimming hole. He managed to muscle enough boulders into place to build a pond worthy of beaver, and it held for a few months until a downpour caused it to burst one day with an explosion that woke us in the middle of the night.

Michael was a powerful leader, and he directed us on every aspect of what our band was going to be. It was like in Russia, where they started Communism by saying, "We've got a five-year plan." He sat us down and said, "Here's what's going to happen in the first five years." Our new group hadn't played a single show, but Michael had already plotted out where we would be if we committed to his vision.

We had to have a name for this new band. We considered several, including going back to Hocus Pocus. Eventually, we settled on a name that Roger and Steve had used before: Heart.

Now that we had a name, we needed a logo. Michael Fisher had already been sketching a Hocus Pocus logo and switched it around a bit. He took the "H" from that drawing, put a heart shape in the serif, and made it "Heart." He drew it in a single afternoon sitting in our cottage over the creek.

We now had a leader, a band, a name, a logo, and a five-year plan that spelled out everything we would do, and all we would become.

All we needed was to make any part of that plan come true.

10

THE IMPOSSIBLE PERFECT THING

A first gig in a cave. A bucktoothed Texan. And a search for something that was right there all along.

ANN WILSON

Heart's first gig was at a Vancouver, B.C., club called the Cave. The name was literal: It was decorated with rocks on the walls to look like a cavern. We had to audition to get the gig. During our tryout, a gust of wind blew in when a door opened, and my acoustic guitar fell to the ground. We got the booking anyway, and made sixty dollars. Before the gig, we were so poor that six of us were living off a hundred-pound bag of rice that Roger's wife Mary had purchased with her tax refund.

Vancouver had a sophisticated nightclub scene, and there were dozens of clubs that featured live music. We eventually played them all, plus others in the suburbs and the rest of the province, because we couldn't play downtown every night without cannibalizing our audience. We performed between three and five sets most nights, and sometimes we were onstage for five hours. We paced the show to start with popular radio hits to get the crowd dancing, like the Rolling Stones' "Honky Tonk Woman," before shifting to progressive rock, like "Siberian Khatru" by Yes, or "Highway Star" by Deep Purple. As our club career developed, we'd sneak our originals into the set between two covers. "Here's a little thing we wrote called 'Crazy On You,'" I'd say, trying to soft sell it.

But the part of our show that first gained us fans in Vancouver was our thirty-minute set of Led Zeppelin covers. The interplay between Roger Fisher's guitar and my voice mimicked the dynamics of Jimmy Page and Robert Plant on songs like "Stairway to Heaven" and "Whole Lotta Love." Roger even learned to use a bow on his guitar, so he could play "Dazed and Confused" like Page. Our skill at doing Zeppelin became our calling card and earned us most of our first bookings.

The androgyny of Zeppelin always appealed to me—they had just as much of a feminine side as masculine. And though Heart mostly covered their rock songs, Zeppelin were always more of a folk and blues band to me. I could easily sing their ballads, but it took me a while to learn to do the screamers without getting hoarse. I had quit smoking, and that helped, but the clubs we played were so filled with cigarette smoke that it hardly mattered.

I'd seen Led Zeppelin in concert in Seattle, and everyone in Heart went together to see them in Canada in 1973. When they returned to Vancouver in 1975, we had to miss them since we had a gig that night at Oil Can Harry's, Vancouver's most prestigious club.

I was onstage when the post-concert crowd began to stream in. To my shock, as I was singing "Stairway to Heaven" Led Zeppelin walked into the club. To me this seemed like the ultimate kismet, but this probably happened to Zeppelin all the time, and they never registered that we were playing their signature song. They immediately retreated to the club's private pool table room. During our set break, Steve Fossen and Howard Leese talked to John Bonham and Robert Plant. Jimmy Page didn't talk to anyone because he was being seen to by "his doctor" and was passed out in a booth.

▪ ▪ ▪

In our early days, we were happy if we made a hundred dollars for a booking, though that didn't pay for much partying on our part. When club gigs started to earn us more, Michael Fisher carefully doled out our pay, but used most of our earnings to upgrade our equipment. Michael was obsessed with the band's "surround" sound system, which he designed and built. It became part of our appeal with fans: Whether they liked us or not, we sounded better than any other band on the circuit. Whenever we weren't playing, Michael and Roger were building new speaker systems.

Though I was the front person of the band, I was still confined by the attitudes the other members of the band had toward women, particularly when we all lived together. I was still expected to clean the house, cook the meals, and wash the clothes. Some of these expectations were Michael Fisher's, but some were my own. I would wash the sheets, hang them to dry, and iron them so that when Michael came home there would be fresh sheets for him on the bed. But even if I didn't volunteer, the guys expected that the women would do all the chores.

Two of the band members were married, and Roger's wife had a daughter, so a baby was part of our group. We were like one big commune in principle, but oftentimes there would be a separation of the sexes during social time, and I didn't fit in either group. The guys wanted to just be guys, but I didn't mesh with the other women, either. The girlfriends and wives were sweet and earthy, but their role—being defined only by their support for the men—was not mine.

As we started to play more out-of-town shows, and we'd need hotel rooms, groupies came into the mix. That was the rock guy mentality of the day, and the men in the band took women, and road sex, for granted. Roger Fisher, in particular, was the most sexually driven creature I ever met. He had been hitting on Nancy since he met her, often telling me he was in love with her, though he was married and had a daughter.

When we returned from an out-of-town gig, the wives or girlfriends would immediately descend on me, wanting the truth about what went on with their men. I had to pick between the code of the road, and the sisterhood. I always chose to protect the guys, and band unity, as best I could. It was a rotten position because I witnessed the tears and heartache of these faithful young women when they discovered the indiscretions. Early on I had been naive enough before one road trip to suggest the wives come along. It proved to be a terrible idea. The wives had no fun watching groupies flirt with their men, and the guys had no fun ignoring the flirts.

Michael Fisher was, to my knowledge, too disciplined to be a cad in that way, plus I was his girlfriend and on the road with him. I was also onstage singing songs I had written about Michael, like "Magic Man," which became one of our most popular originals that year. For Michael to have cheated would have been a betrayal of me and of everything Heart represented to him. That sidestep wasn't in the five-year plan. Nor was flubbing lyrics, and when that happened Michael didn't wait a minute when I came offstage. He was on me right away, dressing me down in front of everyone else. Michael was our leader, but no one in the band would ever say that he was easy on us. He was just as harsh when criticizing his brother Roger.

His benign dictatorship did have results though. By 1974, we had become "the number one cabaret band in Vancouver," which had been on his five-year plan. Early that year we had signed on with a booking agent named Barry Samuels. We told Barry to get us any gig he could, so we played high school dances, proms, weddings, and private parties, in addition to nightclubs. We had started at the bottom of the rung, but as our reputation grew, Barry eventually got our fee up as high as three thousand dollars for a multi-night booking. Although that seemed like a fortune to us, as usual most of it went to better equipment, gear, or the van we got that year. But it was progress.

We were also trying to save money because one of the parts of the five-year plan we had yet to execute was releasing a record. Michael Fisher had contacted every label or producer in town, without success.

We finally got a break when we ran into an engineer named Rolf Henneman who worked at Mushroom, a recording studio and an independent label. Rolf came to see us play, and invited us to audition at Mushroom. Producer Mike Flicker ran the studio, but he wasn't there the day we arrived. His assistant Howard Leese was, though. Here's how Howard recalled the first day we visited:

HOWARD LEESE

I had first seen them in a club when everyone in Vancouver called them "Little Led Zeppelin." When you saw Ann sing, you'd say, "Holy, crap, her voice is bigger than Robert Plant's." When they came into the studio that day, I was the only one there, but I agreed to record them doing a couple of songs. They played "Willie and the Hand Jive" by Johnny Otis, and a cover of Elton John's "Sixty Years On." Ann was great, but at the time, they didn't seem to have any songs of their own.

Mushroom was interested, but only in Ann. They offered to sign her, alone, to a recording contract. She said it was either the whole band, or nothing, so Mushroom passed.

It would be almost another year, before we'd see them in the studio again.

NANCY WILSON

In the fall of 1972, I moved to Forest Grove, Oregon, to start my freshman year at Pacific University, a private liberal arts school. I wanted to learn about literature, art, and language. When I had to declare a major, I picked art and German, the latter because the Beatles spoke a tiny bit of German, of course.

Even as I reveled in all my higher learning, I was placing flyers in the student union looking for other musicians. I found a gig at a coffeehouse, where I played solo, which was a first for me. I did songs by Joni Mitchell, Paul Simon, and even an occasional original. Eventually, a guitarist named

John Farrell became my duet partner, much as Geoff had been, but this time minus the romance. I made enough from gigging that I was able to buy a Gibson J-55 acoustic guitar and D'Angelico strings. It had a rosewood neck, a spruce top, and a mahogany back. It immediately became my favorite possession.

My school had practice spaces where I could sign out a room with a piano, and I began to practice more. I felt like such a bohemian intellectual, but I also felt lonely being away from home for the first time. I wrote a friend that first month to say, "I'm learning so much, but have no one to share it with."

I would still travel to visit Ann in Vancouver on school breaks, and a few times I sat in with Heart for a song, or two. "You should join the band," Ann said. I knew one day we'd again be in a band together, but I was still in the college mindset.

Pacific was a relatively expensive school, and when the year ended my parents asked if I was serious enough to continue. College always felt temporary, but I wasn't ready to give it up. I decided to transfer to Portland State University, in downtown Portland, because I thought being in a big city would give me more music opportunities. I was trying to play both sides I guess, music and school, to see where each might go.

In the fall of 1973, I started at Portland State. I liked the school, but I still felt isolated. To fight that, on one of my trips to Vancouver to visit Ann, I rescued a black lab. I named him Zooey, after the J. D. Salinger book *Frannie and Zooey.* Zooey became the charter member of my "small but appreciative audience," coming to any gig I had, and loyally listening to me play for hours each day. Zooey wasn't supposed to live in the dorm with me, but I smuggled him in and hid him the way other girls were hiding boyfriends.

The week I started classes, I also began searching for a musical partner. As I began to audition players, I wrote a friend a letter outlining what I was looking for. It read, in part:

"I've posted some notices around school asking for anyone who sings and plays acoustic guitar or bass well, because I intend, as soon as possible, to form a trio of excellent musicians, especially excellent singers, who can help me do what I'm longing to do with my music. Every day I receive an audition candidate or two into my dorm room, and serve them tea, and talk to them for a short time, and hand them a guitar, and then sit and listen. So far, all I've heard, as you might have predicted, is sheer bullshit trash. Every day I get more impatient for *my person* to walk in.

"It's a comical experiment to invite strangers from the outside into your territory, and challenge them. I've found strange pleasure in it, and several times it has become so laughable that I had to look out my window, as if I could hear better in that pose, to contain my laughter. Last night, I was visited by a 'long tall Texan' with buckteeth and filthy hands. The gentleness, and timidness of his eyes contradicted his entire countenance, and he played songs which I could have mastered at age twelve, thumping each loafer-clad foot, thump-click-thump (like Captain Hook), which immediately intrigued Zooey, who began to chew on the distracting shoes, each in turn. His original songs were full of such lyrics as, 'going steady with the sun,' 'wish you were my sister, and had sucked from my mom.' MOM! I couldn't believe it. He finally left, after playing five or six 'just one mores.'

"I want ideally to have two other flexible and talented people, who would be willing to make an intensely serious project out of creating music with me. As always, I expect the impossible perfect thing to simply find me, and introduce itself. I want it to be a vocal-oriented trio with everything from the daintiest subtle breathtaking beauty to the hardest, meanest, dirtiest release. Please give me a miracle with no onions. I would be clean without mud. No more of this now: It only serves to frustrate me more."

I never found a consistent musical partner in Portland, though I did play solo a few times at the student union. My attempt to simultaneously pursue music and college increased my frustration with both. Every time I visited my parents in Bellevue, they questioned me on whether I should continue at my college. Every time I visited Ann in Vancouver, she entreated me to join the band, which was becoming more popular by the day.

In another letter I wrote a friend that spring, I summed up my quandary, noting that my parents had suggested I attend the University of Washington, where in-state tuition was less. On the idea of joining Heart, I wrote, "I could join Ann in her musical endeavors, which judging by the present state of things, would entail ample monetary gain, and the certainty of immediate travel. I don't know if I'm ready to take upon the bond of membership, which would be indefinite. My calling in music also seems to be of an acoustic nature." I wrote another friend a similar letter, but put it more succinctly, in all caps: "SHOULD I JOIN THE BAND?" She wrote back, "YES, YES, YES."

That spring, on my next trip to Vancouver, I asked Ann if we could include more acoustic songs if I joined the band. "That's what I've always imagined" she said. "That's why I want you to join."

I made the decision that I was leaving Portland, but I still wasn't sure whether I was headed to Seattle for the University of Washington, or to Vancouver. Ann wrote me that week to announce she, Michael, Roger, and Roger's wife, Mary, had moved to a home on Water Lane in West Vancouver. She described it as the most beautiful setting she'd ever seen—the house backed up against a huge park filled with ancient trees, and a rocky beach. The keyboard player in Heart had quit, and Ann said if I came up I could have his waterbed.

Ann also reported that the new house had reignited her creative streak, and she was writing more than ever. "I want you to be part of that," she said. Seeing those words in my sister's handwriting made me realize that just as I was looking for "my person" in music, so was Ann. We were both seeking the same thing. Ever since Ann had moved to Vancouver to be with Michael, I had been telling friends how I needed to find "my person," my musical partner, and I put up flyers all over Oregon seeking that connection.

What I had temporarily forgotten was that "my person," my "impossible perfect thing," was right here next to me, and always had been.

11

THE NORTHERN LIGHTS

Nancy joins Heart but faces a frozen bed and questions on whether her guitar is plugged in. Heart completes their debut album and survives a run-in with a moose. . . .

NANCY WILSON

I arrived in Vancouver in mid-1974 to join Heart. I moved in with Ann, Michael Fisher, and Roger Fisher in that picturesque house on Water Lane. Though Ann was ecstatic to have me join the band, there were complications. Roger had recently separated from his wife, and he began hitting on me right away. I turned down his advances, and in my basement room, slept on the promised waterbed alone. The bed proved less comfy than expected. It was an old-fashioned waterbed without baffles, and it sloshed with any movement. The only time the bed didn't shift was in the winter when it froze into a solid block of ice.

Moving to Canada required that I apply for status as a "landed emigrant," and that took time. Ann and the rest of the band had been approved the previous year, which meant they could work in Canada. I was on hold waiting for my application to be considered—and even once it was considered, my acceptance wasn't a sure thing.

Yet the biggest complication came from the band members. Though Ann wanted me in the group, some of the guys resisted. They didn't like my idea that we might play more acoustic music, and they were afraid there would be a shift in power with two sisters in the band. The band insisted that I "audition" to join, and so I began to sit in for a few songs every night to see how it worked with two females, and another acoustic guitar, onstage. I was given the assignment to work up the introduction to the Yes song "The Clap." It was very complicated, but I learned it and played it with Heart at a tavern one night. I passed, and for Heart's next show, at Starvin' Marvin's Bump City, I was onstage for an entire set. Within three months, I was a permanent part of the band.

Steering Heart toward more acoustic material proved to be a bigger challenge. The group's reputation was based on playing radio hits, songs that the crowd could dance to. We began to include an occasional Seals and Croft song, or Elton John number, and those were places for me to shine. My love for Elton John was so strong that when his Vancouver show sold out that year, I insisted on going, even though we only arrived back in town after an all-night drive and no sleep. I had no ticket and no money, so I begged our booking agent Barry Samuels to front me money to try to buy one from a scalper. Barry agreed, but only if I got on my knees and promised I would repay him. With my borrowed money, I bought a scalped ticket outside the hall. At the entrance hall I was turned away and nearly arrested when the ticket I purchased turned out to be counterfeit. I was not going to be turned away, though. I found a place in the loading area where two sections of the chain-link fence were locked together, and I climbed over the fence and ran into the crowd. I stood up through the entire concert because I didn't have a seat, but then so did everyone else. The concert was worth the humiliation, the financial cost, and the pain in my fingers from climbing the fence.

It was almost as hard to get the rest of the band to embrace the folk music I wanted. Ann and I soon realized the easiest way to get them to play acoustic numbers was to write original songs for the band in that format. Heart was already talking about putting together enough material for an album, and that's what Ann and I set to work on that fall.

ANN WILSON

I had always wanted Nancy in the band, but there was an unintended result that was also beneficial to our marketing: The idea that our band had two sisters in it became part of our calling card and changed forever the way we were perceived. There were plenty of bands with a female singer, but in that era it was extremely rare for a band to have two women, rarer still for them to play guitar, and almost unheard of for them to be sisters. The "sister act" jokes started immediately. As a veteran of clubs, I was used to sexist and sexual comments, but it was hard to watch Nancy suffer them. She was also asked every night if her guitar was really plugged in, or if she really knew how to play it.

Heart was not a huge financial success then. Though Heart was the most popular band in Vancouver, we were greatly limited by geography in the bookings we could accept. The most lucrative market was still the States, but due to Michael Fisher's draft status we couldn't travel there. We found ourselves forced to head deeper and deeper into the Canadian prairie simply to find a gig playing for a school prom.

The only way to break out of the chains of the club circuit was to record, and that's what we concentrated on during the next year. Michael Fisher approached every label in Canada and in the United States, but failed to land any offers. He had, however, continued to foster a relationship with Mushroom and producer Mike Flicker. Flicker finally came and saw us almost a year after I'd recorded our first demo at Mushroom.

Here's how Flicker recalled that period:

MIKE FLICKER

Nancy had just joined the band and was still a diamond in the rough, and not quite comfortable onstage. But it was the first time I had ever seen a female onstage playing a guitar, so I was impressed with that. I was just blown away by Ann's voice, though. A few of the other guys in the band were not cutting it, and I couldn't imagine bringing them in to record the type of album I was used to making. But I saw the politics of it, so I came to the group with an odd offer. I said I'd be interested in signing Ann, Nancy, and Roger Fisher. I wanted to sign Roger, frankly, for the only reason that without Roger, Michael Fisher wouldn't go for it. Because Michael was Ann's boyfriend, it was strictly a political decision, as it was my shot to get the two girls. They went for it. And so the contract, which became a hugely disputed contract later on, only consisted of those three members.

The band came into the studio and we chose to do one song, "How Deep It Goes." This was customary in those days, to make sure you could get enough radio attention to warrant recording a full album. I brought in a studio drummer, and Howard Leese arranged a string part. When we were done, we released it as a single.

The single only got a small amount of airplay. Ann later told me that she and Nancy would call up the local station using different accents and request it multiple times. We were all disappointed it hadn't become a hit, and it looked like Mushroom's relationship with Heart would end there. I had a boss at the label, and he wasn't interested. In the meantime, Ann and Nancy started writing together more, and those results were impressive. When they sat down with me and played songs like "Crazy On You," "Magic Man," and "Soul of the Sea," I knew we had to make an album. Then my boss had a heart attack, and I was able to make the album my way. In a bizarre twist of fate, a heart attack saved Heart.

Initially, as the studio sessions began, it felt like we were simply recording singles, and the songs lacked cohesion to each other. Singles were important still, but this was the era of the album, and I told them that. Ann came by a few days later to say she had a song she thought could frame the record. She played me "Dreamboat Annie." That, I told her, was a thread we could build a whole album around. It immediately became the album title—there was nothing else considered.

From there, *Dreamboat Annie* came together easily in the studio. Howard Leese had such a great time working on the record, they offered him a job in the band, and he took it. Mushroom released a single of "Magic Man" before the album was done, with high expectations. It started to get airplay around Vancouver and in a few other markets, but it wasn't a hit the way I had imagined it would be. It took some time to grow.

The single benefited greatly at the time from the Canadian content law. That was a requirement that Canadian radio stations devote at least one fourth of their content to Canadian artists. It was passed to stop the domination of U.S. acts, but when it came to Heart it had unintended consequences. I was originally from the states, but I had immigrant status, as did Ann, so *Dreamboat Annie* qualified as a Canadian album, and a significant portion of the early airplay came from that. But the law also hurt Heart when they tried to break the record in the United States, since broadcasters there were suspicious of any Canadian record, since it might have only gotten airplay due to the content regulation.

Having "Magic Man" on the radio helped the band in Vancouver, but they were already popular there. To survive, the band had to take every live gig they could. They would play these shows deep in the interior of British Columbia, braving snowy roads to get to the gigs.

And then I got a phone call that their van had hit a moose.

NANCY

We were on our way to an out-of-town show in the interior of British Columbia. Michael Fisher was driving, Ann was in the passenger seat, and Roger and I were in the back. It was a clear night, though the roads were icy. I looked out the window, and on the horizon I saw these eerie green lights, and thought, "What's that?" Then I realized I was seeing the aurora borealis.

"Wow, oh, my God!" I said. "The Northern Lights! Ann, come look out the window." Ann had just moved from the front passenger's seat to the back, when there was a loud explosion. I looked up to see a shattered windshield, and a moose bouncing off the van. The van struck the moose at exactly the point where Ann had been sitting just moments before, and the result was a big gash in the van. The glass from the windshield covered the passenger seat, which was thankfully empty. I don't know if I was more shocked by the sight of the magnificent animal bleeding on the side of the road, or the idea that my sister had come inches from being killed or at least seriously injured, with a face full of glass. An angel was watching over us that night. The accident could have changed the whole course of everything. There might have been no musical career, no band, no *Dreamboat Annie*, but instead a whole other life.

As it was everyone in Heart survived and, after shaking glass off our clothes, we were no worse for the wear. Our van was another story—it required expensive repairs. But the moose suffered the direst consequences, dying by the side of the road. As our van limped to the nearest service station, I noticed tufts of the moose's fur still adhered to the spot in the van where Ann had once been sitting.

Dreamboat Annie came out in Canada in October 1975. We had released "Crazy On You" as a single, and it had received airplay, but our circumstances changed little. Mushroom was a tiny label and had been unable to convince any U.S. company to pick up the album, so only a few thousand copies were sent to stores there, the biggest music market in the world, and our homeland. And though we still sold out most of our Vancouver club dates, we couldn't play there every weekend. This explains why, when the offer came in for two weeks in Calgary at Lucifer's, we jumped at the gig. The club even ran an ad in the *Calgary Herald* announcing, "Lucifer's is proud to present 'Heart,' Dynamic Recording Stars, featuring the latest hit *Dreamboat Annie*," along with a picture of Ann and me.

The Lucifer's gig was almost as damaging to us as hitting the moose. We were fired after Ann criticized the club's food and became temporarily stuck in the middle of the Canadian prairie. But that opportunity to open up for Rod Stewart became available, and we were stunned. We found we were suddenly stars in Montreal, where "Magic Man" had become an FM radio hit, and soon the rest of the album was a certified smash on Canadian radio. We didn't immediately become rich—having a hit album in Canada, on a tiny independent label, didn't translate into riches, but it was a start.

Mushroom's director of promotions, one of only three employees, was Shelley Siegel. He tried to capitalize on our airplay that fall and drove Ann and me to what seemed like every radio station in Canada. We'd go in, meet the DJ, maybe do a station ID, and then Shelley would tell us to go wait in the car for him. We had no idea what was going on, and what the music industry was really driven by.

ANN

Though we were stars in Canada, the United States was a tough nut for us to crack. We had to break the States manually, by taking opening slots on tours, and traveling to radio stations with Shelley Siegel to shake hands, just as we had already done in Canada. We slowly made progress and got airplay at KSHE in St. Louis, WLUP in Chicago, and WMMS in Cleveland. After the Rod Stewart tour, we did a month of dates with ZZ Top, which brought us even more exposure. It was eye-opening for Nancy and me because we witnessed firsthand how masculine guitar rock wooed audiences. The guys in ZZ Top were supportive, though, and taught us how to balance our soft side with the hard. We became a better live band after only a few of those dates. Other tours that year found us opening up for Jefferson Starship, Strawbs, and the Bee Gees.

Our first real success in the States came from border cities like Detroit, Seattle, Buffalo, or any place that could pick up Canadian radio. But soon radio airplay in the Midwest brought us to the heartland. Some of that came because of our music, but Shelley's promotion efforts were also crucial. Shelley would take us to these radio stations, introduce us to the DJs, and send us to the car. When we were out of the way, he'd pass the DJs a gram of cocaine, or maybe the number of a hooker he'd lined up, and say,

"She's yours, on Heart." We suspected the drugs when Shelley's own issues became apparent, but we never knew about the hookers until years later. We were pretty sheltered, but if we had known, it would have been a difficult ethical situation for us. We were so intensely serious about our music, and thought our political message was one of love and purity. We had no idea how corrupt the industry was.

Shelley also lined up the first few stories in the press done on Heart. When we complained that the facts were wrong in some of those pieces, Shelley just waved us off as if we knew nothing about the ways of the world. "Ink is ink," Shelley always said.

If Heart was going to build on the success of *Dreamboat Annie* in Canada, we needed to play regularly and tour in the United States. Faced with that, Michael Fisher decided to turn himself in to the authorities. He did it for me, but he also did it because he believed in the band, and he didn't want to be the obstacle to our success.

Michael had met my parents one time when he'd snuck down to the States with me. I had imagined that my Marine major father might not be crazy about my draft-evading boyfriend, but Dotes surprised me. Dotes, a man with a Purple Heart, and a revolver in the drawer by his bed, not only accepted Michael, he supported him evading the draft. Dotes said he might have done the same if the "dirty war of Vietnam" had been happening when he enlisted. When Michael's draft-dodging case was close to going to trial, Dotes wrote letters to the judge and to the president, asking for leniency. It was impossible to know how much that correspondence had to do with the fact that Michael settled his case without jail time—Michael had also uncovered massive corruption in his local draft board where deferments were given to anyone wealthy, or connected. Still, I'm sure a letter from war hero Major Wilson had an effect.

Now that we could play in the States, Heart began to tour there regularly, a pattern that would continue for the next several years. It was with some sadness that we eventually left Vancouver, which had been an adopted home to me for almost four years, and a city where I felt loved and accepted by our fans. But the United States was where we all grew up, and where the biggest success was possible. Once *Dreamboat Annie* hit the U.S. album charts it stayed there for two years. We found an audience because our songs touched a nerve, but some of it was also timing, and hard rock stations were ready for more female voices at the moment we were coming up.

Just a few months before, our record had been so slow to catch on in Canada that Nancy and I had phoned radio station request lines with foreign accents, thinking that might jumpstart our struggling career. Now, with a hit album that would sell two million copies in the States over the next two years, we didn't have to do that anymore. Our mother couldn't let go, though. She thought phoning the request lines and getting us played one more time on Seattle radio might make or break our career. Unlike our attempt to hide our identities, Mama had no shame in her calls.

"This is Lou Wilson," she'd proudly announce to whatever DJ answered the phone. "Can you play another track from my daughters' album, please? They're called Heart."

12

BURN TO THE WICK

Nancy makes a decision, and the Wil-Shers begin. An ad by Mushroom launches a war. And Ann is confronted by a man with bad cologne named Tone-Knee who inspires a song. . . .

NANCY WILSON

In the fall of 1975, just as *Dreamboat Annie* was becoming a hit, I made a decision to get involved with our guitar player Roger Fisher. It wasn't that I ever said "yes" to Roger, but I simply stopped saying "no." He had pursued me for years with lyrics, songs, notes, appearances out of the blue, and by being extremely forward about his sexual interest in me. I held him off for a long time, but finally gave in. Initially it helped bond the band, and with two brothers dating two sisters, we truly were one big family now.

Ours was never a deep soul love, but a relationship of convenience for me. We were traveling together, and having a boyfriend in the band to bunk with made sense. We saved money on hotel rooms, and it was as if Ann, Michael, Roger, and I were on a never-ending double date. Ann and I even came up with a combination of our last names that represented our two-sisters-two-brothers relationship: We were the Wil-Shers.

Within the Wil-Shers, however, I always felt Roger and I were the mascots to Ann and Michael. They seemed a really solid couple, like adults, while Roger and I were silly and adolescent. If we went somewhere together, they drove, both literally and metaphorically, while Roger and I were in the backseat.

My relationship with Roger did have significant musical highpoints. He was a gifted guitarist, and onstage we fed off each other. We pushed each other artistically offstage as well, and for someone who was never happier than when I was playing guitar, Roger was my ever-ready duet partner. We both discovered the mandolin at the same time, and when Heart went into the studio to cut *Little Queen*, that shared interest helped shape "Dream of the Archer" and "Sylvan Song."

Roger was handsome, athletic, and muscular and had no qualms about showing off his great body. To someone as shy and inexperienced as I was, it was an education. I had to almost beg Roger to put clothes on. Sometimes I got with the hippie plan, and we would sit around nude playing guitar. There was a downside to Roger's physicality, however, in that I was not the only female he had his eye on, even when we were living together. I discovered that fact early in our relationship when I caught him with his ex-wife. I initially had felt tremendous guilt that I was with a guy who had only recently separated from his wife, so in a way maybe that incident was my penance. There would be more painful lessons to come on this front.

But being with Roger did cut down on most, if not all, of the unwanted male energy directed toward me. Ann initially had her reservations about our relationship—having spent several years on the road with Roger, she knew his ways too well. But our brother-sister relationships had unintended positive effects on the band: It became a news story of sorts and was yet another unique aspect of Heart in the press. Fleetwood Mac had inter-band romances, as well, but not among siblings.

The story of Heart became the story of the Wil-Shers. But in another way that was similar to Fleetwood Mac, these were not relationships without drama or pain.

ANN WILSON

The success of *Dreamboat Annie* changed everything. We still weren't seeing much money from our success, though, because Mushroom was so small that cash flow was a huge issue, and their slowness in paying us became increasingly frustrating. Other record labels, some who had previously turned us down, approached us in the meantime. We put the other suitors off out of loyalty to Mushroom. We ended up touring to make money, and we played over two hundred dates that year alone.

In 1976, we were on tour in the States, opening up for the Beach Boys, when our relationship with Mushroom changed forever. The label had attempted to leverage our success by signing more bands, adding U.S. distribution, and raising their industry profile. Sometimes they did that with money that might have gone toward paying us royalties we were owed. So we weren't surprised when they bought a full-page ad in *Rolling Stone* touting our success. "Million to One Shot Sells a Million," read the headline. They had mocked up the ad to look like it was the front page of the *National Enquirer.* The main headline read: "Exclusive—the Heartbreaking Story, Regional Hit Mushrooms into Million Seller."

But what *was* surprising, and heartbreaking, to Nancy and me was the headline that ran farther down the page. Under a photograph of us, an outtake from the *Dreamboat Annie* cover sessions that shows us back to back with bare shoulders, the caption read: "Heart's Wilson Sisters Confess: 'It Was Only Our First Time!' "

It was a moment when I thought that my mother's warnings had come true—we *had* turned into something tragic like Judy Garland, corrupted by the entertainment industry. The ad went against everything we had hoped to achieve, against our ideals, and against all the intent and beauty in our songs. What steamed us the most was that our *own* record label had put out an ad that implied we were incestuous lesbian lovers.

We angrily called up Shelley Siegel. He answered the phone as he always did, "Mushroom, home-a-duh-hits." As we had become more successful,

Shelley had become more arrogant. On his wall he framed a quote from our first *Rolling Stone* article where he said, "I've sold a million fucking albums, and nobody in L.A. knows who I am, so when they find out, I'll sell a million point two." As we might have expected, Shelley tried to blame the ad on someone else, but we knew it was him. He later would admit to placing the ad but claimed we had approved it. Shelley had developed a serious cocaine problem by then, which affected his already questionable judgment. "Don't worry," Shelley said on the phone that day, giving us his typical sales job. "Ink is ink."

There was one headline that was part of the *Rolling Stone* ad that was true. It read, "New LP on Its Way." With the success of *Dreamboat Annie* we were rushing to finish our second album, and we had nearly completed five songs, including "Heartless." It was more of a concept album than our debut. We planned to call it *Magazine* and have it fold out like a publication. "Heartless" contained some of my favorite lyrics ever ("Never realize the way love dies when you crucify its soul"), and I was convinced our second album was going to be our best so far.

Michael Fisher had been Heart's de facto manager, but as *Dreamboat Annie* became a hit, Michael realized that for the sake of our relationship we needed an outsider. We hired Ken Kinnear out of Seattle to represent us. One of the first tasks we gave Ken was to renegotiate our royalty rate with Mushroom because it was not in line with what a platinum band should earn. Those negotiations were ongoing, but Mushroom was holding tough. Mike Flicker, who had been an employee of Mushroom, as well as our producer, later told us the owners of the label thought we might be one-hit wonders and so refused to budge. The negotiations proved a difficult point for Flicker, who eventually resigned from Mushroom to continue to produce us. The line-up of Heart then was me, Nancy, Roger Fisher, keyboardist and guitarist Howard Leese, bassist Steve Fossen, and drummer Michael

Derosier, who had joined after *Dreamboat Annie*. But producer Mike Flicker could have been the seventh member of Heart.

The renegotiations had been difficult, but the "It Was Only Our First Time" ad was the final straw in our relationship with Mushroom. We hired a lawyer and eventually our contract dispute ended up in federal court. Over the next year, Heart would become nationally known for something Mushroom certainly never expected when they placed their advertisement: Mushroom and Heart became involved in one of the nastiest legal battles in the music industry that decade.

As the case wound on, we began negotiating with other labels and eventually signed with Portrait, a division of CBS Records. Mushroom was adamant that they weren't willing to let us out of our original contract, which called for two albums. We argued that since Mike Flicker was listed in that agreement, and Mushroom could no longer provide Flicker, their contract was invalid. They threatened to release the material we'd already recorded without our approval.

And that's exactly what Mushroom did. They took the few tracks that were nearly done and completed them without our involvement, using our rough vocals. To that they added a few outtakes and live tracks, and rushed the album into stores, trying to beat our first Portrait album, *Little Queen*. The Mushroom album had a disclaimer on the back that read, "Mushroom Records regrets that a contractual dispute has made it necessary to complete this record without the cooperation or endorsement of the group Heart, who had expressly disclaimed artistic involvement in completing this record. We did not feel that a contractual dispute should prevent the public from hearing and enjoying these incredible tunes and recordings." It was one of the oddest chapters in the record business, and unfortunately it involved us.

We received a federal injunction that recalled *Magazine*, but not before fifty thousand copies were sold in stores in New York and Los Angeles. And though we were unhappy with the mixes, the song selection, and the shoddy design that stripped away our original concept, the songs on *Magazine* were immediate radio hits. We found ourselves in the uncomfortable situation of asking radio stations *not* to play our record. Most played it anyway.

Although it took some time for the court case to settle, in the end we won the right to sign with Portrait if we gave Mushroom a second album. We decided to make *Magazine* that album but insisted we finish the vocals and mixes. We did that in a Seattle studio later that year, as an armed security guard stood by. The court had ordered the guard because Mushroom was afraid we would erase our original multi-track recordings out of spite.

Mushroom re-released *Magazine*, our ill-fated second album, in April 1978. It was a project we had begun with high hopes, but it had ended so painfully. But our name was attached, and *Magazine* vaulted up the charts. It sold a million copies in just three weeks. It was a huge infusion of cash for Mushroom, but much of that was eaten up by legal bills, of which we had a mountain of our own.

A few months after the re-release of *Magazine*, Shelley Siegel collapsed and died of a brain aneurysm brought on by cocaine abuse. We were on the Washington coast with Sue Ennis on a writing retreat in a cabin with no telephone when it happened. We heard a pounding at the cabin door and discovered a police officer, who had been sent out to tell us to call our office, which is how we heard. Shelley, even with his faults and his sleazy ad, had been one of our original disciples.

We felt less grief a few years later when Mushroom Records went bankrupt. The owners had failed to find another group who did as well for them as Heart, a band they thought would be a one-hit wonder.

Not long after the "It's Only Our First Time" ad appeared, I had an incident in Detroit with a radio promo guy. His name was Tony, but he bellowed it out as "Tone-Knee," stretching the syllables like an opera aria. We had met plenty of these promo guys by then, all with the same sexist jokes, all who called us "girls." Shelley Siegel was the same kind of guy.

I had just come offstage when I met Tone-Knee. "Hey, Ann, it's 'Tone-Knee,'" he shouted. He was wearing a red satin promotional baseball jacket with HEART stitched on the back. "Where's ya lover, Ann?" Tone-Knee said as he pushed a meaty elbow into me. He had a wide smirk on his face.

I thought he was asking about Michael, but even with that interpretation the use of the word "lover" was too familiar. "Michael's back at the mixing board," I said. "He'll be there for another hour, breaking gear down, if you need him."

"Nah, nah, nah, not him," Tone-Knee said. "Nah, ya lover! Your sista! Where's your lover?"

Tone-Knee had seen the "It's Only Our First Time" ad, and he apparently thought Nancy and I had taken it out to announce our incestuous love to the world. To Tone-Knee, it was the most natural thing in the world to walk up and ask me where my lesbian-lover-sister happened to be. If Nancy had been there, she might have smacked him with her guitar. I, however, was immobilized with rage.

Tone-Knee continued on. "Hey, look at my watch, Ann," he said. He pulled back the sleeve of his Heart satin jacket, to display his wristwatch. On the face was an image of a buxom Marilyn Monroe–type in her underwear. It was the image that every woman in the entertainment industry would forever be compared to: You were either Marilyn Monroe, or you were not. I was not.

"Look at this, Ann," Tone-Knee said. "Ya push this button, and her undies fall down, and shows her tushie!" As if on command, Tone-Knee pushed the button, the dial shifted, and Marilyn's naked body, from the front, appeared. If I could have found words, I might have informed Tone-Knee that if he thought a woman's vagina was her "tushie," he was terribly confused.

Instead I left, thinking that if I made a quick retreat, the encounter would slip from memory. But Tone-Knee's essence would stick with me the way his bad cologne hung in the air.

■ ■ ■

I ran into Nancy in our dressing room. I was so embarrassed I could barely get the words out. As I tried to tell Nancy what Tone-Knee said, she started screaming, "He said WHAT?" She later described him as "like Artie Fufkin from *This Is Spinal Tap*." These radio promo guys were so archetypal there were movie characters based on them. It was one step away from *Goodfellas*, but it was the way business was done in that era, with a wink, and a nudge, and a flash of a naked body on a watch.

I left the venue and went back to the hotel. I sat down with pen and paper, and started writing a song. No song is completely about any one person, and what later came to be known as "Barracuda" was not just about Tone-Knee: It was about a million Tone-Knees, some in the record industry, and some outside it. It was about how this thing we thought was about art was, when mixed with sexuality and marketing, just a sleazy commodity. It went in part:

You lying so low in the weeds
I bet you gonna ambush me
You'd have me down, down, down, down on my knees, wouldn't you?
Barracuda! Ohh!
Back over time we were all trying for free
You met the porpoise and me, aha
No right, no wrong, selling a song
A name whisper game.
If the real thing don't do the trick
You better make up something quick
You gonna burn, burn, burn, burn to the wick
Ohh, Barracuda! Oh yeah.

I had never written lyrics so quickly. We didn't even know the meaning of the word "misogyny" at the time, but we felt it loud and clear, and reacted with anger. Nancy came back to the hotel and joined in, and her anger mixed with mine. She supplied the melodies, and the bridge. The rest of the sound was provided by Michael Derosier's beat, and Roger Fisher's riff. The song has a crazy bar-of-five that made "Barracuda" interesting. If you were dancing to it, it suddenly shifted, and you had your good foot in the air.

It wasn't the only song that season with a galloping beat, though. Long after "Barracuda" came together, a tiny brouhaha erupted when we toured with Nazareth, who had scored a hit with a cover of Joni Mitchell's "This Flight Tonight." Nazareth's Manny Charlton came to our dressing room after our first show with them and gently, but tersely, suggested we had ripped their gallop off. I told Manny we were "channeling Led Zeppelin," who had stolen it from Joan Baez's "Babe, I'm Gonna Leave You," who had taken it from the bluesmen, who had taken it from Old Stinky Rag Jackson, who had taken it from drummers in Kenya, who had taken it from gypsies, who had learned it from Adam. And Adam got it from Lilith. She got it from the horses. That shut him up.

When we went into the studio to record "Barracuda," Roger was experimenting with feedback. His guitar cord brushed against his amp, and it made a bizarre sound. It was a brilliant accident, and exactly the kind of inventiveness that only a non-linear player like Roger could pull off. You could never ever do something like that today with ProTools. Here's how Roger recalled how his contribution to "Barracuda" came together:

ROGER FISHER

We were at a soundcheck, probably in the Midwest somewhere. Derosier and I would get there first, so we could have some time to play. And we'd get down, shred, while they were setting up the gear. We were locked in that gallop mode. My brother said, "That's a pretty good riff, you should make a song around that." So we kept developing that. . . .

There was one point during the [studio] session, when I leaned over the amp, and I had a flanger on for an effect, and all of a sudden, this wah-wah-type sound came out of the amp. So I took the plug for the guitar out, and put that metal plug next to the amplifier tubes. . . . What you're hearing is a cord plugged into the amplifier, but the guitar itself was not even plugged in. The other end of the cord was next to the amplifier tubes. It's called oscillation. I said, "record this." We stopped and started a few times so we could get the cycle in just the right place. Mike Flicker said, "What should we call it?" I said, "Alien Attack." It became "Barracuda."

13

NATURAL FANTASIES

A goat and a wagon mark the debut of *Little Queen.* Heart's mother comments on the evils of taverns. And the Wilsons become accidental babysitters for a southern drummer. . . .

NANCY WILSON

Our first album on Portrait Records, *Little Queen*, came out May 14, 1977. It became our second Top Ten and would sell over three million copies in the next year. "Barracuda," "Kick It Out," and "Little Queen" all were hit singles, with "Barracuda" going to number eleven on *Billboard*. When *Magazine* later was re-released, we had the distinction of having all three of our albums on the charts at the same time.

The cover of *Little Queen* became one of our most iconographic images, even though it wasn't our favorite. Ann once told me she could smile in a thousand pictures but it was always the photograph with the pout that was chosen and would live forever. She had smiled in most of the other pictures that day, but they picked the one with her pout. There was a kernel of reality in the photo, but only a kernel. Ann and I had a joke that no matter what we did, the press would always imagine her as fierce and raw, and me as ethereal and angelic; even though those roles had little basis in reality, they had more to do with our hair color than our personalities. We were still new enough on the scene that promoters often would reverse our names, and so as a joke we made up buttons that read, "Ann's the brunette. Nancy's the blonde."

On the *Little Queen* album cover we were chasing the gypsy vibe on songs like "Dream of the Archer." We were on the road so much, we felt like gypsies, so we threw out the idea to the record label that we could dress like that. We were in Los Angeles at the time and discovered that in Hollywood we could rent anything, including a gypsy wagon and a goat.

We shot the album cover in Elysian Park in Los Angeles. The guys in the band had fun doing it because it was different from how they usually dressed onstage. With their beards and long hair, they looked like they already belonged to a different century. Nothing that we rented looked good on Ann, so she just wore her own clothes. We wanted it to be completely authentic, but there is one place you can see a zipper on Ann's boot. And though the cover looked "back to nature," even that was a bit of a façade. Elysian Park surrounds Dodger Stadium, so our gypsy camp was right next door to the ballpark.

Ann and I felt like we had our own fashion sense, long before the days when rock stars hired stylists. The clothes we wore onstage, and off, we usually sewed ourselves. If we didn't make something, we bought it off the rack and doctored it. For a time Ann wore an outfit onstage that was a bathrobe she purchased at Nordstrom's. After she sewed rhinestones on it and wore it with purple tights and knee-high boots, it was fashion.

Everyone in Heart had a unique fashion sense, and if we walked down the street together, we looked like a band. The poster of us that came out in the *Little Queen* era showing us arm-in-arm at the end of a show was emblematic. Ann wore a red and black corset, while I had on a long red dress with a black ribbon around my neck. Steve Fossen wore a white hippie shirt, with necklaces around his neck (he often wore a unitard onstage to show off his third nipple!). Roger wore a buckskin vest, tied at his waist. Michael Derosier was shirtless, in pajama-style drawstring pants. And Howard Leese wore pajama pants, a karate-type robe, and a purple sash around his neck—an outfit that could have belonged to Obi-Wan Kenobi. Howard would often dress in a blousy shirt and carry a saber, or in chaps and boots with pirate feathers in his hair. A few years later, he became fond of one-piece Spandex jumpsuits, which he had in several colors with matching amplifiers. Howard came by it honestly—his parents were in the fur and jewelry businesses.

Because all of the members of Heart liked showy clothes, and those were hard to find in 1977, the guys sometimes had to buy women's clothes. In just over a year, we'd all shift into more Asian-inspired fashion for *Dog and Butterfly*. But *Little Queen* was pure gypsy.

ANN WILSON

In July 1977, we appeared on the cover of *Rolling Stone* for the first time. The magazine used a photograph of just Nancy and me, and this became a sticking point with the guys in the band. It had become a common theme, the guys feeling jealous when so much attention was paid to us. We tried to be inclusive, but often they didn't want to attend the interview sessions, arguing that there would only be questions for us. The *Rolling Stone* piece addressed this tension. "All the time," I told the magazine, "I say, 'Today, I'm going to do four interviews and if you guys want to come along, follow on, present yourselves.' They always choose not to because it's too much work; they'd rather sit in the sun."

Heart had begun as a democracy, but in truth as the band moved along it shifted, particularly after Nancy joined. The transition wasn't just due to the fact that the press zeroed in on Nancy and me: It also had much to do with songwriting. As our success grew, the demand for new songs was constant, and the pressure fell almost exclusively on us. The guys loved to jam, particularly at soundcheck, but there was a big difference between crafting a riff and writing an entire song. The distractions of stardom were powerful, and Nancy and I had to retreat to the Oregon Coast, often with Sue Ennis, to write. That was the kind of discipline that most of the guys in the band, all brilliant improvisational players onstage, found hard to come by. "By being so creative, and coming up with such good ideas, they've challenged us males to do the same," Roger told *Rolling Stone*.

That *Rolling Stone* cover was a perfect example of how getting press was a mixed blessing. Most of the story focused on inane questions the writer had about groupies, sexuality, and gender, with very little emphasis on music. The cover headline, "Natural Fantasies, Natural Acts," was not quite as explicit as "It Was Only Our First Time," but the implication wasn't lost on anyone. One pull quote read, "The sexual fantasy we give onstage is a very natural one." I did say that, but it was in response to repeated questions about sexuality. We knew sexiness was an element of rock 'n' roll, but we were already exhausted by this topic because it was always being raised. The writer also played up our physical stereotypes, but with a higher brow than usual: "[The Wilsons] look strikingly like the good (blond) and evil (dark) sisters in Ingmar Berman's *The Virgin Spring*."

If these were the topics of a story on Heart in *Rolling Stone*, imagine what the articles were like in down market publications. *Circus* and *Hit Parader* seemed to be obsessed with us, and while it was rewarding when *Circus* named me the female vocalist of the year several times in a row, the sensationalism of their coverage was maddening. One *Circus* cover doctored a photo to make it appear that I was staring up adoringly at Robert Plant. The only time I'd ever even been in the same room with Plant was back in our Vancouver club days when he walked into the venue while I was onstage singing.

Even the storied *New York Times* couldn't resist talking about our appearance. John Rockwell noted our "striking good looks," but also mentioned what Rockwell thought was our "conformance to expected feminine archetypes in such matters." We could not escape the expectations of male critics.

Creem was the worst offender. Being sophomoric was part of the magazine's appeal, and for several years we were their favorite whipping posts. One profile of us was headlined "Heart of My Piece," began with the word "sex" and ended with the writer's suggestion that he was leaving our interview to go have sex with his girlfriend while fantasizing about us. Another *Creem* article was a massive feature that used the word "sex" dozens of times, including the last paragraph, which simply read "sex, sex, sex, sex. . . ." That writer asked us exactly how much "to the nearest ten thousand dollars" we would ask to pose in the nude for him (we didn't answer, but he nonetheless put his question in the article). He also asked if we would date him.

We would not.

There was one feature article that year we truly enjoyed reading because it wasn't focused on us, but instead was about our parents. It appeared in the *Bellevue Journal-American*, our hometown paper, and ran with large photographs of Mama and Dotes. Our parents were unguarded and spoke with the kind of clarity you rarely found in our other clippings. Mama said when I first began to practice the flute "it sounded awful." Our dad said he listened to our music, but no other "hard rock." In the previous year, Nancy and I had stopped in to Dotes's classes a few times to talk about lyrics, until the crowd grew too large. Dotes said our appearances made him so popular with his students, "they no longer love me for myself."

Both parents mentioned how proud they were of us, and particularly how our early life in the Congregational Church had shaped our values, but there was a hint of trepidation from Mama. She said the rock world was "a strange way to live," and that when we played "taverns" it "frightened [her] to death." Mama said people occasionally called her "Heart's mother." "Sometimes I resent it," she said, "but other times I'm proud."

Mama was right when she said that returning home for us was like coming back to the "womb." The more we toured, the more we valued being home, but the fewer days we had off, the less time we spent in Seattle. With money we had earned from our Portrait Records advance, Michael and I purchased a house on the shores of Lake Washington, and Nancy bought a place in the area, too. They were lovely homes, but we felt like we rarely enjoyed them.

In a few years time, we also bought our parents a new home on Lake Washington. We had worked so hard for our success, with their absolute support, and buying them a beautiful house seemed right. But when we packed up everything from our old home in Lake Hills, it was more than bittersweet. As the final boxes were gathered from a house we had lived in longer than any other, it felt like the end of childhood. I said good-bye to our handprints on the back cement. As the movers drove away, we all said good-bye and dusted off our shoes a final time.

I had another Bellevue experience that year which also brought back memories of childhood: I attended my ten-year high school reunion. I rented a limo, got all dressed up, and went with my best friend Sue. I thought I was going to have my moment of glory, but there were so many people coming up who were fans of the band, I felt I was backstage at a concert, signing autographs for a line of people I didn't know.

The few conversations I had didn't go particularly well. One guy who never paid any attention to me in high school started flirting. "Wow," he said. "You're looking really good these days. I always did think of you as someone special." This guy had been so cruel to me in school I could still remember what he told me in tenth grade: "When women stand and put their legs together," he had announced, "you should still be able to see light between their thighs." I had failed his test then, and now. Still, he was sidling up, and acting like he was going to get lucky.

I wasn't having any of it. I was perfectly willing to let the past be the past, and to let high school be a memory. But when he started flirting with someone he had mocked, it went too far, and I wasn't able to let it go. "Give me a break," I told him. "You were so mean to me back in high school. Fuck you." I walked away.

A few minutes later I spotted Red, the boy who back in seventh grade had announced to the whole class that I was "a fat thing" when he'd heard I had a crush on him. It was exactly the sort of scene I had dreamed of all these years, that I would arrive at my high school reunion as a star, on the cover of *Rolling Stone*, and prove to everyone that I really mattered. Instead, I walked in the other direction and away from a confrontation with Red. Once I was faced with my old demons, all I wanted to do was escape.

I left my high school reunion as I had left high school most days, wishing the car would move faster so the bad memory might fade quicker. Only this time, I was telling a limo driver to speed it up.

Even when we had a few days at home, Heart was almost immediately back on the road because there were always shows to do. The demands of playing hundreds of concerts a year around the globe quickly outpaced our capacity to travel by bus, so we leased a jet. It sounded luxurious, and in a way it was, but the convenience meant the label and concert promoters could ask more of us. The best part was that with the plane we could take our dogs with us on tour. After a show, we'd all get on the plane, and if you were taking a picture from outside, you would have seen all these people partying in the aisles, with dogs jumping everywhere.

Eventually, some of the guys in the band claimed they were "afraid" to fly at night. We always suspected they just wanted to hook up with women after the show, but a couple of them were actually scared. Michael Derosier was truly afraid to fly in the early days, and Howard Leese was so uneasy that he would carry a motorcycle helmet with him on the plane and wear it during take off and landing. It didn't help matters when our manager Ken Kinnear bought an eight-seat prop jet of his own and would often fly us on short trips. Our old friend Kelly Curtis had begun to work for us as our press agent, but he never let us forget the time Kinnear made Kelly fly with him and the crew to Europe in that prop jet—Nancy and I had flown earlier on a commercial jet. Ken's plane had to stop in Newfoundland on the way, and it took them three days to get to Europe.

We had a few of what seemed like near misses in those days and some very uncomfortable flights. One particular itinerary had us fly from Los Angeles to the Dominican Republic, then to Puerto Rico, then to Chicago, all in three days. We had all our band, crew, and gear in the small plane, and it was overloaded. The cabin began to run out of air. I had one of the first anxiety attacks of my life, and they had to give me a canister of oxygen to calm me down. The only place I could lie down in the crammed plane was in the aisle. As I lay on my back with an oxygen mask on my face looking up at the plane's ceiling, my life felt anything but glamorous.

In the United States we often toured with Southern rock bands, which were odd pairings for us, but concert promoters thought they needed the yin and the yang. The worst of these was the Marshall Tucker Band, who repeatedly made sexist comments toward us. At a show before fifty thousand people at Denver's Mile High Stadium, a member of the Marshall Tucker Band crew pulled the plug on the sound system mid-song to force us off stage. I was right in the middle of singing "Crazy On You" when the sound just disappeared. We were stunned, and so was the audience. As we walked away, the members of Marshall Tucker made catcalls. I never knew whether they were just jerks, or whether they thought we would upstage them, which we did. Our manager got in a fistfight with their manager in a chaotic backstage melee. The concert promoter, Barry Fey, was so embarrassed by Marshall Tucker's actions that he later went onstage, grabbed a microphone, and apologized to the audience. "This is the worst show I've ever done," he told the crowd.

We toured several times with Lynyrd Skynyrd, who were sexist, too, but with mellower good-old-boy overtones. One night there was a knock on my hotel room door in the middle of the night. I mistakenly opened it without looking, and Artimus Pyle, Skynyrd's drummer, did a somersault into my room. He dashed to the balcony—this was in a high-rise hotel on an upper floor—and squatted on the railing. I tried to coax him back, saying things like, "There's some real sweet music here in the bedroom. Come check it out." And he'd respond, "I'm fine here."

This act went on for far too long. I tried to distract Artimus with fabulous things I claimed were inside the hotel room. "Artimus, you wouldn't believe what's on television here! Dancing chickens!" Finally, he came back in, and I managed to push him into the hallway and lock the door. He kept knocking on it all night, but I knew not to open it. I looked through the peek hole once, and he was still right up against the door.

Another night, Nancy and I were in a room together, and I again made the mistake of opening the door without looking. Again it was Artimus, but this time he had a young boy he pushed toward us. "I've got to go see this guy about something," Artimus said. "Ya'll are women. Can you watch my son for a short while, ma'am?" Apparently, since we were the only females on the tour, he figured we were perfectly suited to be babysitters. He ran away before we could speak, so we took the boy in and ordered food for him. Artimus said he'd be back "real soon," but hours went by, and we eventually put the poor kid to bed. Finally, Artimus returned the next morning with a hangdog look on his face. "Real sorry, missus," he said. When his son left, we couldn't tell if the boy was disappointed that Artimus had returned late or that he'd come back at all.

That incident was only a few months before Skynyrd's tragic plane crash, which killed Ronnie Van Zandt and five others. Artimus Pyle survived, but barely. The legend was that Artimus ran to a nearby farmhouse for help, but when the farmer saw the blood all over him, he took a shot at him. Artimus left the band after the crash, but he had other legal problems later. In the coverage of his other issues, the press dug up much of Pyle's past, but our little tiny tangents, as babysitter and counselor squad, were overlooked.

We had a more pleasant experience when we opened some European dates for Queen that year. They were the ultimate English gentlemen and quite a contrast to the Southern yahoos. After one show in Edinburgh, they invited us for dinner at a fancy restaurant that was off an alley near Edinburgh Castle. It had no sign out front, you just had to know what ancient wooden door to knock on. It felt like it had been there for five thousand years. We sat down at a long table covered with fine champagnes, including a rare pink Dom Perignon, and many delicious dishes. Brian May was sweet on Nancy and spent the whole night chatting her up.

In the middle of the dinner, down the candlelit table in this ancient brick cavern, came the booming voice of Freddie Mercury. "Ann, oh Ah-NNN," Freddie bellowed in his unmistakable voice. It sounded so odd to hear my name spoken by one of the true greats in rock. The rest of the table stopped talking, and there was silence. "Ann," Freddie said. "Who is the real 'Magic Man'? It's me, isn't it? You meant me, didn't you, Ann?"

14

OCEAN UPON THE SKY

A visit to San Francisco results in one of Heart's best-loved songs. Dotes's health takes a turn for the worse. The original line-up of Heart implodes amid flying guitars. . . .

NANCY WILSON

With the huge success of *Little Queen* the pressure was on to follow up with another album quickly. We decided we would take the train down to Berkeley, where Sue Ennis was getting her PhD, and convince Sue to become our formal songwriting partner. Grad school was so intense that one of Sue's schoolmates had committed suicide, and we imagined we were saving her. In truth, we were also saving ourselves.

Sue was living in this little apartment with a roommate. We brought our guitars and went into Sue's tiny bedroom, and began to play. I did a riff I'd been working on, and Ann and Sue both said to play it again. We worked on it for an entire day, and it became the intro to "Mistral Wind." Heart fans often cite the song as their favorite, and it's mine as well.

We didn't finish the song before we had to leave for some tour dates. So we came back a few weeks later and rented the penthouse of the Mark Hopkins hotel. It had a commanding view of San Francisco, but we were there for the grand piano. For three days we tried to come up with something. We only ate room service, and we even insisted that the staff leave our food at the door and not disturb us.

The intro I'd written on that last trip was dissonant, and we still weren't sure what the song was about. But as we sat there looking out over San Francisco, I said we were like a sailboat without wind. Sue then told us about the crazy mistral winds in southern France, and lyrics started to come together. It frequently worked that way. We would struggle for days trying to find an idea, or a groove, and then in moments a song would coalesce. Through the course of "Mistral Wind," a storm comes over the audience, until they are washed to the shore. To me, the song always represented how once you've tasted excellence, you can't ever go back. "I have always held the wheel," part of the lyrics go. "But I let the wind steal my power, spin me 'round my course, my nights run by like hours."

When we came to record "Mistral Wind" later in the studio, Roger Fisher and I combined our forces, but the electric guitar riff two minutes into the song was strictly Roger's creation. Ann always called that one musical line the song's "Devil's interval." After we recorded it, she said Roger and I combined "into one guitar machine, together," and I think she was right. It was one of Roger's greatest riffs, and it was part of the signature of the song.

"Mistral Wind" became a cornerstone of our live show. It was one of only two songs we've ever played that had the power to summon the weather (the other was the Who's "Love, Reign o'er Me," which once started a monsoon). Once we were playing "Mistral Wind" somewhere in the middle of America on a perfectly calm evening, when a wind gust hit the stage and lightning struck. We didn't know whether to stop or forge ahead. We played on. Then a torrent of rain came down but stopped the moment the song ended. Everyone in the band, wet from the rain, stood there looking at one another with the hair on our arms standing up. I turned to Ann and said, "That couldn't have just happened that way."

■ ■ ■

"Straight On" never started hail, but it also came together from another one of our writing retreats with Sue. When we brought that tune into the studio, we told bass player Steve Fossen to imagine "I Heard It Through the Grapevine," and to marry that beat with the Eagles' sound. We were never a funk band, but we had spent so much time as a dance band in the early days, everyone could get with that groove when needed.

"Dog and Butterfly" was written one day when the three Connies were sitting in Ann's house in Bellevue. Ann looked out the window and saw her dog Moffa chasing a butterfly. She started on the lyrics. The three of us later went to Lake Washington, sat on a picnic table, and wrote the rest. It has always been one of Ann's favorite songs, one of the few she thought was perfect. We decided it would be the name of our next album. Some of the lyrics went "we're balanced together, ocean upon the sky." Moffa inspired the song, but those lyrics were also shaped by how Ann felt about Michael Fisher. For me, though, the "ocean upon the sky" line always felt like it was more about my relationship with Ann. We were balanced together, ocean upon the sky, always had been, and always would be.

Michael Fisher was jealous of the friendship of the three Connies, particularly when Sue and I took Ann away for extended periods. But when we came back to him with "Dog and Butterfly," he softened. "Okay," he said. "Keep doing that. Go write some more of those."

Roger had less of a problem with us going away, which I should have seen as a sign, but it was one of many warnings I ignored. We were so busy with our career, there was little time to sit down and talk about our relationship. The band always seemed to have a bigger life than our individual selves.

Dog and Butterfly came out in October 1978 and sold a million copies the first month. It stayed on the album charts for the better part of a year. It would eventually go on to be a triple platinum album, our fourth multimillion seller in a row. The album also earned us some of our strongest notices. In a rave review in *Rolling Stone*, under the headline "Silk onto Steel," Ariel Swartley called it our first "great album" and noted that

"Mistral Wind" was a stunner. The review ended, "Heart knows what it wants, and exactly how to go after it."

ANN WILSON

While we were on tour in 1979, we had a distressing phone call that shaded the success we were enjoying. Our dad was in the hospital, after a stroke. Mama hoped he would recover, but Dotes was never quite the same. Neither were we.

Even with his war wounds, Dotes had always been in generally good health, and he was so big and strong we thought he'd always be there. He'd had some dental work done that month and was taking antibiotics, when he got the flu. His regular doctor was out of town, and he was prescribed a medication that interacted with another he was on. He had a stroke and stopped breathing. Mama tried to give him CPR, but too much time passed before the medics arrived, and he'd lost oxygen to his brain. He spent several weeks in the hospital, but even with extensive physical therapy his teaching career was over, and so was his ability to walk. He'd spend the rest of his life in a wheelchair, unable to do much of anything for himself.

He was able to communicate to us, though his speech was difficult for anyone outside the family to understand. Underneath, we knew he was there. Once he got out of the hospital, he listened to music on headphones and soon learned to request a beer. With so few joys left for him, none of us wanted to deny Dotes his cups.

We initially brought in caregivers and tried to pay for full-time assistance, but Mama would only accept an occasional helper. She had imagined they would travel in their retirement, but that was not to be. She insisted she be Dotes's primary caregiver, and that became her life. Back in March of 1942, she had gotten his proposal letter on Marine Corps stationary—"This command loves your command"—and nothing, not even a stroke, was going to stop her from being faithful.

Dotes's accident wasn't something that was going to stop the Big Five from being a family, either. We took him to restaurants, and he attended our concerts whenever we played in Seattle. Few in the audience knew that the man in the wheelchair accessible area was our dad. For years we had a tradition of having dinners every Sunday whenever we weren't on tour, and those didn't stop just because of his stroke either. And every time a new album of ours arrived, we'd play it for him, our first fan. Dotes would listen, look at us, and give the big thumbs up. It was the only review that truly mattered.

Eventually, there were also troubles within the band. Nancy's relationship with Roger fractured when his philandering ways became more obvious. By that point, drugs were commonplace in the music scene and common among the members of Heart. Partying might have started out fun, but many decisions were made that didn't look so joyous in the next dawn.

It was embarrassing to everyone that Roger was so open about his dalliances, and it was particularly embarrassing to me, since he was with my sister. I was infuriated, not only for Nancy, but because it was his own incredible recklessness that made things get so out of control. If he was going to be an asshole, he should have been a private asshole, and not one in the middle of the whole band.

I loved Roger like family, but there was a basic misunderstanding we had with him. He didn't understand that when we wrote those lyrics about fidelity, and love, we meant them. A lot of people in the rock world, and even in our band, never paid attention to the lyrics. But when "Dog and Butterfly" spoke to the ocean and the sky, there was only one ocean in that song, and only one sky.

NANCY

The year just seemed to get crazier and crazier, as we toured behind our hit album. When the tour took us to New York, a promoter suggested we might want to check out Studio 54. "Can we get in?" I asked. "You can get anywhere now," he said. We soon discovered it was as decadent as we'd heard. There were secret rooms everywhere, with lusty stuff happening left and right. We were eventually led downstairs to private offices where piles of exotic drugs were spread out. It was the age when the music industry was shifting from the marijuana that dominated Seattle, into a world of cocaine and more. I turned down the offers. As we tried to leave the club, we literally ran into a completely wasted Liza Minnelli. When she saw our road manager Dick Adams trying to get us out, she threw her arms around him and said, "Hey, do you work for me?" He didn't, but being the good egg he was, he also got her a car before she fell over.

Not long after that we went to Japan for the first time where screaming hordes of teenage girls chased me everywhere trying to grab my hair as if it was a talisman to them, shouting, "Non-Sea." It was as close as I ever came to living out the scene in "A Hard Day's Night" when the Beatles are chased by screaming throngs of girls. When we escaped, we snuck into a department store and bought kimonos.

My relationship with Roger was transitioning, but Japan was a brief reprieve for us. Everyone in Heart partied in those days, but Roger partied more than anyone, and he was really rolling high that year. There were many nights during our relationship when all I wanted was a little peace and quiet, but I couldn't find it. He was hyper already and didn't need to medicate, but in Japan he couldn't find anything to medicate with, so his old self returned.

When Roger was sober, there we times when I felt a deep sweetness from him. He was always writing poems for me, though I never knew if they were strictly for me or for girls in general. His poems always had a feel as if they were written for "sexy girls that I like." He was simply unable to be monogamous, and after a time that made me move away emotionally.

That fall I developed a crush on our drummer Michael Derosier and told Roger I couldn't see him anymore. Roger had been unfaithful to me so many times that I felt justified in my feelings for Derosier, and vindicated. But it was the stupidest thing I have ever done—getting involved with someone else in our band, thinking Heart could still continue as a musical unit after that. It was ugly, and it got uglier still.

Roger did not take the news well. He was angry, hurt, and he told me that all the other women he'd been with hadn't mattered to him. None of that swayed me. I was completely infatuated with Derosier, and I wasn't with Roger anymore. We were a band of six including my sister, and in short order I'd been involved with two of the four men. When I told Kelly Curtis, he rolled his eyes. "This is so incestuous, it's crazy," Kelly said. "This has disaster written all over it." Kelly was right. I was now bunking with Derosier on tour, but anytime the entire band was together, it was uncomfortable for everyone.

Some of the tension between Roger and the rest of Heart was musical. We were under such intense pressure to keep cranking out hit albums that when a studio session didn't go well, fingers were quickly pointed, and usually at Roger. He was a brilliant live player, but when he had to play one part over and over, he often folded, particularly if he was partying. During one session for *Dog and Butterfly*, each band member had headphones on for playback on one song. Roger walked in late and examined how everyone had set their headphone mixes, and he became angry. "You all turned me off!" he said. It wasn't meant to be hurtful, but his erratic playing was confusing all of us.

I tried not to mix our professional and personal relationships, but I'm sure I failed. I know I wasn't a good friend to Roger in that period. I should have said, "take some time off, go work on yourself, and I'll be there to help you when you want the help." But I didn't say anything at all.

It all came to a head at one show in Oregon. Roger was clearly on something that night, and his guitar kept going out of tune. He later told *Behind the Music* it was heartbreaking for him to be with "this beautiful gifted person next to you, who is in love with the drummer." I know it was hard, but

I never understood how Roger, who was repeatedly unfaithful, could know anything about "heartbreak."

The show ended with Roger smashing his guitar. Backstage he threw part of the guitar at me, and it whizzed by, just missing my head. Roger later claimed that if he had intended to hit me, he would have, and that he was in control. From what I witnessed, he seemed out of control, and, at that point, so was our band.

I had left college to move to Vancouver to join Heart when everyone lived in one tiny house together and ate meals of brown rice as a communal family. Now our band was partying at Studio 54, smashing guitars onstage, and screaming at each other. Heart was falling apart, and there were times it seemed it was all due to my relationships.

A few days later, there was a band meeting where we voted on whether to kick Roger out of Heart. He had helped form the band, so we knew it was a serious decision. I was also aware that if we kicked Roger out, we were seriously complicating Ann's relationship with Michael Fisher. But Michael had been a leader who always taught us to put the whole of the band above any individual. In the early days, Michael Fisher might have insisted that he produce Heart, but he ceded that, knowing that Mike Flicker was a better choice. Michael might have insisted that he continue on as the band's manager, but he knew that for the good of his relationship with Ann we needed an outsider. So when it came to the matter of whether we should vote out Roger, Michael Fisher's stewardship was on all our minds.

The vote was unanimous, and Roger was out. Steve Fossen had been Roger's best friend for fifteen years, but even Steve felt it was best for Roger, and for Heart. Roger ultimately made it easier for all of us when he started telling everyone he was the one who had broken up with Heart because he wanted to start another band. And maybe he did. But in October 1979, Heart became a five-piece for the first time since I had joined.

■ ■ ■

My relationship with Roger was doomed long before I developed a crush on Michael Derosier, but my new relationship didn't last either. I always felt like I was chasing after Derosier, and I never got anything back. I had begun to feel the tick of my biological clock, and since Derosier had French heritage, as did I, I thought we might make beautiful babies together one day. He was tall, good-looking, and had a French last name. Those were hardly sane reasons to start a love affair, but my hormones were making the decisions for me then.

Even the physical aspect of our relationship was unfulfilling. Derosier had an obsession with cleanliness, and seconds after we were intimate, he would jump up to take a shower. Whereas Roger had wanted me naked all the time, Derosier made me self-conscious. He was more refined than Roger, but maybe a little too much. He was a bit aristocratic and had a lot of sarcasm, which always looks good on young people. But I was twenty-six the year we were together, and soon that aloofness made me think he was a snob. I was vulnerable, and all I got for my openness was pain. We were together a year before we broke up.

In the end, I felt like I had three strikes against me when it came to men. That next fall at Ann's annual Halloween party, it was Ann who came dressed like a nun, but the costume should have been mine.

With Roger's departure, there was the matter of what would we do to replace him in the band. Howard Leese ended up stepping into that role, though I took on a few more lead parts. I never seriously considered becoming our permanent lead guitar player, not because I couldn't play the leads, but because I loved rhythm guitar. It is the lost instrument of rock 'n' roll, the backbone which is rarely discussed. There is no Who without Pete Townshend's rhythm, and no Beatles without John Lennon's guitar. Rhythm guitar is what other guitar players notice, but few listeners do. Musicians appreciate rhythm players, even if the readers of guitar magazines don't.

But there was also a gender aspect to the decision. There were still so few female guitarists in rock that if I'd become our lead player, it would have shifted even more attention to our gender, and away from our songs. Lead guitarists are almost exclusively males with a strong alpha vibe. Guys are drawn to those flashy solos, although the heart of the song is always in the rhythm guitar. It's the stuff you don't necessarily hear, but that you feel, that makes a song work. If I'd played lead, Heart might have been too feminine because the lead player is like another singer, and in our band that meant counterplay with Ann. I was Ann's harmony, not her contrast. Heart's strength was always our yin and yang, how the feminine played off the masculine.

Howard Leese was also an exceptional player, and having him handle those duties opened me up to play piano on some songs. Many of our tunes were complicated, built like a Rubik's cube, and we had a difficult enough time with one less player onstage. We had gone through a major shake-up, and I'm not sure the rest of the band would have supported me as the lead player—plus I was just too timid then. It was the right decision, but five years later, I might have chosen differently.

In 1979, power was still a new concept to us. We were just beginning to feel confident about getting out from under the thumb of the Fisher kings. They were both very controlling, Michael Fisher in particular, and although they wanted only the best for us, the power had to shift if Heart was to go on. Since *Dreamboat Annie* the public had always conceived of Heart as my sister and me, even when we didn't think of it that way ourselves.

Before I joined the band, when Heart was a Vancouver club group, Ann would play until two in the morning, and then on the next day, she'd get up wash all the sheets, and make dinner for everyone in the group. Those days were no more.

SUE ENNIS

When Nancy and Roger broke up, the power in Heart shifted forever. Nancy and Ann hadn't really claimed it before, but with Roger out of the band, and Michael Fisher's influence on the wane, it was if they were hurled toward it. Heart had always been their band, but now they owned it in ways they hadn't before.

Nancy already had bought a couple of houses. When she and Roger broke up, she and I moved together into a home she had in Redmond. The house earned the nickname, "The House of the Rising Sun" after we went away for a weekend, and our house sitter trashed the place—it looked and smelled like a brothel when we returned.

The slow split with the Fishers also forever changed the personalities of Ann and Nancy. They had both inherited a sense that a woman's place is to support her man, her wonderful, elegant, warrior man, which is what they had seen their mom do all those years. And each of them idealized the men they were with, until they didn't anymore. For years they pushed themselves down to elevate their guy, and they quashed their own sense of self.

That started to change in "The House of the Rising Sun." And once it shifted, it never went back.

15

BLOWS AGAINST THE EMPIRE

The Wil-Shers come to an end. Elton's lyricist tries to seduce Nancy. The Wilsons finally get to meet "Joni." And Keith Richards can't be located, anywhere. . . .

ANN WILSON

The end of Nancy's relationship with Roger was a significant turning point for Heart, but another shift occurred just a few weeks later. We had begun working on the album we would call *Bebe Le Strange*. Since Roger had been a cornerstone of our sound, there were plenty who wondered, maybe some even inside the band, if we could still succeed.

We had a band meeting at the end of October to talk about preproduction with Mike Flicker. Michael Fisher was usually at these meetings because he was still running our sound and therefore was still a big part of the group. This time, though, Michael couldn't make the meeting. Someone in the band made a joke that implied Michael was running around on me. After the meeting, I sat down with Mike Flicker and our manager Ken Kinnear and said, "Michael would never do something like that." Ken just looked at me silently. Then he said, "Well, he is." Everyone in the band knew about it, everyone but me, Flicker and Kinnear told me. Years later, Flicker would tell me it was the worst thing he ever had to do in his career.

I asked Nancy. She said someone must have confused Roger and Michael, and that Michael wasn't like his brother. Michael and I were too tight, she said, living together, and traveling on tour together. It didn't seem there was time for an affair, other than when he went skiing, or when I went away to write.

I went home and confronted Michael. "Are you cheating on me?" The look on his face said it all. Michael believed in the principle of always telling the truth. It was part of the high moral standard he held himself to, though that standard apparently didn't apply to being faithful. "Yes, I was," he said. I asked if he was still seeing her, and he said no. Michael was very honest, even in his duplicity. I said, "Do you love her?" He said, "Yes." Michael tried to talk his way out of it, but this was one thing I didn't need to try to understand. We'd been together for nine years, and I thought we had built this beautiful, perfect union. For a time, maybe we had.

In six hours, Sue, Nancy, Lynn, and my mom moved everything I owned out of the house. I now lived with Nancy and Sue in the "House of the Rising Sun." We were suddenly just as we had been together in high school—three single women.

My songwriting muse had, in many ways, already predicted my break-up with Michael. Just a few months before, I had crafted a song called "Break," but it could just as easily have been called "The End of the Wil-Shers." I wrote it at the beach, and when I played it for Michael upon my return, I could see a light bulb going off for him that told him I was unhappy. There was no mistaking how boxed in I felt. I'm not sure whether the song was naive, or unaware, or gutsy, but it was one that I had to scream out and let everyone, even Michael, hear what was going on inside me. When you write an honest song, you often hurt people. "Break" was another example of the song writing me.

When we performed it live on our next tour, I would introduce it with sarcasm: "This is a very sweet and tender song. I can barely make it through this love song without crying." Part of it went: "The dust is gathering where I stand / Now I know there's a crack in this plan / After a while there just ain't no more magic, man / I got a need, I got to know / Give me the truth who is running my show / Tell them I'm sorry, but I just had to go / My patience ran out / I gotta run / Out of a habit that used to be fun / I just wanna break / Shake it, shake it, shake it off / Take off, break it off / Break, break, break me outta here."

The photo shoot for *Bebe Le Strange* produced my favorite album cover. The picture captured us at a moment after I had whispered a secret joke to Nancy. Both the music and the cover seemed to connect with audiences, and it became our fourth platinum album in a row, going to number five on the *Billboard* charts, and staying on the charts for half the year. *Little Queen* sold slightly more, but the success of *Bebe Le Strange*, without either Fisher involved, felt more our own.

Maybe it was our gallows humor, but we released *Bebe Le Strange* on Valentine's Day, 1980. The album also earned us some of the best reviews of our career. We wouldn't have wished our break-ups on anyone, but they helped create a juicy back story. "Healing a Broken Heart," one review headline read. Critics loved songs like "Down on Me," "Break," and "Even It Up," which were often cited as examples of us finding fire again. As a songwriter, seeing a critic quote a line you really felt, like "I don't want to burn it all, no, but this axe she, she got to fall," from "Even It Up" felt rewarding, as if I had connected with the audience.

One of the only publications that panned the album was *Rolling Stone*. Just a year earlier, female journalist Ariel Swartley reviewed *Dog and Butterfly* by writing about how that album represented "blows against the empire," meaning against the male-dominated world of rock. But when male Tom Carson tackled us a year later in the same publication, our music was now "cock rock without the cock." To Ariel Swartley, we were "fresh and welcome," but to Tom Carson our approach was "the same as on all previous Heart records: Mix together enough styles simultaneously, and maybe you'll be mistaken for an original." While different critics often have contrasting views, the number of times sexual organs were referenced in our reviews was truly extraordinary. In the *Rolling Stone Record Guide*, Mikal Gilmore wrote, "Take Ian Anderson and Robert Plant, endow them with mammaries, and you have the essence of Heart."

Though *Rolling Stone* panned the album, they still featured us on their cover that spring. The headline was lurid as usual ("Rock's Hot Sister Act"), but the article was a fair and detailed examination of our roots. The writer convinced me to take her back to my old high school, and to the house we grew up in. Our Lake Hills home was still empty, two years after our parents moved out, and it was eerie to visit. My mom was quoted about my break-up with Michael, and as usual Lou didn't mince words: "Michael used to walk her out every night [on stage]. I wonder who will walk her out now?" Nancy addressed our new singlehood by announcing, "We'll be each other's keepers." We had always had been.

Daisann McLane wrote the *Rolling Stone* profile and, thankfully, left out the usual references to our sex appeal. But the issue was not without a sensationalistic element. The photographer Annie Leibovitz had been assigned to shoot the cover. We were on tour in Biloxi, Mississippi, and Annie wanted to photograph us on the beach, as an update to the *Dreamboat Annie* cover. We arrived, and there were alcohol and drugs aplenty. As the shoot went on, she asked if we'd pull our shirts down a bit so she could get our collarbones. Then she asked us to pull them down farther, and we said no. Then she said, "Ann, your top is reacting with my lighter meter, so would you mind taking your top off?" I took my top off, and put a towel over me. Then she claimed the towel was messing up her light meter. Our tour manager Dick Adams was standing holding this big sheet so that no one else on the beach could see us. Finally, after Annie's nagging, I took the towel away. Though it was framed on the magazine so you couldn't see, in the photograph of us on the cover of *Rolling Stone* I'm topless. I'm not sure why I agreed to it. Maybe it was the rebel in me, maybe that fact that Annie had shot so many artists I'd respected, or maybe I just wanted to get off the hot beach.

The topless pictures were not enough for Annie Leibovitz. In the middle of the night, there was a knock on our hotel room door. It was Annie with a bottle of vodka, a tray of cocaine, and her camera gear. I should have just gone back to bed, but I let her in, and we had another photo session. She was obsessed with getting us naked, but the best she got that night was us looking tired in rumpled clothes.

The next day, I had second thoughts. I had allowed myself to be sexualized, and it was exactly the opposite of what Heart represented. I think part of it was that because Annie was female, I trusted her not to objectify us, which had been a mistake.

We asked Annie to destroy the film. She refused. A behind-the-scenes brouhaha ensued, and the matter ended up in court. Though a judge wouldn't order the photos destroyed, he decreed they be stored in a safety deposit box that could only be opened with two keys, one in Annie's possession, and one in ours. She couldn't get to the photographs, and neither could we.

My topless photos are still there today in that safety deposit box. I've long ago lost the key.

NANCY WILSON

I never took my top off for Annie Leibovitz. Maybe I remembered when my mother slapped me when Lynn's husband shot me naked all those years ago. But though I wasn't actually naked on the *Rolling Stone* cover, the photo might not have been the best decision for a newly single woman. It was the first time since we'd been stars I'd been single, and there was unwanted male attention in every direction. Some of it even came from legends.

The same month as our Annie Leibovitz photo session, we were invited to Elton John's birthday party at Le Dome restaurant in West Hollywood. We had met Elton a couple of years before, backstage at one of his shows. I thought about telling him the story of how when I'd first moved to Vancouver I had to beg on my knees for the money to buy a scalped ticket to his concert, but I was so nervous that all I managed to do was to shake his hand. We heard someone call Elton "Eo" backstage that time, and Ann named her next dog Eo after Elton.

The invitation to Elton's birthday party was a dream come true, but the event itself was surreal. Elton had purchased an interest in Le Dome, and he wanted to show the restaurant off, so the lavish spread of food and drink was fit for a king. The party was filled with movie and music stars, including Sean Connery, who impressed us more than anyone else. The news that I was single seemed to bring attention from all sides, and I had two of the Eagles, Don Henley and Glen Frey, flirt with me that night. But the one gent who was attached to my side all night was Bernie Taupin, almost the guest of honor considering he was Elton's songwriting partner.

Elton, of course, couldn't have been more gay, though he wasn't out at the time. Bernie, however, was extremely interested in women, and that night extremely interested in me. He may have been married at the time, but that certainly wasn't stopping him. Bernie was convinced that getting me high was the key to seducing me. He repeatedly pulled me into the bathroom, telling me he had to talk to me about songwriting. Then he'd pull out of a vial of cocaine from his suit pocket and dump it on a mirror. I kept saying, "no thanks," but Bernie kept tapping the glass vial to get the coke to come out. Only he'd already snorted all the drugs, so his vial was empty. We'd sit down, and two minutes later he'd be pulling me into the bathroom again, having remembered he had another vial in his other pocket. Only it turned out that vial was empty as well. This went on until Bernie had pulled empty vials from every pocket of his suit. He still tried to seduce me. It was always hard for me to know how to handle such delicate situations, as I wanted to be polite—maybe one day Bernie and I would write a song together, I thought—but I was not a pushover.

Thankfully Kelly Curtis grabbed me. "We have to get out of here," Kelly said. Kelly was having romantic problems of his own. Elton's manager, John Reid, had a crush on Kelly, and though Kelly kept insisting he wasn't gay,

John Reid wasn't listening. Reid had been Elton's boyfriend for the first part of his career.

When Kelly had just been a neighbor kid I met because I gave him guitar lessons in my suburban home, I'd taught him how to play Elton's "Sixty Years On." Just ten years later, we were in this fancy West Hollywood restaurant, at Elton John's birthday party, with the "Sixty Years On" lyricist trying to seduce me with cocaine, while Kelly was putting off the advances of Elton's lover. It was a shift in our lives that seemed almost impossible, but it was true.

As Kelly took my hand, we fled the restaurant looking like two actors in a horror movie running from a monster. But our movie had a twist: As we ran onto the Sunset Strip, a giant billboard loomed over me. It was the cover of *Bebe Le Strange*, and my own face, fifty feet high, was looking at me, as if to ask, "What are you really running from, Nancy?"

We flew out of Los Angeles the next day to start the *Bebe Le Strange* tour, which would be our biggest yet. We played all over the world, to sold-out crowds in almost every market. We came off the tour feeling exhilarated, but that soon dissipated in December 1980 when John Lennon died. It destroyed Ann and me both. John's death was the greatest tragedy that ever happened to rock 'n' roll, but it felt personal to us, and I couldn't help but think of us sitting in front of Maudie's tiny black-and-white television watching the Ed Sullivan show in 1964. Because we were women, we'd always had increased security concerns. John's death changed the way we interacted with fans and increased our isolation, and that of every rock star. Ann and Sue Ennis wrote the song "Angels" a few days after John was shot. It was Ann's way to reclaim some of the love that during that month seemed gone forever.

We had begun 1980 still in relationships with the Fisher brothers, with a unified Heart, and awaiting John Lennon's great new solo album. We ended the year with grief on all fronts.

ANN

We spent most of the next year on tour, but eventually I put thought to buying a new house. Both Nancy and I had purchased cabins on the Oregon Coast as getaway retreats—across the street from each other—but I needed a more permanent home base. While I was on tour I asked Kathy Cox, a real estate agent and the wife of our good friend Frank Cox, to look for places for me. She called a few weeks later to say she'd located the perfect spot: A hundred-year-old former hotel and speakeasy that had been renovated into a three-bedroom house. It had a ballroom that was perfect for parties, and the house was very private, tucked into a hillside in a leafy Seattle neighborhood. Kathy said it would sell quickly, and that I needed to buy it immediately if I wanted it, but I still had weeks to go on the tour. The solution was that she videotaped the home and sent me the tape. I bought the house based on a video without ever seeing it in person.

When I first drove up and saw my new house, I knew it was home. It felt like me—roomy, beautiful, complicated, full of soul, always needing attention and love, but giving it back when you lit a fire or lit a candle. Some of the neighbors thought it was haunted because of its former history as a speakeasy and brothel, but it felt like a family house to me.

A few years after I bought my home, Nancy bought a new house herself in the Seattle area, but she opted for a farm instead. It had stables, horses, and a long gravel road. Eventually, she'd buy up the houses around her farm, and our parents and Lynn would live next door. Nancy had always wanted to be like Neil Young and live on a big farm, and her dream had come true. She wanted a family compound, with all of us near. Living on a farm never appealed to me—one of the many differences between us.

Neither of us had much time to enjoy our homes, though, because the demands of touring were ever present. That year we played on three continents and did almost two hundred shows. Our manager then decided we would barnstorm Canada in a salute to where our careers began. Only this time, he rented a C-130 transport plane plus a 737 jet to carry the band, seventy-five thousand pounds of equipment, and all the crew for three dates in three days. It was almost as crazy as us driving on snowy back roads in a van trying to avoid moose, but it was also a remarkable contrast to how we used to tour.

In October, we took a brief break from that madness to play the "Bread and Roses" Benefit in Berkeley. When Mimi Farina, one of the organizers had approached us, we immediately said yes, both because it was a good cause, and because Paul Simon was on the bill. The night before the show, there was a dinner at the Claremont Hotel for the performers. We were looking everywhere for Paul Simon, when Mimi Farina came up to us and said, "Joni wants to know if she can come over and say hi." The look on Nancy's face was priceless: Finally, she thought, she was going to meet Joni Mitchell. Mimi goes away and comes back with Joan Baez, her sister, and "Joanie" to her friends. Joan Baez was another idol, and she sang with us at the concert the next day, but Nancy couldn't hide her disappointment.

The day after the Bread and Roses show, Heart opened up for two dates with the Rolling Stones in Boulder, Colorado. It was one of the biggest stages we had ever played, and even the backstage was a maze of sorts. Even as the opening act, there were places we weren't allowed to go, but you could see these rooms filled with hundreds of bottles of every kind of liquor imaginable. When we performed, we played on the giant tongue. At one point during the show, Nancy came and whispered to me, "I can't believe I belong here!"

Just a few minutes after we came off stage, all full of adrenaline and covered in sweat someone came and said that Mick Jagger wanted to meet us. We had no time to look great for Mick. He came in, sat down, and said, "You guys were really great." And we were like, "No, you are." It was so strange listening to Mick Jagger talk about me. I could barely understand what he was saying since all I could think the whole time was, "*Mick Jagger's* lips are moving." We told him how much the Stones meant to us, and he said, "Wow, God, thanks," and it sounded like it really mattered to him.

Mick looked perfectly relaxed, until he brought up the topic of Keith

Richards. "We're supposed to go on in thirty minutes," Mick said, "and I have no idea where Keith is. He hasn't shown up. No one has seen him all day." Every so often a roadie would come in the room, whisper something in his ear, and Mick would repeat, "They still haven't found Keith yet." Eventually Keith was located, and Mick left us for the stage. The first time either we, or Mick Jagger, saw Keith Richards that day was when Keith walked onstage.

In late 1981, we began to work on our next album, which we planned to call *Private Audition.* We'd parted ways with producer Mike Flicker and had hired Bob Ezrin, who had done wonders with Pink Floyd. But Ezrin pulled out, so we brought in Jimmy Iovine, and did a few sessions with him, before that fell apart, as well. We finally finished the record with the band listed as producer, but the resulting album suffered as a result.

When it came out in June 1982, *Private Audition* sold only 400,000 copies, far fewer than our previous albums. And while our concert tickets were still selling well, even in a recession (we had the eighth highest grossing tour of the year), our singles hadn't performed. "This Man Is Mine" only hit number thirty-three in *Billboard.* In show business, if you are not gaining ground, your critics quickly sharpen the knives.

On our fall tour, one of our biggest problems was our opening act John Cougar (this was before he went by Mellencamp). While we were on the tour, his single, "Jack and Diane," hit number one. He was still a newcomer, and we had almost ten years of hits under our belts, but a few weeks into the tour he showed us how he earned the nickname "the little bastard."

He told a journalist one day he "felt sorry" for us. He said he planned to "be extremely nice to [the Wilsons], and not in any way, shape or form throw it up in their face. You know, 'my record's doing better than yours,' that sort of thing. . . . I'm going to downplay my success around them. Who knows? Maybe next year they'll have a number one record and mine won't even go top ten."

UNITED STATES MARINE CORPS

Corvallis, Oregon
30 March, 1942

rom: J.B. Wilson Jr., Pfc., USMCR.
o : Miss Lois Mary Dustin, Alpha Delta Pi,
Corvallis, Oregon.
ubject: Request and orders.

1. It is requested by this command that you comply in all respects with the wishes of said command concerning matters of close attachment and eventual marriage.

2. It is further requested that you enter into a state of relaxation concerning the matter of this command's deep feeling for you.

3. This command loves your command.

4. You are herebye ordered (Paragraph 908, Section 17, Article 3b, Landing Force Manual)to remain on active duty with your present organization and commandant. This command will absolutely not tolerate any evidences of lack of"esprit de corps".

5. The foregoing are herebye directed and ordered for immediate carrying out, ~~barring the exingencies of the service,~~ within reason, at your discretion.

By order of,

JBWilson Jr.

Pfc., USMCR.,
Commanding.

ANN: To our mother, this letter from our dad asking for her hand in "eventual marriage" was the most romantic thing she owned.

(1942, courtesy of the Wilson family archives)

NANCY: At the Hannah Dustin statue in Haverhill, Massachusetts. Hannah was the original axe woman of the family.

(2008, courtesy of Julie Bergman)

ANN: In the Hannah Dustin family tradition.

(1980s © Roger Ressmeyer/ CORBIS)

ANN: Nancy and me in our parents' car in Taiwan. Our dad was stationed all over the world, and we followed.

(1956, courtesy of the Wilson family archives)

ANN: On a camping trip with "the Big Five" plus one more. Mama, Nancy, me, Lynn, Grandma Dustin, and Dotes.

(1956, courtesy of the Wilson family archives)

NANCY: This is Ann and me, performing for our friends.

(1966, courtesy of the Wilson family archives)

NANCY: Our mom and dad on the way to a Marine officers' ball. He was dashing; she was gorgeous.

(1960, courtesy of the Wilson family archives)

NANCY: Another one of "the Big Five": Ann, Dotes, Mama, Lynn, and me — this time with our dog Trumpie. Taken when we were living in Bellevue, Washington.

(1970, courtesy of Roger Keagle)

ANN: Doing some serious hanging out in a hotel room with Nancy in the early seventies.
(Courtesy of the Wilson family archives)

NANCY: One of our first Heart promo photos, from the early seventies.

ANN: The promo photo for one of my first bands, Hocus Pocus. Back row: Nick Etchoe and Chris Blaine. Behind me, Gary Humphries and Roger Fisher. Next to me is Steve Fossen. I would play with Fisher and Fossen for the next decade.
(1972, courtesy of Roger Keagle)

ANN: The first photo of Heart, in Vancouver, B.C. Left to right: John Hannah, Roger Fisher, Brian Johnstone, me, and Steve Fossen in the early seventies.

ANN: Michael Fisher and me on a train in Japan.
(1976, courtesy of Kelly Curtis)

ANN: Backstage with Queen in 1978.
(Courtesy of Kelly Curtis)

ANN: First class! *Bebe Le Strange*, 1980. (© 2012 Neal Preston)

NANCY: On the wing of our first plane. Roger, Steve Fossen, Howard Leese, Michael Derosier, Ann, and me. (1979, courtesy of Kelly Curtis)

NANCY: March 25, 1980.
am on the way to Elton John'
thirty-third birthday party a
Le Dome. A billboard with ou
album cover on it looked dow
over the restaurant
(Courtesy of Kelly Curtis

ANN: Backstage before a show in 1980.
(© 2012 Neal Preston)

NANCY: Me, Ann, and Winny on the farm in Washington.

(1980 © Roger Ressmeyer/CORBIS)

ANN: Here are the Connies: me, Sue Ennis, and Nancy. "The Mighty Three."

(1980 © Roger Ressmeyer/CORBIS)

NANCY: Hamming it up with Bernie Taupin.
(1980 © Roger Ressmeyer/CORBIS)

ANN: At Studio 54 in New York City with our great friend Kelly Curtis.
(© Marcia Resnick 1979)

NANCY: I had begged for tickets to see Elton John just a few years prior. Now we were hanging out at Studio 54.
(© Marcia Resnick 1979)

NANCY: Shooting some footage of our fans in Orlando, Florida. We were on tour with Cheap Trick.

(1980; © 2012 Neal Preston)

ANN: Here we are in 1980.

(1980 © Roger Ressmeyer/CORBIS)

NANCY: In 1979 our dad had a debilitating stroke, but his love of music never waned. He always loved to hear us play.

(1984, courtesy of the Wilson family archives)

ANN: At Cher's show at Caesars Palace.

(1981; courtesy of Kelly Curtis)

NANCY: Just before "I do."

(1986, courtesy of the Wilson family archives)

ANN: Bad Animals!

(Late 1980s)

NANCY: At the Bridge Show Benefit in 1993. Graham Nash, Art Garfunkel, Paul Simon, Eddie Van Halen, Neil Young, Sammy Hagar, and Bonnie Raitt.

ANN: The Lovemongers meet Hilary Clinton in Portland, Oregon. Me (with my daughter, Marie), Nancy, the First Lady, Sue Ennis, Frank Cox, and Barb Hoyt (kneeling).

(1996, courtesy of Eric Johnson)

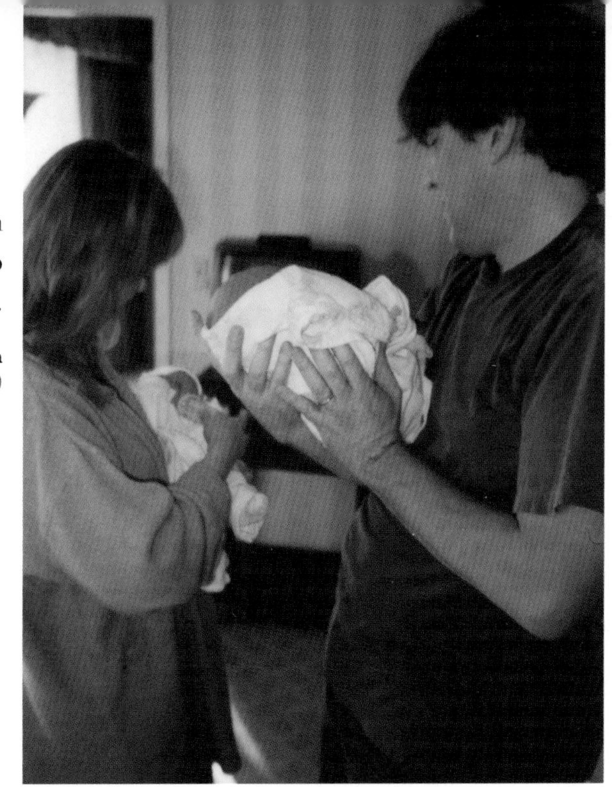

NANCY: With Cameron and our two boys, Billy and Curtis.

(2000, courtesy of the Wilson family archives)

ANN: My family on tour: daughter Marie, me, Nancy, Gretchen Gove, my son, Dustin, and our sister, Lynn.

(Early 2000s, courtesy of Eric Johnson)

ANN: Onstage together.

(2011, courtesy of Sue Wood)

NANCY: Starting a new life with Geoff. Geoff, me, Kelly Curtis, and Ann.

(2012, courtesy of S. Anderson)

The next day, he came to us backstage and did the opposite. "Seeing as how your album is a turkey, and mine is a hit, care to swap places on the tour?" he asked. We told him no, and reminded him that some shows had sold out before he'd been announced as an opening act.

But ultimately, John Cougar was the least of our worries that year. We had other problems brewing, as tension within the band had reached the boiling point. Heart was fracturing, and where we once had been a unified family, everyone now had a contrasting opinion on every decision. The internal differences had been easier to overlook when we were a multi-platinum band, and piles of cash made everything easier, but as album sales stalled, debates erupted about who contributed to songwriting, to the live show, and who didn't. There had been more cohesion when Roger was still in the group because his behavior was always such that most eyes were on him. Our partnership model was no longer working when it came to band decisions, as *Private Audition* proved.

It wasn't an easy choice, but we decided it was time for Michael Derosier and Steve Fossen to leave. Derosier wasn't an original member of Heart, but he'd been with us since our *Dreamboat Annie* tour and was a cornerstone of our sound. But ever since Derosier and Nancy had broken up, his presence in the band was uncomfortable for everyone, and the tension between him and Nancy was obvious. Fossen had been in Heart longer than anyone, dating back to the earlier incarnations as the Army and White Heart. Steve was also the only bass player I had played with for over ten years, but he was dissatisfied with many things by then. Howard Leese would stay, and he immediately began to help us audition new players.

That next year we would add Mark Andes, formerly of Spirit, on bass; and Denny Carmassi on drums, who had played in Montrose. There was even a new look onstage for Heart: With the additional of Mark Andes, we now had more blondes than brunettes for the first time. We hoped it would prove fortuitous.

16

HEARTLESS

A Wimbledon winner chases Nancy. A Van Halen gets his first guitar. Ann finds romance with the original young dude. And both women become "Coffee Achievers" for a huge payday. . . .

NANCY WILSON

After Derosier and I broke up, I found myself single and adrift. I'd gone out with two members of our band, but dating within our cocoon had proven to be a terrible idea, and I swore it off. Still, we lived in such a bubble that meeting someone on the outside also seemed impossible.

There was plenty of male interest toward both Ann and me, but most of it was from inappropriate fans or pushy celebrities who thought seducing us would be a notch on their bedpost. Our road crew insulated us from many of these suitors, but not all of them. There would be so many gifts and flowers left for us that one of our crew drew a sarcastic cartoon about them. In the first panel, a starry-eyed fan says, "I'm in love with Nancy Wilson. Those eyes, those lips, those golden-blonde tresses. Maybe she'll marry me." In the next panel, a delivery guy asks where to put the diamonds. A roadie responds, "Just throw them near the Porsche, or the Rolls, or the furs that someone else sent." It was an exaggeration, but only slightly.

Though we loved that our fans felt a connection, many notes we received were too personal, and, at times, disturbingly sexual. Ann's were usually fans who felt some intimate soul connection with our lyrics, whereas mine saw me as a pure sexual conquest.

One of the most aggressive men who chased me was the professional tennis player Vitas Gerulaitis. He had won a double's trophy at Wimbledon and didn't like to lose. He came to a few of our shows and tried to talk his way backstage, but the crew kept him out. But at one show he got through, and as he approached my dressing room, a roadie told him not to go in because I was getting dressed. That didn't stop Vitas, who tried to open the door. Our road manager Dick Adams tackled him. It took Dick and another roadie to throw out this "all muscle" tennis pro. They told him he'd be arrested if he came back again.

There were many celebrities whom I enjoyed meeting, including Larry David, who later created *Seinfeld*, and Michael Richards (Kramer!). Both were in the cast of *Fridays*, a late night ABC comedy show that for a time got higher ratings than *Saturday Night Live*.

We played on *Fridays* a few times. A cast member named Bruce Mahler made a major play for me. Mahler is best known for his role as Elaine's over-sharing Rabbi Kirschbaum on "Seinfeld." He kissed me one night after we had all gone to dinner. It was not what I wanted, although years later it would be an interesting story to say I had been kissed by the rabbi from *Seinfeld*.

One night when we were in Los Angeles at a *Fridays* taping, Kelly Curtis said he had someone to introduce to me. "Nancy, meet Cameron Crowe. He's a writer." Cameron and I spoke only a few words to each other, and I didn't get much of an impression because he was so shy. He seemed a little pale and pasty, as if he had been indoors writing for months.

Kelly and the photographer Neal Preston, Cameron's roommate, kept asking me if I wanted to meet Cameron again. Kelly set up a dinner with Cameron and a few other friends and asked if I would go. I agreed.

The dinner was at the West Hollywood restaurant Le Dome, where we'd gone to Elton John's birthday party. Kelly saved the seat next to me for Cameron. Cameron never came. I ate my dinner next to an empty chair.

That was my first date with the man I would eventually marry and have children with.

Kelly and Neal kept on me about Cameron. They explained that he was shy like me. A few weeks later we were on *Fridays* again, and Cameron came. He was charming, and cordial, but also hysterically funny. He made me laugh the way no other man had. And at that moment, I decided I wanted this man in my life.

After the taping, we went our separate ways, but a few days later a letter arrived from Cameron. He said he might like to see me again. He mentioned a magazine piece he was working on about Joni Mitchell. He later told me that when he put that letter in the mailbox, he knew it was a commitment. My parents had instilled in us that the pursuit of excellence in any artistic form was something to be cherished; Cameron had that. A fantasy developed in my mind about what a relationship with Cameron might be like. I imagined sweet letters like this would come almost every day.

We started hanging out. He'd gotten some sun playing softball since the first time we'd met, and he looked good. We didn't go on any traditional dates. We just hung out and traded mix tapes. Cameron was living from project to project and was barely able to pay his rent, though he was working on a movie script. I was a rich rock star, and he was a starving artist.

After I'd been seeing Cameron for a couple of months, I wrote a letter to a friend about him. It showed that my break-up with Derosier was fresh enough I still referenced that as well. It gives an insight into how ready I was to fall in love. Part of it read:

> I'm on a night flight heading into L.A. on my way to visit Cameron Crowe. Some love is seemingly just not put together in the stars, but I believe rare moments do occur where stars align just so, and two magnetisms combine into one conscious and unconscious force. But that's also my damned outdated idealism again for you. I can't help it. It's my lot in life to believe love can really exist and even last—survive our wonderful world of today. It's in the stars for some, but not for many. I've been disenchanted for a long time, way too long, and finally had the courage to call it off. So now I've been lately visiting this guy Cameron, who's the ex–*Rolling Stone* journalist who also did the Joni interview, and a few other heavies. He says Joni is brilliant, and extremely wary of "the press," like any smart person learns to be eventually. He's just finished a book about the high school experience, which was supposed to be called *Stairway to Heaven*, but it had to be changed since some new book about pyramids was just released by that title. Now it's called *Fast Times at Ridgemont High*, which he hates, but the company chose (he has only partial artistic control). It should be released as a movie by next summer with some new Heart material for part of the soundtrack. I'm also looking forward to the possibility of meeting Joni on one of my visits, but it could be a totally intimidating experience. I, for now, will survive off many amazing firsthand stories from Cameron (who's just twenty-four, and a "whiz kid," who's more sensitive than many women I've known). We've become addicted to each other's conversations, and we have big fun. It's such a new thing for me to know a guy who is actually this great.

I was ready to fall in love. And I did. Totally. It completely took me away.

Sue Ennis once observed that my romance gene was "deadly." If so, I got the gene from my mother, and so did Lynn and Ann. But everyone in my family would agree that I got it the worst. And when it came to Cameron, I got it bad.

▪ ▪ ▪

Cameron asked if I wanted to do a walk-on in *Fast Times at Ridgemont High*. I had no lines for my "Beautiful-Girl-in-a-Car" role. I wore a pink sweater, drove up in a convertible next to Judge Reinhold, and gave a flirtatious smile.

My relationship with Cameron didn't stop male attention from other celebrities, though. That same year Ted Nugent tried to woo me. He came to our dressing room wearing a vest made of the hides of animals he'd killed and skinned. He picked up my dog Wombie, thinking he could win his way to my heart by impressing my dog. But Wombie didn't like the smell of the hides, or of Ted, and started growling and barking. Ted Nugent, the big-game hunter, retreated from a little dog.

At one hotel, we met Eddie and Alex Van Halen. Over the course of a few hours, they had a Kamikaze-drinking contest, followed by a cocaine-snorting fest. Once they were good and loose, they got into a fistfight. Moments later, they were hugging each other and falling down, saying, "I love you so much, man." They would cycle through this pattern every hour.

Eddie and Alex let it be known that if Ann and I wanted to sleep with them, they would be amenable to that. Their concept was two brothers with two sisters: Instead of the Wil-Shers, we could now be the Wil-Halens, except they wanted us in one bed. It wasn't the only time we had that offer, and as with every other request, we turned it down.

Talking with Eddie that night, he said he really admired my acoustic playing.

"You should play your acoustic guitar onstage," I said.

"I don't own an acoustic guitar," Eddie said.

Eddie Van Halen—at that point one of the greatest living guitar players, when he wasn't punching his brother in the face—didn't own a single acoustic guitar. I couldn't believe it. But he swore it was true.

"I'm going to *buy* you an acoustic guitar right now," I announced.

I went and woke up our road manager. He told me that at midnight instrument stores were closed. "Then let's give him one of mine," I declared. We went to our gear truck, and I took my favorite Ovation. I walked up to Eddie's room and handed it to him.

He started crying. "That's the nicest thing anyone has ever done for me," Eddie said.

I went to my room to sleep. But at seven in the morning, my phone rang. It was Eddie.

"Nancy, Nance, sweet Nancy, sweetest Nancy," he said. He was obviously still high and had been up all night. "I wrote a song for you on my Nancy-Nancy acoustic guitar." He put the phone down and started to play. He was only a few rooms down the hall, so I could also hear him through the walls.

The song went on for many minutes and was truly amazing. It was more of a suite than a song, but it was beautiful. Eventually, the line went dead—I think Eddie had passed out. I don't know if he ever played the song again, or even if, when he sobered up, he remembered anything about the night, except that he and Alex didn't manage to take the Wilsons to bed. But it was the best thing I ever heard Eddie Van Halen play. I only wish I could hear it again.

ANN WILSON

In the fall of 1982, we were on the road when our manager Ken Kinnear called to tell us there was a full-page story in the *Seattle Times* about how our tour was "bombing." It ran under the headline "Heart Trouble" and said that *Private Audition* was a "flop." It ended with the suggestion that our career was over, we'd soon be a "local band," but that we should "be thankful [we] had five good years." Ken read parts of the story to me on the phone, but not all of it. Ken was planning the highly unusual step of running a full-page newspaper ad to contest the many factual errors.

We had never received a bad review in Seattle before, and this article panned a show we'd done there a few months prior. Under a picture of me, the caption read: "The usually spirited Ann Wilson was so reserved that the show never caught fire."

Patrick MacDonald wrote the piece. He often lazily cited the reporting of rock critics from other cities, instead of doing his own legwork. The piece on us had some of that, but also cited "unnamed" sources. I shrugged it off. I tried to tell myself it came with the territory.

But then I talked to my mother, and she was distraught. She told me the article blamed my weight for our career struggles. I was stunned.

I finally managed to read the whole article. One section read: "The audience . . . may have been shocked by Ann Wilson's appearance. Often cited as one of rock's most attractive sex symbols, she had gained considerable weight, emphasized by a tight–fitting black dress that covered her from neck to knee. Perhaps because of that, the usually high-spirited singer was reserved to the point of almost hiding behind other band members. Without her spark, the show never caught fire."

There had been comments in the press on my physical appearance from the moment our career started. As a woman in the male-dominated world of rock 'n' roll, I knew it came with job, but it wasn't easy to live with. Whether it was criticism of how much I weighed, or lustful comments about how "sexy" I was, they were always disturbing because they weren't about our music. When I was the thinnest in my life, during the first few years of Heart, there were times I was still called "chubby" in the press. You couldn't be too thin, too young, or too good-looking if you were a woman in music. The standards were entirely different for any man in rock 'n' roll. John Bonham could go onstage with a three-month beard, unshowered for weeks, fucked up, shirtless, and have the confidence that the only thing that would be written about him was how he played the drums.

As a woman, I lived in a different world. It was a world where I was judged constantly, on and offstage. Patrick MacDonald was right. I had gained weight, although not much at that point, but the show he reviewed was often cited by fans as our most energetic that year. He had the right to think our show sucked, but even if it did, was it fair for him to blame it on my "tight-fitting black dress"?

The article stung because it had upset my mother. But there was another reason it burned: Although I didn't know many of the rock critics who threw barbs at us, I knew Patrick MacDonald. He was far more overweight than I was or would ever be. Here was an overweight man who felt it his job to suggest that because I'd gained weight—at that point, only a few pounds—I wasn't good at my job. Furthermore, MacDonald had written a piece just a year before in which he described me as "slim," though even that story mentioned that I had a "tendency to gain weight." It was true; I did have struggles with my weight, but Patrick MacDonald had more struggles than I ever would. The hypocrisy was fucking heartless.

I wish I could say this was the last time my mother ever had to feel that kind of pain. I wish I could say that article, or others like it, successfully shamed me into losing weight and or getting the figure that male critics wanted me to have, and, that many times I wanted to have myself. But my issues with weight had been very complicated my whole life.

They would remain so.

After my relationship with Michael Fisher ended, it was some time before I began dating again. I told *Circus* that year, "The rock 'n' roll life isn't designed to keep couples together." Fans might have thought that I'd joined a convent, but I was far from chaste. I did learn to keep my relationships private because as a high-profile woman in the music industry, I was under a microscope. I learned that lesson the hard way.

I had watched the guys in the band have many casual relationships on the road, so I decided to try it as well. Though I missed Michael tremendously, there was a freedom in being single, and I decided to take advantage of it. I told one magazine that year "I went from my father's table to my boyfriend's table without knowing what it was like to be alone. So in one sense, it's fun to be single for a while." I decided to explore what that meant. After one concert, the whole band went out to a club to unwind. A good-looking young guy began talking to me. We eventually ended up in my hotel suite for a wild night of passion. It felt great to be alive again in that way.

The next morning, I was going in and out of sleep when I felt a stirring on the other side of the bed. Then I heard my bedmate on the phone.

"Hey, you are not going to believe who I am laying here next to," he whispered into the receiver. "Yep, the hottest woman in rock 'n' roll, Ann Wilson of Heart, is in bed with me right now." He was trying to speak quietly so as not to wake me, but the person he was talking to on the phone was extremely loud, and I recognized this voice: My new paramour was on the phone with the morning shift DJ at the biggest radio station in town. It was a painful way to find out that the groupie-star dynamic was not gender neutral. If a woman had called up the station to announce she'd slept with Steven Tyler, the jocks would have said, "you and twenty other women in every city, big deal." But for a male fan to bed Ann Wilson was an accomplishment, and worthy of bragging about on the radio, apparently. Humiliated, I threw his clothes at him and kicked my groupie out of my room.

I had a few other brief road romances, some with members of the crew because they were discrete, though they never lasted long. But my first real relationship after Michael came with another singer. There was no power imbalance in this, except for the fact that the man, Ian Hunter, was our opening act.

I had long been a fan of Mott the Hoople, and watching Ian the first night of our tour I could see he was an incredible musician. After the show, we looked at each other, and an intense sexual thing grabbed us both. I never even asked if he was married, and he never mentioned anyone else, but soon Ian was in my suite every night. Kelly Curtis found out when he had to knock on my door with an emergency and found us in the throes. The next day Kelly said he wasn't sure whether he was more surprised by our romance or the fact that he'd finally gotten to see Ian without his trademark sunglasses. The glasses were Ian's barrier to the world, and when he took them off, I knew I was seeing the real him.

Kelly's emergency was one of many we had that tour, which apart from my romance with Ian, was perhaps the craziest, wildest jaunt we ever had. I was single, and drinking a lot, and Kelly was often my co-conspirator. Fire extinguishers would be set off in hallways, televisions would be tossed off balconies, and much alcohol was consumed in hotel lobbies. That night when Kelly interrupted me the emergency was real: Kelly was in the process of being arrested after he had driven the motel's riding lawn mower into the pool and covered it with all the recliners in the patio. I had to pay for Kelly's bail. It was one of the many times we ended up with an IOU from Kelly.

It was a few days later, after everyone sobered up, that Kelly told me Ian Hunter was married. That was against everything I believed, but the power of my own unguarded sexuality had me by surprise. It was my first visitation into sexuality without someone leading the way, and it consumed me. I realized that when I had sung previously about "going crazy on you," I hadn't understood the half of it.

When the tour was over, we parted, but I couldn't stop thinking about Ian, and I missed him. I tried reaching him at other venues he was playing at, but failed. Finally, I tracked down his home phone number. I was now the "other woman," a place I never thought I'd be, particularly considering the pain that infidelity had caused Nancy and me, but I decided I was going to call Ian at home and tell him how I felt. If his wife answered the phone, I was going to tell her we were going off together.

I looked at the phone for a long time. I never dialed. Ian's number was pinned to my wall for years, before I finally threw it away.

NANCY

In the wake of *Private Audition*'s sales, our record label put pressure on us to "rock" on our next album. In 1983, we recorded *Passionworks* in Los

Angeles with producer Keith Olsen. The sessions were awash with cocaine, used by all of us, but especially by Olsen. He was hitting his bottom, and he immediately went into treatment when the album was done.

Everything we did in those years had a white sheen of powder over it. There were only a few people on our crew, or band, who resisted. Cocaine was sprinkled over the albums, the videos, and our lives. Cocaine stripped all the humor out of our music. The videos we made were completely without intentional comedy, but were so serious they had an almost comedic feel.

The label wanted us to bring in outside writers to produce hits, and we acquiesced. We did a cover of the Jonathan Cain song "Allies," and it was released as the first single from the album. It only went to Number 83.

I began to wonder if Patrick MacDonald's "Heart Trouble" article hadn't gotten it right and we had truly outlived our expiration date. Only a handful of bands had ever been able to have careers that lasted for more than five years, and we were three years past that.

That tour still did well, however, even though it was accident-prone. Howard Leese sprained his ankle, Ann broke her arm, and even a guy in our opening band Kansas broke a bone. We nicknamed it the "Crash and Burn" tour because of those mishaps, but that could have described our career at that point, too.

Our second single, "How Can I Refuse," only went to number forty-four on *Billboard*, but it became a staple of AOR radio and helped the album sell better then its predecessor. But even though *Passionworks* stayed in the charts for twenty-one weeks, our record label was disappointed.

After seven albums, and with over twelve million records sold, CBS Records dropped us. We were without a label for the first time since we were a struggling band on the Vancouver club scene.

Early that next year we were offered to appear in a coffee commercial for a fee of one million dollars. It was an incredible amount of money, but also an incredible sell-out. With multiple homes, a large crew, and a big payroll, we felt we needed it. We flew to New York and filmed the thirty-second "Coffee Achievers" commercial on a soundstage in Queens. It wasn't even our music in the background; it was "Hold on Tight" by ELO. David Bowie, Kurt Vonnegut, and Cicely Tyson had also taken the big paycheck, and they appeared in the same commercial with us. It was really bad. It might have been the biggest mistake in our career, but thankfully it wasn't on the air for long.

In early 1984, Ann and I went to see *This Is Spinal Tap* at a cinema. With the cocaine, the sleazy "Barracuda"-like promo guys, the multiple drummers, and the unethical record labels, it felt as if we were watching a documentary about our career. When I walked out of the theater, the first thing I said to Ann was "Ouch."

I had no idea at the time the second act of our career was about to begin, and it would be an even wilder ride.

17

LEAVE IT TO CLEAVAGE

A new manager, new record label, and new direction lead to corsets, smoke machines, and gold records. "True Blue Lou" keeps a love story alive. . . .

NANCY WILSON

By the middle of 1984, our "Crash and Burn" tour was over, and it felt like so was our career. We did what most entertainers do when things languish: We fired our manager. Ken Kinnear had been with us since 1975, and he'd taken us far, but we were without a label, and, in some ways, without direction. We hired HK Management out of Los Angeles and were set up with a five-foot-two Englishwoman named Trudy Green.

We thought that a woman manager might better relate to us. We were entirely wrong. A journalist once asked Trudy what a nice girl was doing in this business. Her response: "I'm not a nice girl. You can't afford to be a nice girl in this job. You've got to be a shark." That we understood and respected, but Trudy had more testosterone than most men we worked with. Her favorite expression was, "Sooo sex-say," as if she were seducing us like a skin magazine photographer. Trudy was obsessed with breasts, and every video or photo shoot we did that year emphasized cleavage.

Our in-band nickname for the tour we launched that year was the "Leave

It to Cleavage" tour. For the crew laminate pass that year, they used a photo of Ann and my cleavage side by side. Beautiful, voluptuous, natural breasts were a Wilson family endowment, but we had no idea the Pandora's box we were opening by putting that on our laminate. It was a joke to us, but it seemed to make the almost all-male crew smirk constantly.

We weren't naive, but we were lost and no longer trusting our gut. We wanted to please Trudy because we believed that she could right our ship. Any resolve we had left dissolved once we began shopping for a new label, and we struck out. We went to five different labels and were rejected by each one.

Capitol Records was interested, but only if we were willing to cover songs written by others, or if we would cowrite with hit factory songwriters. We agreed, reluctantly, and signed with Capitol. The joke Ann and I made was that we delivered "songs written to order as you require them." Some of them, as Bernie Taupin once wrote, were songs written "with bitter fingers."

Capitol brought in cowriters and appointed Ron Nevison as producer. He was brash, arrogant, and highly opinionated. He had had a lot of success making pop records, but he'd also been the engineer for Led Zeppelin's *Physical Graffiti*. Capitol originally had only hired Ron to produce a few singles, but once we met with him, we decided he was the guy to do the whole album. We were ready to have a strong producer with a vision, even if it wasn't always a vision we shared.

In one of our first sessions he told me, "The acoustic guitars are so old-fashioned and out-of-date. Can we lose those?" My acoustic was my muse, my wheels, me. Still, I said, "Sure."

ANN WILSON

Before we began working on our first Capitol album, I was convinced to sing a duet with Mike Reno on "Almost Paradise" for the soundtrack to the movie *Footloose*. I didn't want to do it, but I felt I had to. I flew to Chicago for the session, and in my hotel I cut my wrist on a broken mirror.

At the emergency room, I refused painkillers while they stitched me up. It was an era of hard partying, but I had an ironclad rule that before a session or concert I was always completely sober because I never wanted my voice to be compromised. I sang the session in pain. When the track was released, it went to number seven on the charts, my biggest success in years.

When it came time to do the album, there were intense debates between Trudy Green, Capitol's A&R head Don Grierson, Ron Nevison, the rest of the band, Nancy, and me about what songs to include. Many demos were traded back and forth. Some songs we had to be convinced to try, while others were rejected outright because I couldn't feel them.

"Never" was one of our best experiences because we cowrote it with Holly Knight. It was one of the few times, along with "All Eyes," where our songwriting was just as important as the hired talent. We didn't write "If Looks Could Kill." It originally had been written for Tina Turner, but she had passed on the song. We grabbed it up, and it worked.

"What About Love" had a more difficult birth. Nancy disliked the demo so much that when it was first played, she got up and left the room. But Ron Nevison kept at us, telling us the demo was just "notes on paper to be worked with." "You guys have the best fucking voices in music," he said. "Don't worry about what the demo sounds like, because you're going to sing it *your* way." We trusted Ron, and he was right.

"What About Love" was one of the first tracks we cut in the studio, and one of the first the brass at Capitol heard. Don Grierson told me that as he played it to a conference room of suits, many of whom had been reluctant to sign us in the first place, the song won them over. "You just positively killed that," Don said. When I complained that I didn't write it, he said, "No one in the audience will know that." We trusted Don, and when we finally played the song in concert, he was right. "What About Love" became, and remained, the showstopper of our live set.

We had reluctantly agreed to try out material from other songwriters, but some of them were great songs. "These Dreams" was a gem that Ron Nevison brought to us. His manager had handed him a cassette that contained two songs by Bernie Taupin and Martin Page, "We Built This City," and "These Dreams." The first song went to Jefferson Starship, but Ron had grabbed "These Dreams" thinking it would work for Nancy. It was really a song Nancy could have written herself.

NANCY

Bernie Taupin told me later "These Dreams" had originally been presented to Stevie Nicks, but Stevie wasn't considering new material then. Ron Nevison didn't have to work hard to convince me to do it. I knew it was a great song, and being an Elton John fanatic, I loved anything Bernie did.

I did have to fight to do the song, though. A couple of band members complained that it didn't sound like a Heart song, and I had to fight with Capitol because not everyone was behind the idea of me singing this ballad. The song had trippy words, but they seemed like my words.

We had decided to record the album in Sausalito, so we'd be away from the influences of Los Angeles. During the sessions, we received a letter from the family of a young fan named Sharon Hess, who was dying of leukemia. She had only a little time left, and one of her last wishes was to meet us. She arrived at the studio on the day I was recording the first vocal run through of "These Dreams." Sharon was this feisty twenty-two-year-old who was courageously fighting this horrible disease. It was also very emotional having her in the studio and seeing such a young life facing death. I had a bad cold that day, and my voice was cracking when I had to hit the high notes of the chorus.

Sharon fell in love with "These Dreams." It was a transcendent, ethereal song, and it touched her as it had touched me. We cut the final vocals a couple of months later, and my cold was long gone. At first Ron Nevison joked that I needed to "get sick again" to sing it, since my healthy voice didn't have the rawness of the first run through. He convinced me to allow him to use the original where my voice cracked. It wasn't perfect singing, but it added emotion.

On the album notes, I decided to dedicate "These Dreams" to Sharon. Every time I sing it, I think about her. She died only a few days after we finished the final mixes. She was buried wearing a Heart T-shirt and cap, and with her favorite guitar in her arms. It's just the way I'd want to go out.

We had trouble coming up with a title for the album once we were done. Capitol had an idea: We could just call it *Heart* since our band name had never been an album title. It was what many groups did on their debut record. With a new label, and a new sound, in a way *Heart* was also a bit of a debut. We didn't love the idea but we went along with it. The album was completed in the spring. At the start of June we held a listening party in Seattle. We had no idea what to expect. The album could be a rebirth, or the final nail in the coffin of our career. I told one reporter that if it didn't pan out, "we were probably going to have to do something else." It was make, or break.

Jimmy Page happened to be in town, and someone from the label dragged him to the listening party. He was really messed up that night, and it was hard to see one of my biggest idols barely able to stand. It gave the whole evening an ominous feel. But in the end, the crowd loved the album.

The same month as the listening party, "What About Love" went out to rock radio. It was a hit. Within a few weeks it crossed over and charted on the pop charts, and became our first top ten hit in five years. When the album was released, it quickly went up the charts. It would go on to sell over five million copies in the next year alone.

Just a year before, Ann and I had been adrift in our career, without a record label. Even I had questioned if Heart had passed our expiration date. Our first success had been so rooted in the Fisher brothers, in the original line-up of the band, and in the seventies. We had wondered if we ever would break free, but when *Heart* became our biggest album ever, it felt like we had new life without baggage.

Just a year earlier, John Cougar had suggested that we'd be smarter to become his opening act. Cougar, now going by Cougar Mellencamp, also had a huge record in 1985 with *Scarecrow*, which I thought was his best. But when I followed the *Billboard* album charts that fall, a small amount of satisfaction came from the fact that *Scarecrow* never went higher than number two.

It was always right behind *Heart*, our first number one album.

That August, while we were in Los Angeles filming the "Never" video, our mom wrote a letter to a friend about us. Reading it years later, it was fascinating to me that even when we had a number one album, my mom was still handling many of our business and financial affairs, and working with our fan club. She often answered our fan mail. Her letter gave insight into the madness of my life, but also the sweetness that was our parents' relationship. It read in part:

"Any mail sent to Nancy's house has slight chance of ever being read by anyone. She is so very seldom at home, and the piles of mail and papers become so high in her absences that she usually brings them to me in a box to process and collate for her in order of importance and time value.

"Meanwhile John and I continue to live our full and growing life; hating the disability, slugging it out with wheelchairs and all of that, but still making our own small waves in our own direction. All is well."

Our mom had wanted to travel, but instead she was full-time nurse for our dad. We helped get paid assistants, but Mama was adamant that she was going to do most of the care giving. Her meticulousness was also in the letter. She chastised herself on its sloppiness: "I just noticed I'd left out some letters in words. 'If neatness counts, its curtains for Lou.'" She also plugged our album, as if getting one more person to buy it might save the day for Ann and me.

That was "True Blue Lou." It was no exaggeration to say she was our biggest fan.

ANN

The runaway success of *Heart* surprised our family, the record label, and even us. Few bands had ever managed to have a second act in a different decade, but we did. I was thirty-five years old when *Heart* came out, and Nancy was thirty-one. We were hardly teenyboppers in a business that was dominated by youth.

Still, the renewed success came at a cost. We had made a deal with the devil, in that we were singing songs we didn't write, and the devil had been right: They *were* hits. The success put us on a slippery slope. We'd had our first number one album after following the advice of others. And that was a path we stayed on for some time. Things got dizzier, tighter, and more surreal until after a while our feet weren't touching the ground. We were hanging on a meat hook.

In the mid-eighties, labels believed making videos for MTV was integral to success. In the next few years, we made nearly a dozen videos, each one more ridiculous than the next, and every one a small step away from what Nancy and I wanted to be. As the hairdressers and costume designers came in, the image we projected to the world was less and less our own. Apart from an obsession with cleavage in the videos, we sported stiletto heels and hairstyles that had to be carefully coiffed. I turned to Nancy during one shoot and asked, "How big do you think our hair can get?" However big it was, the video producers wanted it bigger. When our natural hair wasn't big enough, they added extensions. If we didn't look like porn starlets, the directors weren't happy. In one video, Nancy rode a horse (better to bounce her breasts). Our joke about the videos was that the name of our band was now "Heart, Featuring Breasts." We were constantly complimented on our excellent boob jobs, when we hadn't done any work and didn't appreciate the fact that our bodies were being marketed as part of our branding.

We always had an appreciation for fashion, and there was a sense of costumery to our videos that was occasionally fun. But the images on the screen became bigger than the real people, and it was the video images fans wanted from then on. If we didn't look like that carefully constructed video clip, with corsets and hair and boobs, people were disappointed. It was hard to move, or even to breathe in those outfits, and it was particularly difficult for Nancy to play guitar when she was sent onstage with stiletto heels. In the seventies, I often wore ballet slippers onstage, and they helped me remain fluid. Many of our seventies outfits were natural fabrics, often made out of suede, which moved with you. But eighties' clothes were synthetic and had no give. Additionally, our hair was teased up so high it often felt as if we were wearing helmets onstage. Our hair was so heavy that, I felt weighted down by it. I had turned into a singing statute.

Most of the songs on the *Heart* album became hits first on radio, and then the videos built on that. But as the album continued to have legs, and as MTV's power grew, videos became more important than radio. We spent a fortune on the videos. Though the record label advanced the costs, they ultimately came out of our royalties. Budgets mushroomed upwards of hundreds of thousands of dollars for a three-minute clip. And as the directors, stylists, choreographers, and hairdressers increased, we'd be on a set with a hundred people all telling us what to do. It was no longer our show. Our own videos increased our objectification a thousand percent, and it was our fault. "Purple Rain" had been a huge influence on the video industry, and we looked more like Prince's band than the Heart we once had been.

I found myself on many video sets listening to dozens of people talk about me as if I wasn't even there. They talked about how to make me look younger, prettier, but mostly they talked about how to make me appear thinner. It became an obsession with everyone involved with our video productions. One day I overheard a video producer remark, "If only we just had Ann's face and Nancy's butt, we'd have the perfect woman." My younger self would have walked out of the studio upon hearing that, but by the era of MTV excess, those comments came so often, I just sat and listened to them insult Nancy and insult me.

As with many who struggle with weight, the ten pounds I had tried to lose the previous year had turned into twenty I'd gained. I wasn't rail thin, but I was fine with my body. Still, everyone around me acted as if I was betraying them when I gained a pound. Management, executives at Capitol, and sometimes my own bandmates told me that it was unacceptable. The crazy thing was, the more successful we became, and the more we toured, the harder it was for me to make healthy choices. Once the album hit, we didn't have more than two days off for almost a year. We were in the studio, on video set, or onstage every single night. I never ate much until after the show, and then, in the wee small hours, I ate and drank too much as a way to cope with the stress. Having a number one album only made my struggles with weight more difficult.

Critics began to constantly review my weight rather than my singing in our performances. And even when they did review my singing, the fact that I had gained weight made them shift the metaphors they used for my voice. One review linked both stereotypes: "Where she once strolled the stage as a raven-haired siren, now Ann Wilson was a shrieking gargantuan who sang histrionically."

My weight had nothing to do with my singing, with our songcraft, or with my ability to move onstage, but in the MTV-dominated industry, our video directors in particular acted as if how I looked was the only challenge Heart faced as a band. They shot me standing on a box in one video while the camera looked up at me; in another they used expensive postproduction effects to shrink the image size. There was so much smoke in another video, which they thought would take five pounds off me, that it took them six hours to get the "air" right before we were even asked to come to the set. It was crazy, and it increased into a spiral of dysfunction.

The shackles of video didn't just bind me: My sister also felt the pressure. That ratcheted up considerably in early 1986 when we shot a video of "These Dreams." Though blessed with a different physique than me, Nancy felt *she* wasn't thin enough. The stylists around us constantly compared me to Nancy, but Nancy was herself compared to every fashion model or younger video starlet on MTV. One video director told Nancy that everything about her was perfect except her "huge thighs." He told her, "you really have to do some work on those thighs." Every aspect of our bodies was open to discussion, or improvement, on the video stage.

On March 22, 1986, "These Dreams" hit number one on the *Billboard* pop charts, the first Heart single ever to reach that pinnacle. We were elated. And no one was more elated than Nancy. In the wake of that success, many asked if I was jealous that it was a song my sister sang that became our first number one. The truth was I *had* been disappointed that "What About Love" and "Never" hadn't reached that mark. The success of everything Heart did, though, was shared by Nancy, me, and the rest of the band. It was never a competition, no matter what people on the outside thought. We shared the same blood harmony, and almost every song Heart recorded included a vocal mix of both of us somewhere in the song, as did "These Dreams."

When "These Dreams" had first surfaced, I had tried to sing a verse of the song, but it didn't work for my voice. Later on in our career, I did sing it a few times when we did karaoke in a bar, but it never was right. Once onstage, when we were bored and trying to shake things up, I tackled it again, but I had to change the key to get through it. It just didn't break with my voice the right way.

It was Nancy's song from the start.

As 1986 continued, our tour never seemed to end. In ten months, we had played 148 concerts, plus countless days of travel, interviews, or video shoots. When we arrived in Japan that summer, we were greeted by hordes of fanatical fans wherever we went.

On tour that year, we felt imprisoned by the fame that a hit album and videos had created. Before MTV, people only knew what we looked like from our album covers and concerts, and it was still possible to live a normal life. We could go out, go to the gym, or go for a walk in a city on the tour.

But a hit video, and a chart-topping album, made it virtually impossible for Nancy and me to go anywhere without being swarmed. As soon as we'd play a show, we'd retreat to our hotel room and order room service. We no longer called them hotel rooms—we called them "our cells." The guys in the band had enough anonymity that they could eat out, or go see another band. But even when Nancy and I went to the hotel lobby, there would be fans, paparazzi, or people who wanted something out of us. Our road managers were afraid for our safety and hid us under assumed names with guards at the doors of our suites. We also had death threats that year from crazies, and we had to have bodyguards.

It was a time when we should have been enjoying our success the most, and yet we were living the lives of recluses. Many celebrities before and after us have felt this isolation. I was grateful for our success, but living this way was very hard. Our only post-show entertainment was watching old movies in our hotel room. In our luggage, we carried a VCR, VHS tapes like *Gone with the Wind*, needle-nose pliers, and wire cutters. We learned how to splice our VCR player into any hotel television. Other bands would get huge bills for the televisions they threw off balconies. We had damage bills, too, but ours were for cutting the wires to our hotel televisions so we could hook up a VCR.

When I recorded that very first single in 1968, "Through Eyes and Glass," I had waited in vain to hear my voice on the radio. Now my voice was on nearly every station, and a video of me in a tightly bound corset was on MTV every hour. I had thought fame would make my life bigger. Instead, it had shrunk my world.

I found myself with my sister, stuck in a hotel suite with our needle-nose pliers and our favorite VHS tapes, alone.

18

JUNIOR'S FARM

A *Gone with the Wind* wedding competes with million-dollar offers. A sheen of white powder blows through the halls. And the Gherkin Pickle Wagon awakens even the dead in Germany. . . .

NANCY WILSON

It was while we were in the middle of our crazy world tour that I began planning my wedding to Cameron Crowe. We had seen each other over the previous year whenever we could. Cameron had sold a couple of scripts, but the only thing he had directed by then was a Tom Petty music video and documentary called *Heartbreaker's Beach Party.*

It wasn't easy planning a wedding while on tour. We decided on a low-key affair to be held at Ann's Seattle house, but my work life kept conspiring to complicate things. The *Heart* album stayed in the top ten for six months, and offers kept pouring in for us to play that summer. Only a few days after we had settled on a wedding date, we got our biggest offer ever for the date I had planned to marry. It was nearly twice as much for just one concert as our dreaded "Coffee Achievers" commercial. I turned it down. We had made a lot of money the previous year, and we didn't have to say yes to everything. Saying no to that show was one of the most satisfying things I ever did.

Our wedding was July 27, 1986. It was not a big affair, but in the tradition my mother had taught us, it was elegant. We held it at Ann's house, with an outdoor sit-down dinner beforehand. The ceremony began at eleven p.m., when the only light came from hundreds of white candles. Ann was obsessed with *Gone with the Wind* at that point, and no electricity was used during the ceremony. We scattered six hundred roses—in my favorite color, "dusty rose"—around the house. Garlands of flowers lined the staircase, which looked like something Scarlett O'Hara would have waltzed down. White champagne was served before the ceremony, and pink after. Ann, Lynn, and Sue were my bridesmaids. On Cameron's side, there was Neal Preston, Joel Bernstein, and Cameron's mother and father.

We moved inside for our vows and said them before Reverend Lincoln Reed from the Congregational Church. Cameron used Dotes's Marine sword to cut the wedding cake.

There wasn't much time for a honeymoon. We spent the night in a Seattle hotel, and then headed to the Oregon Coast for a week. On our honeymoon, we wrote a bunch of humorous songs together for a project we were calling "Blue Seattle." It seemed like the start of a romantic and creative partnership. I had spent so much of my life walking on the Oregon beach, but now I was taking the same journey with a husband.

We didn't make a big deal out of our marriage in the press. Unlike some entertainers, we never marketed our relationship. We had separate careers in slightly different industries, and we didn't want to become a Hollywood power couple.

Being married didn't stop the machine of Heart, and mere moments after the honeymoon we were planning our next album. In a month we were in intensive band rehearsals. In some marriages, my career would have been a problem, but Cameron was also constantly writing, so the separations weren't an issue. He was working on the script for *Say Anything* during this time.

Heart's last record had been so successful that we decided to have Ron Nevison return as producer. He and Capitol had been searching for more songs for us, and having a number one album helped pull in several A-list writers. Diane Warren contributed "Who Will You Run To," and Holly Knight and I wrote "There's the Girl." Since the big singles last time had been from outside songwriters, it was harder for us to get our own songs considered. Still, we contributed "Bad Animals," written with the band, and "RSVP" and "Easy Target" we crafted with Sue Ennis.

The lyrics to "Bad Animals" reflected where our group was at in those days: We'd all be hung over, strolling into the hotel lobby with sunglasses on, and we moved like a pack. We never were more unified as a band, but it was sad that partying was a big part of why this was true. But the lyrics to that song were also a great example of how something good comes when you least expect it. Ann and I had gone down to the beach to write but had wasted the day instead. We were driving home and nearly to Seattle, when we began writing the song in the car. "We're bad animals, bad animals, got to swim upstream, got a rebel seed." We were screaming the lyrics out the window of the car as we wrote them on Interstate Five.

That year we also started reaching out for writers we liked, and we brought in a Canadian songwriter named Lisa Dalbello. She had a song called "Wait For An Answer," which she had recorded on her own album, and we covered that. The song required Ann to sing through five different keys, quite a feat.

Lisa came out to my farm and we worked on a few tracks with her. It was one of the most rewarding relationships we had with another female songwriter—other than Sue. And when we sang with Lisa, as we did on "Lucky Day," a song we included on the *Strange Euphoria* box set, there was a sisterly blend. It was one of the only times you could ever hear us singing on record with another female, other than our sister Lynn.

"Wait For An Answer" ended up making the album, and so did two songs by Tom Kelly and Billy Steinberg, one of which would end up as our biggest single ever.

ANN WILSON

Tom Kelly and Billy Steinberg were one of the most successful songwriting teams of the eighties. They had written "True Colors" (Cyndi Lauper); "Like a Virgin" (Madonna); "Eternal Flame" (the Bangles); "I'll Stand By You" (the Pretenders); "I Touch Myself" (The Divinyls); and dozens of other big hits.

We were still resistant to the idea of outside writers, but Ron Nevison told me Tom sang as well, and that helped soften me. Once Ron played a cassette of "Alone," I needed no further convincing. I hadn't written it, but it felt like my song. When I sang, "the night goes by so very slow," in "Alone," I didn't have to act.

My sister was never one to mince words. "That is soulful stuff," Nancy said after hearing me run through it. "You speak through that song. The song and your voice really shake hands." Sue Ennis once told me that "Alone" was "more Ann Wilson" than any song in our catalog we didn't write ourselves.

When it came to recording "Alone," Ron Nevison, whose name we had started to sing to the tune of "Bad Medicine" because it rhymed, and because his dictatorial style increasingly clashed with ours, did his magic. He used extreme dynamics between the verse and the chorus, and our excellent drummer Denny Carmassi made the song more dramatic. Ron asked me to delay a moment before singing the chorus after the second verse, and to ad-lib. I wasn't sure what to sing, so I let out a scream. It ended up being exactly the primal emotion the song needed to make it rock. I'd been singing Led Zeppelin songs for years, and now I had my own Robert Plant moment on record.

We named the album *Bad Animals*, a joke on our band, and our pets. It was released on June 6, 1987, a D-Day of sorts because it would determine whether our last album had been a fluke. "Alone" flew up the charts to become our second number one single. It stayed on top for three successive weeks and became our biggest single ever in the U.K. "Alone" ended 1987 as the second-biggest-selling single that year by any group.

The success of "Alone" also gave us something we didn't have going into the release of the *Heart* album two years before. We now had a number one single *before* our tour started, or our album was out. We were following up on success, and not building to it.

We flew to Europe in May 1987 for the start of our tour. All the dates had sold out, including three nights at Wembley. Nancy and I decided we needed a week of vacation before the tour began, so we went early, and we brought along Sue Ennis.

Our intention was to have the three Connies go on a "Magic Mystery Tour" to Beatles landmarks. We spent a couple of days in London, and then drove up to Liverpool. We spent a day sightseeing Beatles neighborhoods, but found our hotel creepy, so we headed to Scotland. We were convinced we could find Paul McCartney's farm. We hadn't discussed what might happen when we got to Paul's door, but with the three of us acting like schoolgirls, we were sure Paul would be happy to see us.

We had no plan, and no hotel reservations. Sue leafed through road maps while Nancy took the wheel of our rented Mercedes, and I provided commentary. We stopped the first night in an inn on the side of the road and drank scotch and ate haggis. The Scottish moors seemed free of the influence of MTV, and we were anonymous for the first time in years. We were one of the biggest bands in the world that year, but at the Headley Hall Country Inn, we were simply three silly American girls stalking Paul McCartney.

We knew Paul's farm was on the "Mull of Kintyre," which had been the title of his 1977 single, but we soon found that navigating Scotland by song title was problematic. Our Connie joke was that we were looking for "Junior's Farm," another McCartney song, but that farm was in Tennessee.

We discovered that the only way to avoid the long drive to the Mull of Kintyre was to take a ferry to the end of the peninsula. We didn't have enough days to make the drive and still make our first show of the tour. After an arduous journey we came to the dock, only to find that the ferry had been cancelled due to bad weather.

The closest we got to Paul McCartney's farm was standing on the ferry dock and looking toward the Mull of Kintyre. We knew Paul was there on the other side somewhere, someplace, somehow. We had made it all the way from the teenage bedroom of our Bellevue, Washington, house to the Scottish coast, but Paul McCartney remained beyond our reach.

The U.S. leg of the *Bad Animals* tour started in Denver in August, and we were then on the road for much of the next two years. The album would go on to sell over three million copies. We sold more tickets than ever, but our isolation on the road continued. Whenever we had more than a day off, Nancy would fly home to Cameron, and I would usually stay with the band.

For a brief while, I took up with a bad boy named Fred, who looked a little bit like Paul McCartney. I liked him because he was a gentleman who opened doors and escorted me places. Cocaine was a constant on that tour, and Fred always had a supply. Fred was wealthy and had his own butler named Master Bates. Fred claimed the source of his wealth was from Oklahoma oil, but everyone else around me thought it was from dealing drugs, something I failed to see, or acknowledge at the time. It was a road romance for me, during a time when I was open to casual sexuality. Cocaine also affected my ability to make smart decisions.

Our relationship fell apart when Fred decided he was going to make a film about Heart. Because of our relationship, Fred had shot a lot of footage. Soon, everyone around me began to freak out that Fred had been given too much access. Once I asked him to give us the film that was the end of Fred and me. It was only then that I realized how shady Fred had been. He died a few years later from drugs. It's amazing to look back and think that I made it through that time in one piece.

Cocaine continued to be an issue in my life. I had never suffered from stage fright before, but I began to occasionally have panic attacks onstage. If anything went wrong with any aspect of the tour, I thought it was my fault because I'd gained weight. If we had a bad review, it would end up on my seat on our bus, left by either someone in the crew or the band. Cocaine was a very powerful appetite suppressant, and too many times I thought it would help cure my problems, and I used too much too often. It made me paranoid, and, at times, physically ill. But I kept at it.

There was so much pressure. When I went onstage, everything was on me, and every eye in the audience was looking at me. I felt I was being silently critiqued on every single song. I couldn't forget any words. Because I felt self-conscious about my weight, I felt I had to prove to myself that I could nail every single high-powered note.

At one show, the panic came upon me all of a sudden, and I lost my focus. I had mixed cocaine and champagne the previous night, and, though I was sober onstage, the mixture had made me sick. I was freezing cold all of sudden, and the only way I was able to continue was because of sheer muscle memory. If I hadn't been onstage, I would have stopped to do breathing exercises, but at that moment, that wasn't possible. What came over me was an uncontrollable surge of adrenaline, pure fight or flight. I wanted to flee from the humiliating criticism, and from the pressure to personify the MTV sex goddess image in real life.

It couldn't have been more than five seconds that I was frozen, but it seemed like a lifetime. But my sister knew me and sensed something was off. She stepped forward, and began a guitar solo that wasn't planned. In that moment, I was able to gather it together and move forward. It didn't happen again that night, and knowing that Nancy had my back at all times gave me the ability to continue with the tour. But it happened many other times on the tour. Nancy learned to look over at me to see whether I was out of control, and she would make goofy faces, or start walking like Gumby, which would immediately bring the attention to her, so I could compose myself. She was trying to make me laugh, so I could catch my breath.

As the *Bad Animals* tour continued, the panic attacks began to happen earlier in the day, before I ever walked onstage. It finally got to the point that they would begin the instant after my wake-up call in the hotel. I would stare at the ceiling and think, "I'm supposed to be onstage tonight, and I can't possibly do it." But I did it.

We had a number of threats that year from crazed fans. Some insane rumor had started that we gave our royalties to Charles Manson, while another said we were in a witches' coven with Stevie Nicks. Those stories pulled out kooks, who felt the need to try to contact us. We began to travel with a bodyguard whose job it was to keep us safe, but that increased our claustrophobic existence.

We never did a single drug until after the show. No one in our band died or overdosed. For that reason, and because all the other bands of the era seemed far more out of control, I thought we were holding it together. But drugs took us away a bit. That is the truth. Most everyone in the band struggled, and we all went far, but I went the furthest.

When the *Bad Animals* tour finally ended in late 1988, I imagined that with rest and peace, I would clean up, and things would improve. I was mistaken. Things got worse. With all the time in the world, and plenty of money, I became the most famous customer for Seattle's cocaine dealers, who were more than happy to deliver, and bring me bottles of pink Dom Perignon as well. They would collect their money and leave me with my drugs and my booze.

It was only years later, looking through a pile of old clippings, when I noticed a 1979 interview I'd done that so clearly illustrated what some of my views were back then in my youth. "Rock and roll contains both beauty and filth," I said. "What Oscar Wilde says—and this is especially true for a rock and roll artist—is that an artist feeds on the fight between vice and virtue. That's true for me. I hate and love the vice, and I hate and love the virtue. I like sin, and I like to get high. I have very untraditional views of motherhood and the family unit. In the world today, that's considered vice."

But as an adult woman, my days of vice were coming to a close, and my family was not about to let me stay in the filth any longer. Nancy and Sue announced that we were all going to Hawaii for a Connie vacation that month. That sounded like fun, but also a great place to party. When we all three sat down on the plane, I asked who had brought the party favors. "There is no more party for you on this trip," Nancy announced. "You're getting off the party." Over the course of our vacation, they helped me get my life back in order. It wasn't an intervention, just more a wake-up call from my two best friends. I was still drinking. It also didn't mark the last time I ever did drugs, just the end of the downward spiral.

NANCY

Part of the reason we didn't question the amount of drugs during the cocaine-infused eighties was because most bands we toured with were worse than us. Some of our touring mates would have roadies whose only job was to line-up bottle caps full of blow on the back of the stage, so they could stay high during their entire set. We never did drugs onstage, and never before a show.

For a brief time earlier that year, Stevie Nicks became our best friend. She came to one of our shows, and she and her girlfriend just sort of became part of our entourage, traveling with us. She brought along a stack of fashion magazines, and her drawing books. We were partying hard that month, but Stevie, with her Courvoisier and blow, outdid us.

When the tour got to Arizona, Stevie invited us to a party at her house. Her home was filled with all these pictures of her, like it was a shrine to Stevie Nicks. We spent most of the night digging through her closets trying on clothes with her. It was fun to be girls together, and her closets were full of millions of shawls and colored tights wedged into teeny drawers. We spent hours there.

When it came to drugs, though, we couldn't keep up with Stevie. She had a system where she could do various substances, and then do other substances to help her sleep. We never knew how to do that, and, at some point, we had to leave to sleep.

But during those years, we did lose track of time, and often, of our behavior. On a scale of one to ten, with ten being Keith Richards, we squeaked in there at the peak as a five. We were half of Keith. Okay, on the Keith scale, maybe we were just a three, but that was plenty awful enough.

In 1989 we began to work on *Brigade*, our third album for Capitol. We switched producers, but the overall concept was the same. The label thought we needed to rock harder, so in addition to the Diane Warren song "I Didn't Want to Need You," they insisted we do a song Mutt Lange had written called "All I Wanna Do Is Make Love to You." It was originally intended for Don Henley, but he passed. The demo was country.

Ann positively hated it. "What does that even mean?" she said during our first run through. She did sing it, and we begrudgingly turned it into a Heart song. It ended up being one of our most controversial songs, even getting banned in Ireland and a few other countries. The label was right about it being a hit, though: It went to number two on the *Billboard* charts and helped made *Brigade* our third multi-platinum album in a row.

But the glory of chart success increasingly came with a price. We did "All I Wanna Do" on the *Brigade* tour, but retired it after that. When years later, I brought it out again as a tour idea, Ann said she'd try it in rehearsal. She got as far as the first verse, but after the line about "lonely boy in the rain," Ann stopped singing and flagged down the band. "Ah, for fucks sake," she said. "I can't do this. I'm grossed out by this song." It was the first time in our entire lives I saw her stop any song once she had started it. Ann has to "be" the song to sing it, but by *Brigade*, we were struggling to figure out how to be ourselves in a multi-platinum world that we didn't make. Still, Ann always possesses a perfect instinct for what's authentic to our band. There have been many times I was truly grateful when she steered us away from artistically compromised situations.

Our favorite part of *Brigade* was the outfits we wore on the album cover. We called them our Cadillacs because they cost almost as much as a new car. We had them made to our specifications, and to look a bit like *Sgt. Pepper's*. But they were also an homage to our dad, who was the one Wilson who had truly been in a brigade.

Another hit album meant another giant tour. We started that tour in Germany, but before rehearsals we were already burned out. We were in the town of Bremen, and our first morning we were woken at the crack of dawn by screaming. We couldn't figure out where it was coming from, but when it happened again the next day, we discovered it was the horse-drawn "Gherkin Pickle" wagon. It went through the streets every dawn loaded with beer-swilling tourists. Our party days were winding down, and the last thing we needed was that kind of local color. We were exhausted, and that was before the tour had even begun.

As kids, Mama had repeatedly told us never to curse. But each morning in Bremen, both Ann and I could be heard to take the Lord's name in vain repeatedly whenever the goddamn-mother-fucking Gherkin Pickle wagon came by, with its incessant horse clip clops and beer stein clanks.

By the time our tour ended six months later, we were brain dead. Even the goddamn-mother-fucking Gherkin Pickle wagon couldn't have woken us.

19

THE BATTLE OF EVERMORE

A legend-in-the-making dies. Motherhood comes on the eve of a party with Alice. And Nancy finally gets her long-dreamed-for acoustic group. . . .

NANCY WILSON

By the late eighties, we were a Seattle band that was never in Seattle. We were on the road so much that we felt disconnected from the local scene just as it began to coalesce. But as the nineties began we started to reenter our home turf. We found that many young grunge bands cited our seventies output as an influence. Kelly Curtis had stopped working for us and had started managing bands. One of the first he signed was Mother Love Bone, fronted by Andy Wood. We saw them a few times, and Andy was a charismatic lead singer who was going places.

That year the Seattle club RKCNDY, so hip it couldn't buy a vowel, organized a "Heart Tribute Night" and asked if we would come. There were nine up-and-coming local bands on the bill, and we agreed. We arrived and went to a table upstairs hoping to watch the show in privacy. Word quickly got out we were in the club, and all the bands played toward us. It was odd to see grunge bands covering our songs, and doing it with sincerity.

Ann seemed particularly out of sorts that night. "This is the ultimate irony," she whispered to me. "It feels like they are sending us up, and I'm not ready to be sent up yet." It didn't seem mean-spirited to me, and some of it was hysterically cool. None of the bands could do the songs well, but they all had the right energy. We had to stay until the end, because if we walked out on our own tribute, it would have been scandalous. As soon as the show was over, we slinked out, slightly embarrassed by the tribute.

In March 1990, Kelly Curtis called and left a message on my answering machine that sounded more distraught than I had heard him in the twenty-five years we'd been friends. Andy Wood had died.

Cameron, Ann, and I immediately drove to Kelly's house. When we arrived, it was as if everyone in Seattle music had gathered there. It was a tragic night, but it was also important. It was one of the first times that a village had formed around the scene, and those bonds affected things in Seattle for decades to come.

All the guys in Mother Love Bone, who would later become Pearl Jam, were there, and Soundgarden's Chris Cornell was comforting them. Cornell told Jeff Ament, "We're gonna ride bikes, and fucking smoke cigarettes." Andy's girlfriend was crying and screaming, claiming his spirit was still in the house. Everyone was just leveled, but they were distraught together. I had brought our dogs, and they shifted the mood. Our three springer spaniels softened everyone's anger with their licks, love, and sweet faces amid the grief.

Over the next few nights many of the same people gathered at Ann's house. Her home became a salon of sorts, where up-and-coming bands knew they were welcome anytime of the day or night. There were always guitars around, and you'd see Chris Cornell singing with Alice in Chains' Jerry Cantrell, or other combinations that rarely happened onstage. Her house began to feel like our parents' house had when it became a crash pad for our church youth group, but Ann was not the den mother.

Though Andy Wood died when he relapsed, his death didn't scare people off their own drug use, unfortunately. Stardom had yet to happen to the class of grunge. Nothing had been gained, so many didn't understand what could be lost.

ANN WILSON

In June 1990 we started yet another tour, our longest ever. We celebrated my fortieth birthday a few weeks early so we could have a party before we got on the road. It was a subdued affair, due to the fact that we weren't excited about the coming months away from home.

My actual birthday came on the day of a sold-out show in Philadelphia at the Spectrum. That was far more memorable, but not in a positive way. We arrived the day before and both Nancy and I had picked up bronchitis. The hotel doctor prescribed cough suppressant and rest. We were used to propping ourselves up to do the shows. We went to bed and assumed we'd feel better by the next day.

The next day came. Nancy attempted to get out of bed and fainted. I could barely stand and couldn't imagine going onstage. The combination of illness and exhaustion was too much. We had to cancel the show. Our crew and band were at the venue, and in the pre–cell phone era, Lynn had to call the backstage production office. Whoever answered the phone got a message that the Wilson sisters were ill, and the giant show had to be cancelled.

We made the performance up a few weeks later, but we knew it had been a huge inconvenience for fans who had traveled to the city just to see us. It was one of the only times we ever cancelled a show, but the rest of the band and crew never let us forget it.

To this day, all I have to do is look at Nancy and say "The Spectrum," and she knows what I mean. It symbolizes not only the cancelled show, but also the end of an era for us, an era of excess. We had hit the wall.

▪ ▪ ▪

The *Brigade* tour ended in the fall of 1990, and we took a few months off. But the biggest news of next year came early, in February, with the birth of my first child.

The night she was born, I was in bed with Jerry Cantrell of Alice in Chains. It was a strictly platonic sleepover—Jerry told me he liked "skinny girls"—and one that was due to inebriation rather than any romantic escapade. There had been a party at my house, and Jerry stayed over because he drank too much, and didn't want to drive. Jerry wore one of my sleep shirts to bed. He was sleek and lanky, and his long blond hair covered my shirt.

The evening's party had been typical of many at my home. In attendance were a dozen or so soon-to-be-famous musicians, the cream of the crop of the Seattle grunge scene. Alcohol was consumed, fine food was eaten, and a bit of cocaine was inhaled. Guitars were broken out, songs were sung, war stories were told. The party only stands out for two reasons: A few hours later, my phone rang and announced the arrival of my daughter; and it was the last night I ever did any drug.

The conversation during the party never touched on sobriety. In the heady early grunge years, sobriety was such a foreign concept it was rarely discussed, even as the damage increased around us. But I was at the end of my dance with drugs.

That night a few of the younger guys asked me to tell road stories about the previous decade, what it was like to headline stadium shows, what it felt like to have a record sell fifteen million copies. "What was happening to you guys while that was going on around you?" Mike Starr, of Alice in Chains, asked.

"Too much hairspray and cocaine," I said. Everyone laughed.

Musicians in Seattle never spoke with the kiss-ass attitude you'd find at an L.A. party. Seattle musicians didn't lie about liking something they hated simply to get more work, or to network. People were real with you, which was one reason we felt centered at home. So when someone announced, "I always loved 'Barracuda,' but I didn't like your eighties stuff," I wasn't surprised. It might have been something Nancy and I could have said. But it was also evidence of a generational divide: The music of the seventies had a powerful nostalgia for those who created grunge, but they held no such affection toward anything from the eighties.

Yet one of the most telling questions that night came from Jerry Cantrell. "How the hell did it go so far?" he asked. "And why did you do those videos?" I could have answered that with the same quip about too much hairspray and cocaine. Instead, I changed the subject.

Jerry's question was ironic, though, considering where his career was headed. I didn't answer it because these young men knew nothing yet about the Devil's bargains that would be handed to them later in their careers. It was similar to the reason my father only talked about his war years with veterans. If you hadn't smelled the napalm, or the video set smoke machines, you wouldn't understand.

Early that next morning, with Jerry Cantrell lightly snoring beside me, the phone rang. It was the hospital telling me that the birth mother carrying the child I was to adopt had gone into labor. It was a week before her due date, and I wasn't prepared, otherwise I wouldn't have had a party the previous night.

I got out of bed, dressed, called a cab, and left Jerry sleeping soundly in my bed. The cab was my first choice toward a new responsibility. I told myself I was already thinking like a parent.

My house is very difficult to find, and cabs have always had a hard time locating it. I'd given explicit directions on the phone, but I still waited forty minutes for the taxi to arrive. When the driver finally arrived, I insisted he needed to hurry because a baby was being born. I directed him to Evergreen Hospital in Kirkland, fifteen miles away. I suspect English was not my driver's first language. Once he began racing in speeds in excess of a seventy miles per hour, I quickly realized that dressed in my big coat, he thought I was the one having the baby.

He made the trip in record time, but as we neared the hospital, he was pulled over by the police for speeding. We both tried to explain to the officer the circumstances. The taxi driver kept pointing at my obviously not pregnant torso and screaming in broken English that I was going to have a baby any second, while I kept trying to explain that my adoptive child was due to arrive in the hospital up the street.

The speeding ticket delayed us by ten minutes. The cab driver dropped me off in front of the hospital, and I ran inside. I breathlessly arrived at the maternity ward, only to discover that I had missed the birth of my daughter by exactly ten minutes.

I had first seriously longed for motherhood during the eighties. The urge initially felt odd, since during the seventies, I had been diligent never to become pregnant. I was never reckless in that department.

The year we started headlining stadium shows, a powerful feeling of wanting a child came over me. I wasn't sure what to make of it. But it took hold of me, and it didn't let go.

My first thought was that I wanted to carry a child. I became less careful in my personal life. And, eventually, I tried to get pregnant, in the natural way, with a sweet consenting man. I never once considered that I would raise a child as part of a partnership. I just thought that I would take it on myself, and I'd figure out how to hire help for things I couldn't do.

When I began to seriously try, and nothing seemed to take, I went to the doctor and had a retinue of tests. When I went back for the results, the doctor sat me down.

"You've been trying to get pregnant," he said, looking at reports on his desk. "You've just turned forty. My advice is don't try. Even if you succeed, you may have so many complications that the results might not be good." He had a way of explaining it that sounded like lyrics from a song: "Your body is not a landscape that can sustain a pregnancy. Don't go there."

Infertility was common in our family. Our mother had three children, but not many Wilsons or Dustins were as lucky. My "landscape" had spoken. "Don't go there," it said.

I contacted an attorney who specialized in adoptions, and I applied to a dozen adoption agencies. Every one turned me down. Their rejections were rarely explicit, but it was clear to me that being a single woman, particularly a single woman in rock 'n' roll, was not what they were looking for in an adoptive parent.

A few times the agencies did offer up their reasoning. "We really are looking for a two-parent situation," one woman told me. The attorney who was helping me translated that to mean they were looking for "only yuppies, and married yuppies, at that." They wanted something that was an old-school, solid thing. That wasn't me.

After so many disappointments, my attorney asked if I wanted to keep trying. I replied, "Well, sure." Then, just a few days later, I got a phone called from the sixteen-year-old friend of a friend. She was young, confused, and pregnant. She had heard I was looking to adopt, and the idea that her child might stay within the extended family appealed to her.

"I need to think about it," I told her. Then, with my next breath I said, "Yes."

It was what they call an "open adoption." I drove her to all her doctor's appointments, and we drew up papers in advance that spelled out the terms. But with an open adoption, the papers are never final until forty-eight hours after the birth. The law in Washington gave the mother a chance to reconsider once the child was born, and that was an uncertainty I had to live with.

When I rushed into the hospital that day, after my cab driver's speeding ticket, I was an emotional mess for many reasons, but that uncertainty was a part of it. It was possible the birth mother would change her mind, and I would leave in a cab by myself. But she didn't, and the nurses took me into the nursery, and I looked at this beautiful baby girl. "Go ahead and hold her," a nurse said. "She's yours."

She handed the baby to me. I rocked her back and forth for what seemed like hours. I didn't want to let her go.

■ ■ ■

I named her Marie Lamoureaux Wilson. She received Nancy's middle name, and there was never any doubt she was a Wilson. Mama, Dotes, Lynn, and Nancy all came to the hospital, and it was a joyous time. I stayed at the hospital those first two days, during the waiting period. And then Marie really was mine.

When it came time to go home, I wasn't sure what to do. I couldn't face being a single mom with a baby by myself yet. So Lynn came and got me, and I spent the first week with her and her second husband Ted. They taught me how to feed, change, and care for Marie. "You are never going to sleep again," Lynn joked. I thought I had proved my ability to stay up all night partying with Stevie Nicks, and the original Heart line-up, but Marie could outlast the bunch. That sweet baby had stamina.

For many new parents, a child marks the end of their extended adolescence, and the start of adulthood. I turned forty-one the year Marie was born, and she made me care about something other than myself. Alcohol was still a part of my life, but I never again did another line of cocaine. I also started to exercise more. I would swim, do Pilates, and I began to work out with a trainer. I wanted to live healthy for my daughter.

A week after Marie was born Lynn drove us to my house very slowly. We saw no police officers, or speeding taxis. When I walked in, Jerry Cantrell was gone, but I had a new baby in bed next to me. My life had renewed itself.

The birth of my daughter not only changed my life, it changed my approach to songwriting. The first example of that was "Two Black Lambs," which I wrote at the beach not long after Marie was born. Most of my previous songs had been about romantic love, or friendship. Marie brought a whole new dimension to the way lyrics moved through me, and she made mother-child love part of what drove me artistically. I hadn't even imagined that would ever be in me, but it just surfaced, and it didn't let go.

I wrote the lyrics to "Two Black Lambs" in one sitting. Every line of the song came from my life: "I lived on an island of self-control / I was free, and so lonely / I saw you wandering from the fold / out where the weather was stormy / we walked off together like two black lambs." The chorus was "I breathe you in / I breathe you out," which was about how I couldn't get enough of the smell of a new baby. "You needed saving, too," was one line that was literal, but the song was also about how Marie saved me.

It was only years later that it came to me that an early chapter of my childhood linked to the song. My mother wrote a poem about me when I was going through a particularly difficult time that she titled "My Little Black Sheep." I hadn't even been conscious of that when I wrote the lyrics of "Two Black Lambs." The mother-daughter link, and the imagery of black sheep, was so deeply rooted in our family that I could not escape it, nor could Mama, nor could Marie.

NANCY

A few weeks before Marie's birth, we had been approached to play at a Red Cross benefit at Seattle's Paramount Theatre. The first Gulf War was going on, and there was much political debate about the conflict.

The organizers told us it would be billed as a "Support Our Troops" concert. As the daughters of a Marine family, how could we refuse? They initially asked if Heart could play the show, but at that time, there no longer was a band called Heart. We had fired most of the band after the end of the *Brigade* tour, and we didn't want to put together a pick-up group just to perform under that name. We also didn't want to play as the two of us, because that would have been compared to Heart, too.

Ever since we were teenagers, back with the Viewpoints, we had wanted Sue Ennis in our band. We had a long running joke of "come join our band, Sue." Back in high school, Sue argued she was too shy, but as the years went on, and she helped write many of our songs, her "too shy" argument didn't hold much water. She had performed with us at countless hootenannies and jam sessions. We told her it was a one-time benefit, "for the good of the troops," and we pulled her in.

Over the previous decade, we'd become friends with Frank Cox, who on the shyness scale sat directly opposite from Sue. Frank was a natural entertainer, who would don an Elvis suit for a party, or sing anywhere anytime. He had a lot of experience playing acoustically, and his voice meshed well with ours. We hatched the idea of an acoustic, harmony group.

From the first few rehearsals at my farm, it was amazing. We jammed on songs by Paul Simon, Bob Dylan, and Peter, Paul and Mary. We only played a few Heart songs, and those we did in very different arrangements. At that first rehearsal, I grabbed a mandolin and played Led Zeppelin's "The Battle of Evermore." The song had been a showstopper when we did a rock version in early Heart in Vancouver clubs, but it was even better acoustic. Sue played keyboards, Frank played acoustic guitar, and Ann played bass or acoustic guitar. Sue programmed a rhythm track into her keyboard, and as a joke we decided to bring a cardboard cutout of Ringo Starr onstage with us.

After all the bloat of the eighties, that very first rehearsal felt liberating. We were making music just for joy, and for no other reason. But there was something the acoustic group gave me that I hadn't even known was missing. In this new band, I was the lead guitar player. It was challenging in a way that Heart had not been for many years, and it created a new interplay with my sister that reinvigorated me. Lead guitar would take over telling a story, and it gave me a way of connecting onstage with Ann that we had lost during the eighties. There was no one telling us to play hits, or to show more cleavage. It was music created for the same reasons we had made music in the beginning.

Marie was born three weeks before the Red Cross benefit. There was a brief pause, when we all waited to see if new mom Ann might reconsider. But Ann said, "It's just one night, let's do it." She'd already hired a family friend to help her, so we marched on with the show.

A few days before, the promoters called us up with a question "What do we call you?" they asked. We had no idea.

At our next rehearsal, I suggested, "Why don't we call ourselves 'The Peace Puppies'?"

"That's good," said Sue. "There are so many war mongers out there right now, and that sounds like the opposite of that."

"Why don't we call ourselves 'the Lovemongers,' then?" Ann suggested. The name stuck.

At the show we followed Artis the Spoonman and Alice in Chains and played six songs. We hadn't played acoustically in public for years, but the crowd responded more positively than they had on the *Brigade* tour. It felt intimate, and scary, but also freeing. It was way more fun than Heart. At the end of our set, I turned my acoustic guitar over and showed the audience a peace symbol I had plastered on the back. "Lovemongers," said Ann pointing to the sticker. "One night only. Better than the Fishmongers." Our new name was public.

Afterward, Ann, now holding Marie backstage, said it was yet another "proof of concept" in our career—proof that she and I could do something away from the major label world that had sold us like a brand. It was our "screw the corporate bullshit" move and incredibly liberating.

I had my two best friends in the world—Sue and Ann—playing with me in a band, something that I had wanted since I had been a teenager. I was reunited with my acoustic guitar, and harmony singing.

I imagined for a moment an alternate reality in my life, one where I never traveled to Vancouver, never joined Heart, never played rock 'n' roll. It was a world where the Lovemongers followed the Viewpoints, where folk music ruled, and where Sue was always in our band. With the Lovemongers, I was playing for the "small, but appreciative audience" I had in my college coffeehouse days. That tiny audience had once been as wide as I imagined my career would ever get.

20

LIVE FROM THE DOUBLETREE INN

The Lovemongers open up for future legends, and Kevin Bacon approves. Opening act Selena steals the show. A meteor brightens a star. . . .

NANCY WILSON

The Lovemongers had been meant to be a one-time thing. At the Red Cross benefit, we'd even been introduced as "for one night only, live from the DoubleTree Inn at Southcenter," which we thought was funny because the DoubleTree was an airport hotel lounge that featured cover bands. The response we got to the Red Cross show was so positive, and we had so much fun, other offers came in, and not from airport hotels.

In May, Cameron asked if the Lovemongers would play at the wrap party for his new movie *Singles*. It was a private party for the cast and crew, held at RKCNDY, so we said yes. We played a short set, and it seemed to go well, but it was a little odd to be playing on the very stage where we had watched a Heart tribute show just a few months before. After we played, Kevin Bacon came up to me with that big grin of his on his face. "You guys are great," he said. "I'm an actor, but I want to do what you do instead."

Another band followed us, but by the time they played, Kevin Bacon and most people at the party had moved to the catering room. I was one of the few who wandered back toward the stage to watch the next band, since they were Kelly's new project. They had an incredible amount of energy, but the lead singer was so shy he didn't look at the audience. They were called Mookie Blaylock at the time but would become famous later with a different name. After that night it became Frank Cox's favorite joke to say, "The Lovemongers opened for Pearl Jam, and wiped them off the stage." Very soon, as Eddie Vedder found confidence, no one would be upstaging them.

A few years later, Kelly Curtis, who then was more famous as Pearl Jam's manager than Heart's one-time publicist, finally was able to pay us back the loans we had given him over the years. He paid us with interest.

ANN WILSON

The Lovemongers performance was so fun we decided we might do a few more shows. We were mixing a new Heart live album then, but we'd decided to take a year off from Heart concerts.

I thought it might be fun to do a club gig, so I called the New Melody Tavern and said, "How would you feel about Nancy and me coming down there and playing?" It held a few hundred people. The owner couldn't believe his luck and asked if we could do three nights.

Chris Cornell came and sang with us at one show; at another Kris Novoselic of Nirvana was in the crowd. The club was so small that during set breaks we had to towel off in a janitor's closet.

We had done these shows just for fun, but after they were over, I found myself in a situation I hadn't been in for twenty years when the club owner didn't pay us all he had promised. It was a small amount, but the principal of it burned me, and I went back the next day to demand it. Just a year before we had sold out Wembley Arena. Now I had to hassle a bar owner for a few hundred bucks?

We kept having fun with the Lovemongers. Frank Cox had a day job working for the phone company, but he was happy to play anytime and anywhere.

We took a few more gigs even a show in New York City. Sean Lennon came to that, and afterward invited us to his apartment. Photographer Bob Gruen and Joey Ramone also came. We had never met John Lennon, but hanging with his son and Joey was the perfect New York experience.

We played quite a few benefits. Our joke was that we became the number one benefit band in town. Nancy and I were paying our tech crew ourselves, so we lost money at every Lovemongers show we played that year, but it was worth it.

It was not a time when we made wise choices with money. We had spent so much on Los Angeles recording studios, we decided we would purchase the Seattle studio where we had done many of our seventies hits. We went in with one partner, Steve Lawson, but we ultimately invested millions to upgrade the facility to state of the art. Our concept was that we could build a world-class studio, and record our albums in a place we owned. Jimi Hendrix had done the same thing with Electric Lady in New York. We decided to call our place Bad Animals, though later it became Studio X.

The only snag was that when the studio was done, we had to charge $1,500 a day to break even. As studio owners, we couldn't afford to give ourselves a family rate. We did record our next album there, but it would be superstar artists who would keep it afloat over time. R.E.M., Neil Young, B.B. King, Johnny Cash, and soon-to-be-Seattle-superstars like Soundgarden, Alice in Chains, and Pearl Jam would all record in our studio.

In 1997 we sold our interest in Studio X. We had built the best recording studio Seattle ever had, but we only did one album there. By the time we sold it, we had lost several million dollars on that dream.

In the summer of 1991 the only recording we did was with the performance artist Sandra Bernhard. She and I had become friends, and she had moved into my house briefly. Sandra was a hilarious comic, and lots of fun to hang out with, though she was a nonstop party animal. Because I was a single mom without a man in my life, crazy rumors circulated that I was gay, and perhaps Sandra had heard them. Not long after she moved in, Sandra began to hit on me. I repeatedly told her that I didn't go that way, but she kept it up until I had to send her packing.

With her outrageousness, Sandra reminded me in a way of another woman who that season began leaving me phone messages. I never knew how Courtney Love got my home number, but she did. The messages were frequent, lengthy, and many times so long they filled my entire machine. I was a night owl myself, but Courtney's messages might be time stamped at five in the morning.

As to what Courtney wanted, I never could quite piece that together. She seemed to have an important need to connect, and she repeatedly called me "the Queen of Seattle rock, the Queen of female rock, the fucking Queen," and it was imperative she spend time with me. While it was always flattering to hear from women rockers that we had been an inspiration, it wasn't recognition we sought. And when that recognition came from Courtney Love, it was hard to know how to take it.

I never returned the calls.

On September 27, 1991, we released our album *Rock the House Live*. It had been recorded at a date on the *Brigade* Tour. We left most of the hits off, and made efforts to make it sound less slick than our last few albums had. We included one new song we loved called "You're the Voice."

We had incredibly bad timing. Our album came out the same day as Nirvana's *Nevermind*, and we got lost in the sea change coming from a few blocks away from our Seattle homes. *Rock the House Live* only went to Number 107 on the *Billboard* charts, our poorest selling record in years.

Over the next year and a half, we decided to double down on Heart. Most of our albums had been recorded in a rush, but with the luxury of our own studio, we'd have enough time to make a quality record. This time we wanted to do it our way: We insisted we record our songs. The label gave in, as long as we included "Will You Be There (In the Morning)," another Mutt Lange tune. This time the song came with a caveat: Mutt Lange got to approve our version. The label also insisted we separately sing it in Spanish, so they could issue that version in Latin America. The song itself was horrible. We did our first run through it, and Howard Leese sent it to Mutt Lange. Lange objected because we'd changed one note.

On the positive side, we had written a batch of our best songs. "Under the Sky," "Rage," "Back to Avalon," "My Crazy Head," and "Two Black Lambs" were all examples of the kind of harmony we were reclaiming. Having our own studio, even if we were paying the day rate, gave us extended time to craft each track. In the end, the record cost us over a million dollars to finish.

When we turned the album in, the president of Capitol was impressed. He thought "My Crazy Head" should be the first single, and he said they would push it hard for a Grammy. One week later, the president was fired, and Mutt Lange's song was put forward as the first single. This time the hit-making machine failed: The track only went to Number 39. Every other studio album we'd done with Capitol had been a multi-platinum success, but *Desire Walks On* became our poorest-selling studio album since *Private Audition*. In 1993, with grunge dominating the charts, we didn't even have the attention of music fans in Seattle.

We did another massive tour, and as usual we pulled in bigger audiences for our live show than we did for the new album. We played on Jay Leno, David Letterman, Jon Stewart, and even live on MTV. It was one of the first times we were grateful for MTV exposure. We had put together a new line-up that included bassist Fernando Saunders and drummer Denny Fongheiser. Howard Leese continued as the only holdover from the seventies Heart. Despite the lack of chart success, the band sounded amazing.

But that tour was especially grueling. This was the first time I had attempted to tour as a mother, and that complicated things considerably. The band would travel on one tour bus, while a second carried Marie, Nancy, a nanny, and me. There was constant illness and crying on the bus. Marie would sometimes freak out when she saw people in the crowd screaming at her mom—she thought something was wrong. She said, "You are *my* mommy, and no one else's." The separation anxiety she felt when I was onstage was difficult for everyone.

Capitol had been right about one thing with their strategy: Recording a song in Spanish had given us a hit in parts of the world we had never played. They consequently booked us for shows in Latin America. One we did was a sold-out show in Mexico City, playing to a sea of wonderful new fans.

Then we booked a massive festival in Santiago, Chile. We had never toured within four thousand miles of there before, and it was uncharted waters. The routing for our flights had us go from Seattle to Miami, to New York, and then to Chile. We were doing all of this with Marie in tow, and all our equipment. We were exhausted by the time we arrived.

We were the headliners of a multi-day festival. We had shifted our fashion that year, wearing what we wore at home in Seattle—Doc Martens and army coats. That might have made us hip in Seattle, but in Chile, we were entirely underdressed. We had to follow Selena, who had her biggest hit that year. As soon as her performance was over, the crowd began to walk out even before we played a note. There was still daylight, and we could see the crowd pouring out as we valiantly tried to go on with our show. It was the first time since First Congregational Church in 1968 that we played to a crowd with so many walkouts.

It was the low of all lows. It was exactly the stuff that rock-mares are made of. We had joked at that first Lovemongers show that we were "live from the DoubleTree Inn, one night only." Staring at the audience in Chile streaming out, it seemed like the DoubleTree might be our next gig.

▪ ▪ ▪

We had one more album due to Capitol under our contract, and we decided that a live album might shift things. After our Lovemongers' shows, we were interested in recording "unplugged," which we thought might become a new direction for Heart. We'd done live albums before, but this time we wanted it to sound fabulous, so we booked the tiny Backstage club in Seattle for three nights in August and hired the best producer and arranger we knew: John Paul Jones of Led Zeppelin.

We had met Jonesy before, but the project gave us an entire month with him, and he proved to be a prince among men. He told a few funny Zeppelin touring stories, but generally he wasn't catty. He wrote charts for our songs and proved himself to be a brilliant arranger. He was one of the most down-to-earth, sweetest guys we ever met in the music business, so much so that at times I'd even forget that he was John Paul Jones of Led Zeppelin.

John Paul even sat in with us on a few songs at our concerts. The entire run of shows felt like a breath of fresh air as we explored Heart in the acoustic setting. John Paul arranged some of our most bombastic eighties hits in a way that made them shine. It helped me imagine that a new direction for Heart was possible, and I held out hope our label would feel the same. Capitol scheduled the live album, which we decided to call *The Road Home*, for the following year.

If there was an upside to what ultimately was the commercial failure of *Desire Walks On*, it was that it gave us opportunities to record with two of Seattle's legendary voices. We wanted a male voice to harmonize with on Bob Dylan's "Ring Them Bells." Chris Cornell sang it with us at a Lovemongers show, so we asked him, and he agreed. It came out great, but his label wouldn't let us release it.

I called up Layne Staley of Alice in Chains, who had been a friend for years, and he agreed to step in. He was wearing wraparound sunglasses when he came into the studio, and he didn't want anyone else in the control room when he sang. The engineer mixed his take with our vocals, and it sounded perfect. Layne had the blood harmony with us, too.

You could see that day, though, that his struggles with drug addiction had taken away part of Layne. He had become smaller and smaller, inside and out, even hunched over. He was little to start with, but when I gave him a hug, I was afraid I might break his bones.

I had seen some of Alice's first shows when Layne was luminous onstage, whiter than white, as if he was lit from within. It was like he didn't have a body when he was performing. His voice was the template for what everyone else did after him. A lot of other guys buzzed around Layne like bees. He was full of humor, but serious, too. Sometimes he would look me in the eye, and say, "Ann, exactly how are you *really* doing?"

As the years went on, he shifted, and by "Ring Them Bells," his light was flickering. But he would still come to parties at my house then. When his girlfriend Demri was around, Layne was different. He'd lose her, and then we'd have to search for her, and we'd find her curled up in a closet. When she died in 1996, it really took away his essence.

The last time I saw Layne was a couple of years after Demri's death, when he came to a party at my home. He wasn't quite yet the recluse he would become in the months before he died in 2002, but it was still rare enough to see him that his presence was the talk of the party. Eventually, the rest of the crowd left, and it was just Layne and me together on a clear summer night. I decided I wanted to swim, and he followed me to my pool. He didn't get in, but sat there in a lounge chair looking at the sky, sipping on a beer, while I swam laps. He told me that as a kid he had excelled at swimming and diving. "I loved to dive into water," he said. It was a whole different world in water he said.

Suddenly, a huge meteor went over us. It looked like a bright piece of burning coal, and for a second it lit up Layne's face. He looked young again, like a kid who loved nothing better than to dive into water. In that moment, there was nothing dark in his life.

"Did you see that?" he said excitedly. "How close do you think that was to us, Ann? Do you think that almost hit us, Ann? How lucky are we to have seen that?"

"It *was* really beautiful," I said.

"Do you have any idea," Layne asked, "how rare it is for a meteor that big, and that bright, to come that close to us? We *are* really, really lucky people, Ann. You and me."

21

THE OTHER HALF OF THE SKY

A turning point for a duo. Mrs. Clinton plays Mom. Plus a very different view from the audience. . . .

ANN WILSON

In the spring of 1995, Nancy called and said she wanted to talk. She was living part of the time in Los Angeles with Cameron, but also still coming up to work on Heart projects. I knew they were trying to start a family, without success. She had also begun to work on film scores, and I was excited to see her find another avenue for her creativity.

I thought she might want to discuss where a new Heart album could go, and how we could follow *The Road Home*, set for release that summer. It was our last album in our current contract, and there were already indications Capitol may not want to renew. In fact, a few weeks later, after having sold twenty million albums for them, Capitol dropped us.

It was an unseasonably warm spring Seattle day, when Nancy and I met, and we sat on my back patio. The cherry trees were blooming, and little pink blossoms floated by. She sat down and came to the point. "I don't want to do Heart anymore," she said. "At least for a while. I need to take a break and put Heart on hold."

I was speechless. It felt like she had leaned over and stabbed me in the chest with a knife. To me, her announcement was also the end of Heart. For three decades, we had been more than sisters: We had been partners in creativity, business, and a force of two against the world.

Nancy explained she wanted to work with Cameron on more film scores; she wanted to get off the road and put time into starting a family. What she didn't say, but what I thought, was that she didn't want to keep coming back to Seattle to witness the withering and dying of Heart. Though we had been a unified force in Heart for most of our history, there had been times when I wanted to tour more than Nancy did, but we'd always gotten over that. This was the first time I had come up against anyone in the band, or in my family, who didn't believe in Heart. It was particularly hurtful because it was my sister who no longer believed. It was the other half of the sky.

We went round and round that afternoon. It felt like she was leaving me with this incredible mess of dismantling our thirty-person crew. We had a lawsuit pending—someone had been injured in the crowd at one of our concerts and sued us. We had a ton of bills coming in. We even had *The Road Home* we needed to promote. I was going to have to clean up all of this mess, and she was going to walk off with Cameron, and have a different career. It felt like a betrayal. I begged with her, I pleaded. I cried. After an hour of heartbreaking words, she still just walked away. Sitting there on my patio after she left, I wondered what Paul McCartney would have done. Should I start Wings? Should I tour on my own? Would anyone want to see me if Nancy weren't by my side?

Then I stopped thinking about myself, or Heart, or the slew of people who worked for us, and I started thinking about my sister. I had always been the dominant one in Heart. From the start, Nancy had been dreaming a dream I dreamed first. Because I was four years older, I even had a head start on the language of that dream, its parameters, scope, and length. My dream had no end, but Nancy's had a stop, or at least a pause.

I knew she felt she couldn't breathe, that I was smothering her, that it was all my ambition, and that she was sick of that. She wanted to get out and breathe her own air, and maybe explore her own kind of music, and not be beholden to Heart.

I could support her decision as her sister, even if it meant the end of the band. I could love her and forgive her. We were family, after all. When you love someone, you forgive, even if a scar remains. Our words had been ugly, but an hour after that ugliness I remembered that my sister and I were more than just Heart.

NANCY WILSON

When I left Ann's that day, I felt like a murderer. I was surprised I'd actually had the courage to do it, but it still felt awful. I wanted to put Heart on hold for me, but in doing so, I knew I was taking the wind out of her sails, too. I knew I was taking food out of the band and crew's mouths as well. Heart had to be on the road to make money—it was the only way it worked for any us. Ann did not want to hear what I had to say, and I did not want to tell her. It was not fun. It was one of the hardest things that ever went on between us.

I had started working on scores to Cameron's movies the year before, and I was deep into fertility treatments. I thought I could be everything to everyone all the time, but that wasn't working. The demands of being on the road with Heart were pulling me away from the other parts of my life. I was trying to get pregnant, but I was failing at that, and setting up appointments with fertility clinics wasn't easy when you were in Dallas one day, and New Orleans the next.

Ann defined herself by her work, which was similar to Cameron. There is almost no other thing they define themselves by. They both are driven, committed to art, and brilliant. Lynn and I had joked since our childhood that we were on "Ann's staff," and in a way I found myself in the same relationship with Cameron, but happy for it.

The previous year, I turned forty, and a panic ensued that I wasn't a mom. Cameron and I hadn't discussed starting a family before we married.

We had many strengths in our relationship, but talking about important issues was never one of them. We always managed to find time to discuss a new Joni Mitchell album, but our own relationship was the last topic brought up. We had been together for five years before we discussed marriage, and we were married for five years before the idea of having kids was seriously discussed.

We didn't decide to have kids at first; we just decided to stop trying *not* to have them. That was like a lot of our relationship: fluid, loose, and sometimes dysfunctional. All those Joni Mitchell records affected me: I thought true love should be natural, and effortless.

Because both Cameron and I had jobs in entertainment, we had an unorthodox relationship. But when I wasn't on the road with Heart, it was more traditional. I became the stay-at-home wife, working in my husband's world, and making dinner every night. Even when I was home, I hardly saw him, because he was always writing, but at least there was comfort because he was right in the next room.

It was a creative partnership: He wrote his scripts, but he read me every word, and we discussed every line. Cameron was always dissecting the ways rock and film intersect, and it was exciting to be a part of that. I got to be in an eagle's nest in Hollywood, and see the process of moviemaking from scripts to editing.

After *Fast Times*, I next worked with Cameron on *The Wild Life*, a 1984 film he wrote. I played a pregnant cop's wife who found out her husband was cheating when another woman knocked at the door. I wasn't born to be an actor.

I first worked on a score for one of Cameron's films with 1992's *Say Anything*. I even went on the road with him to help publicize the movie. My contributions were small guitar bits, but Cameron was kind to point out in our joint interviews that I had added "Seattle" to the sound of the movie. Anne Dudley, of the band Art of Noise, composed that score, and she was a huge help to me. Creating a score meant working with sheet music, and that initially scared me because it was different from anything I'd done with a rock band. But Anne told me to count the measures out, play where I was supposed to, and feel it.

When we went to the first screening of *Say Anything*, and I heard stuff I'd played coming out of those speakers, it was an amazing thrill. It felt great to find my sea legs in something other than being in a rock band. I a little off the grid, but I was in Hollywood, and my music was heard inside a movie theater. That felt big time, whether or not I was the director's wife.

I had slept with the director, of course. That was my bad joke during those years. It wasn't a good joke, since there were people working on Cameron's films with more Hollywood experience, and surely there were resentments because of our relationship. I didn't have it easy, though, because Cameron was super picky about what he wanted. He would say, "This here doesn't kill me, and I want something else, so keep working on it." And he'd be right.

When Cameron started *Jerry McGuire* in 1994, he asked if I'd do the score. It was an easy fit because Cameron wanted a Paul Simon–like sound, and that was my whole history. I decided to do it inexpensively because I didn't want to be the typical director's wife who expected a big budget for my role. I found a young engineer named Vaughn Verdi, who had a house in Universal City with no soundproofing, or video equipment. I went to Costco and bought a small television with a VCR built in. We'd count the scenes, and press play on the VCR at the right spot, and then I'd play the music. We'd rewind, and do it again. We made the score without syncing. It was so low-tech, it was no-tech.

I did have really good microphones, and I played my Libra Sunrise guitar, the same one I'd used on "Mistral Wind," into a sixteen-track reel-to-reel. We wanted it to sound analog, but sometimes we got a more natural sound than we expected. The house wasn't always quiet, and when the garbage cans would get banged outside, I'd play louder to drown it out. A tree had fallen on the air conditioner so it was broken. Some days it would be 103 degrees, but we couldn't open the doors or windows because we needed the soundproofing. I was playing my guitar in a sweatbox and trying to keep it in tune. It was so un-Hollywood, and so unprofessional, and so edgy. You'd never imagine that the soundtrack to a Tom Cruise movie was made in that environment.

It was through Cameron that I finally had my chance to meet Joni Mitchell. We planned dinner at a restaurant called the Four Oaks in Bel-Air. I knew it wasn't far from her house, because when Cameron and I first dated, we took our picture in front of the gates to her home. And now a dozen years later, I was to meet her. I was so nervous walking into the restaurant that my knees were vibrating. And there, before me, were the actual molecules that made up Joni.

Joni, however, could not have been a cooler cat. She was drinking a cappuccino, and she was a stellar storyteller. She liked to talk about herself a lot, which was perfect since I wanted nothing more in the world than to listen to her talk. She told stories of her relationships with men, of her wild gypsy girl days, and how she ran with wolves, so to speak. She knew how to love, and how not have to have ownership of men. When I left the restaurant hours later, I still didn't have my fill of Joni. I immediately sat down and wrote my old friend Jan Drew, the woman who I had gone searching for Joni with on Sechelt Island years ago. "I actually *met Joni!*" my letter screamed. Joni was one of the few celebrities I ever met who was more inspiring in person than in my imagination.

ANN

Even when Nancy was working with Cameron on movies, she came back to the fold for the occasional Lovemongers gig, or for a benefit. We did a benefit for health care reform in Portland where we met Hilary Clinton, who was then the first lady. Our mom had raised us to be proper young ladies, and she expected us to be able to meet the first lady and present ourselves appropriately. Sadly, our first meeting with Hillary would not have lived up to Mama's expectations for us.

It was a hot day, and we were playing outside before a large crowd in

Pioneer Park. Our dressing room was a little curtained area in the middle of the street. Our road manager was tackled by the Portland Police, and handcuffed when they failed to notice the credentials around his neck. The event went downhill from there.

Marie was three years old and in the active toddler stage when she didn't like her mommy onstage. While we played, she wept, and the instant I came offstage, she was in my arms weeping. My face was covered with sweat from performing. And at that moment, with Marie weeping, Hillary walked into our partition. She looked at me, and then Marie, and announced, "You should get that child out of the sun." I had been "mom-ed" by the First Lady.

The year before, I had met Hillary's husband, President Bill Clinton, but there was no "mom-ing" involved. He was on the docket at a fundraiser at Seattle's Paramount Theatre, and I'd been asked to come do a blues song. As I was singing, Clinton came and stood on the side of the stage listening, with that Bill Clinton smirk on his face. During my guitar solo, he walked out onstage, and whispered in my ear, "You are *real* good." I joked, "You ought to pull out your saxophone, Mr. President." He laughed and said he couldn't do that.

Later that night in the reception line, Clinton pulled me over to him. "What is your name?" he asked. He had no idea who I was. "I'm Ann Wilson," I said. "You are very, very, very good," he said. He smelled and looked Washington-tailored, and being that close to him I could feel the power he had over people, particularly over women. He kept saying that I was "very, very, very good." When he repeated it, he sounded like Elvis.

A few months after Nancy announced she needed a break, I went back on the road billed as "The Ann Wilson Band." Howard Leese remained, but the rest of the group was new, including Scotty Olson on guitar, Jon Bayless on bass, and Ben Smith on drums. Musically, I didn't want it to be "Heart without Nancy," so we built an R&B revue with a local horn section in every city. Our set included songs like "It's a Man's World," "Strong, Strong

Winds," "Gimme Shelter." Musically it was rewarding, but the rest of the tour was chaos.

First, it felt very odd not having my sister on my tour bus. Instead, I had toddler Marie, plus a nanny, Pat, originally from Trinidad, who was large, soulful, and loud in a small space. Pat wasn't a wet nurse, but on a few occasions, I walked to the back of the bus to find Marie's head comfortably cuddled in her enormous breasts.

Not having Nancy in the band had an immediate effect on our finances. When bookers found out she wasn't with us, the offers came down considerably, less than half in many cases. We were booked at state fairs, military bases, and casinos.

One of our gigs was in the Dakotas. We drove nineteen hours on the bus to get there, hauling our gear behind us in a U-Haul. The stage was in the middle of a field, and it was pouring rain. When the show was over, and we tried to leave, our bus got stuck in the mud, and we had to be towed out.

The next show was in Wisconsin. When we arrived, our bus driver took a cash draw, and went on a bender. After our gig, we went to the bus expecting to leave for the next show. We waited hours. Finally, our road manager had to kick his hotel door down to get him.

I normally have a streak of optimism, but by that point, I felt embarrassed that I'd dragged the rest of the band on this hellish trip, thinking I could tour without Nancy. At one show, a sign behind me read "MARLBORO PRESENTS ANN WILSON." Every fan I met asked, "Where's Nancy?" Many of the gigs were on military bases, including Camp Lejeune and Quantico. The officer's clubs we played were the same facilities that had been there twenty-five years before when I had lived on base. I imagined I had forever escaped the clapboard housing of Quantico and the sound of young Marines marching in the parade fields.

But without my sister, I was back where I began.

NANCY

Even while I was working on film scores, my main focus was on becoming pregnant. It consumed me, but it did not go well. Eventually, I began to take fertility drugs. I took those shots thinking they were going to bring me to the thing I wanted the most in the world, but their effects were severe, and often I was an emotional mess.

That year the Ann Wilson Band came to Los Angeles, and I went to the show. It felt so very strange to be driving to a concert that Ann was giving without me. Watching her show from the audience, a part of me was sad I wasn't onstage, but it was also a bit of a thrill. I hadn't watched Ann from the audience since the days I was trying out for Heart in Vancouver.

She was just shredding it onstage, closing it down with her voice. It felt so different to be in the audience listening to her amazing voice. It made me want to be in Ann's band because she was such a good singer. It was like a religious experience.

We had talked on the phone before the show, and she asked if I wanted to sit in, but my fingers weren't itching to play. I was so out of practice, and so hormonally challenged that I didn't want to be onstage and be rusty. I didn't think she could see me in the audience, but when I went backstage after, she told me she had spied me immediately.

"It was hard to pay attention to anything else," Ann said. "My connection with you is greater than any connection with the audience could ever be."

22

THE BOYS MARCH IN

A Lovemongers album. A princess dies, and so does a dream. And the family grows with a different sort of tour, on a crazy bus. . . .

NANCY WILSON

While Ann was doing her tour, I started a musical adventure of my own. McCabe's Guitar Shop in Santa Monica asked if I wanted to do an acoustic show. In March 1997, I did my first solo show in thirty years. It was my college-girl-self, back to the idea that I would play folk clubs, and have that "small but appreciative following."

I played a handful of Heart songs, but also Peter Gabriel's "In Your Eyes," and Joni Mitchell's "A Case of You." Astrid Young, Neil's sister, and Kristen Barry sang backup on a few songs, but it was mostly just me and my guitar. The gig went so well, Kelly Curtis suggested we release it as a CD. He arranged things with Epic, and it was released a year later.

And though I wasn't willing to tip my toe in the Heart waters, the Lovemongers were a different matter altogether. That year we recorded a Lovemongers album for tiny Will Records.

But most of 1997 was consumed, as was every year that decade, by trying to get pregnant. When one technique didn't work, I sought out different doctors and cutting-edge technology. It was very expensive and I spent more than a hundred thousand dollars. It was only considered safe to keep doing fertility injections for a short while, but I went way past the recommendations.

Adoption was also a consideration, though Cameron was mixed on that option. I had always thought I'd have one child from my body, and adopt a second. Infertility ran in our family, but I kept thinking I could beat my age, and DNA, to achieve my goal. I wasn't willing to rule anything out then—my doctor even brought up the idea of using a surrogate.

Everything changed in August 1997. I had just finished a round of fertility treatments, and I went to the Oregon Coast with Ann and Sue to recover. The injections had begun to feel metallic, as if there was metal in my blood for days afterward. Each treatment took more and more out of me.

This time my metal blood had a payoff. I took a pregnancy test the evening we got to the beach, and the results were pink, which meant I was pregnant. The next few days I woke up every morning feeling the hormones of motherhood pouring through my body.

I always had the deepest dreams at the beach, falling asleep to the sound of the surf. Then one night I dreamed I was pregnant, but the dream shifted, and I was not pregnant. It was the worst kind of nightmare, where nothing really happens, but the emotions of dread and panic are there.

I woke up in a sweat. The sun was up, and it was morning. I had to clear my mind, so I turned on the television. A news anchor announced that Princess Diana had been killed in a car crash. It was a horrible end to a beautiful woman. I went to the bathroom and took another pregnancy test. My dream had been real, and I was no longer pregnant. I collapsed on the floor.

Ann and Sue came to me. I was distraught. I told them, and I told myself, I couldn't do it again. "I can't put that poison in my body anymore," I wailed.

It was the roughest day of my life. It was the end of one dream, but it wasn't the end of me, or me being a mother.

ANN WILSON

We told Nancy that the best thing to clear her head, as she explored her options, would be to go on the road with the Lovemongers and play the music she loved. Nancy agreed, and we went on a twelve-date tour in a van in November 1997. We called it the "Don't Blink" tour because if you blinked, it was over. Still, it was the first time Nancy and I had been on the road together in several years.

Our first show was at San Francisco's legendary Fillmore, and it didn't even sell out. The rest of the tour fared better, but since Nancy and I were paying the crew, and the rest of the band, we lost money on the tour. It was worth it, though, since it helped things shift for both of us. I told one reporter I felt like we were "refugees" from Heart.

That next spring, my own family took a surprising turn. A friend called up to say that a Seattle girl she knew was pregnant and was looking for an adoptive mother. Was I interested?

It took me two seconds to say yes. The birth mother was once again a young sixteen-year-old, and I took her to her doctor's appointments. Marie was seven, and overjoyed she was going to have a little sister. But the baby sister Marie wanted ended up being a baby brother. I named him John Dustin Wilson, after my dad, and the Hannah Dustin lineage. We called him Dustin.

As soon as both my children were old enough to understand, I told them they were adopted. When Marie was little, she created her own legend around it. "You went shopping for me in Heaven at the Mommy Store," she would tell me. "And you picked me, and we were together." Dustin was quizzical as he grew older, and he wanted to know if he was part of our family tree. "You were grafted onto our family tree," I told him. "Now you are a true Wilson." I put both of them into progressive schools where they were taught that families come in all forms, and that being adopted was a special distinction.

I never shied away from talking about adopting in the press, but I was annoyed when kids were described as my "adoptive children," as if they weren't really mine. That language made adoption sound like less of a bond. There were many options in the Mommy Store. I just felt blessed the store had opened for me.

In the summer of 1998, I toured again without Nancy. It was mostly the same band, but this time we were billed as "Heart Featuring Ann Wilson." We did three-dozen dates, playing everywhere from the House of Blues to the Louisville Motor Speedway.

Marie and Dustin both were on my tour bus. Drummer Ben Smith had just become a father, and his wife and newborn were on the bus with us, too. I brought Pat, the nanny from Trinidad, again, and she tried to corral the children, who at times outnumbered the adults. One of the babies was usually crying, and there was always someone moving around. We might as well have had chickens and goats in the aisles.

We sold more tickets billed as Heart, but Nancy's absence was mentioned constantly. "Where's Nancy?" was asked so frequently, I considered making up a sign. We eventually had Nancy record a greeting that we played before each show. Few reviews of the tour failed to mention that my sister was missing. And with Nancy gone, there was increased attention to how I looked on stage, how old I was, and how much I weighed. Roger Catlin's preview in the *Hartford Courant* was meaner than most, but not atypical:

"I know what you're thinking: She ate the other one. No, no, no. That's rude. Svelte sister and guitarist Nancy Wilson is taking a break from the summer Heart tour so she can work on starting a family. So it's up to singing sister Ann Wilson to front the same band."

This would never be written about a man, but it was the kind of meanness critics thought was clever when applied to me.

The prior year, the Lovemongers had played a one-off acoustic benefit, and after the show my old nemesis Patrick MacDonald of the *Seattle Times* came up to me. "We just did this benefit to raise money for Puget Sound," I told him, "and you'll probably now filet me in your paper about how much I weigh."

"Maybe I will," he said coyly.

I then did something that was so unlike me that Nancy's eyes about popped out of her head: I punched MacDonald on the arm. It was a real punch, and he flinched. "It hurts my mom's feelings," I said as I slugged him. Patrick MacDonald ran away. He wasn't afraid to criticize my weight in his newspaper, but he was afraid of a girl singer. In his review of that concert, he didn't mention the incident, but he did give us one of the first positive notices for us he'd had in years.

It was the only time in my adult life I ever punched a man. It, too, felt like a blow against the empire.

NANCY

In February 1999, my *Live at McCabe's Guitar Shop* album came out. I did a short tour to promote it, including a show at Seattle's Crocodile Café. It felt so odd to be playing solo in my hometown. Ann had taken a job singing with Teatro Zinanni that season as a nightclub singer. It was a musical theater production, and she got to sing every night and still get home to her kids. It had been strange when I watched Ann's band onstage in Los Angeles, but it was even more bizarre to be playing at a Seattle club on the same night my sister was doing her gig across town.

When I wasn't touring, I was working with Cameron on *Almost Famous*. I loved every one of Cameron's movies, but *Almost Famous* is my favorite because it told both our stories in a way—he being the youngest journalist in the rock world, and me being the youngest member of a band. Kate Hudson and I became friends during the shoot, and we would sneak off set for a cigarette together. She was a really square girl, and was always grilling me for stories on wild rock guys, or drugs and parties. I didn't have much to offer, but I think she wanted to absorb what she imagined was my wildness for her role as Penny Lane. I told her she reminded me of the silent film actress Clara Bow, so Kate got a dog, and named it Clara Bow.

Earlier that year, Cameron and I had made the decision to find a surrogate to carry the child that I couldn't have. It was still a cutting-edge procedure, and we tried a few options, first using my eggs. That failed. After a decade of hormone treatments, and fertility injections, it ended up that another woman would have to provide the egg for my child, and Cameron and I would only have children together through the alchemy of modern science. There was terrible grief in that, but also wonder, and acceptance, mystery, and even awe when I thought of the magic of it all. And I felt immense gratitude that there was another option available to us, because there isn't for many.

I remember when I first told Ann that this was the only option we were left with, after everything else had failed. "I'm so proud of you," Ann said. "You are able to find acceptance because you went to the end. You tried everything. You had to jump through hoops that few other parents have had to. You left no stone unturned, and once you did all that, it became easier to accept what once had seemed unacceptable."

My big sister was right. I always follow everything to the end. I had learned an awful lot about fertility from the best doctors in nation, and I had learned that I couldn't carry children in my own belly. It had made me want to go back to college to study microbiology.

We discovered that our surrogate was carrying twin boys. Now we'd have an instant and large family. I had struggled for so long wanting just one child, and now two were due. To me those were the same souls of the children that I had once carried, but that I had temporarily lost. Now they were finally coming to me. Those were the most wanted children in any family. They were mine.

My boys arrived in January 2000, two days early. The entire Wilson clan flew immediately from Seattle and gathered around the Sacramento hospital where they were born. Ann, Lynn, Kelly Curtis, and many other friends all came to the hospital and got there just after the boys had arrived. The only one who didn't leave immediately was Cameron. We were in Los Angeles, where he was working on a script. The car was packed and everything was ready, but when I told him the boys were coming he delayed leaving. So I drove off to Sacramento without him. By the time our sons were born they had met everyone but their father. It was a great day of celebration and healing, so I was quick to forgive him for being late.

We decided to name them Curtis Wilson Crowe and Billy James Crowe. Curtis came from Kelly Curtis, my old friend, Cameron's friend, and Pearl Jam's manager. Kelly also was appointed the godfather of the boys. Billy came from two places: First he was named for William Miller, the character in *Almost Famous*, who is a loosely drawn version of Cameron himself. But William immediately, and forever after, was called "Billy" after the director Billy Wilder.

When we told Billy Wilder that we named one of the twins after him, he asked us what they each were like. "One is very serious, and the other is a comedian," I said.

"Which one did you name after me?" he asked.

"The comedian."

Billy Wilder comically pretended to be hurt.

Though they are fraternal twins, the boys are so different, there was comedy from the moment they were born. The way they negotiate and compete has always been funny. Curtis is one minute older. He has never let Billy forget that fact, and he also insists that he is one minute taller, when in fact Billy has a slight height advantage.

I had wanted children for so long, but growing up in a house with two sisters, I had no idea what boy energy was like, and particularly twin boy energy. Not long after the boys were born, we gave them the nickname "the Pilkers." I took the name from a favorite Roz Chast cartoon titled "Parallel Universes." It showed a normal mom baking cookies in one panel, and then an alien mom baking "Pilkers" in another. As a mom, I sometimes felt a bit like an alien.

Since my husband was a filmmaker, the Pilkers had elaborate home movies from babyhood. Our home movies, though, occasionally included cameos by Orlando Bloom, Kristen Dunst, and Billy Wilder. But other than the guest stars, they captured typical scenes of the Pilkers during holidays, first steps, and eventually, their first day of school. The school they attended required them to wear uniforms, so their first school day video captured their tiny jackets and ties. We set that short film to the Beach Boys' "Wouldn't It Be Nice."

From a very young age, the twins were a club unto themselves. Even Cameron found himself amazed at the bond they formed. "I find myself wanting to be cool enough to hang with them," he said in the voiceover to one of our videos. "It's the same cycle as high school, but you find yourself cast out by your own children." Cameron took them to his movie sets. The big trucks on the studio lot, rather than A-list movie stars, fascinated them.

They turned five the year Cameron's *Elizabethtown* came out, and we made a video of them talking about the film. "What's the name of Daddy's new movie?" we asked.

"Bang Bang, Boom Boom," Curtis said.

In that footage, Cameron asked Billy if he was into "the kind of movies that Daddy and Mommy work on, soulful, romantic movies." Billy's response: a yawn. We knew they were true boys, though, when they watched "Spiderman II," and their eyes got wide when they saw Spiderman kissing Kristen Dunst, whom they knew from the *Elizabethtown* set.

They don't even call each other by their names when they need to signal each other. Instead they scream out, "My brother."

Around the time the Pilkers turned ten, we decided to tell them the unusual story of how they came into this world. I didn't want them to hear it from anyone else. They were starting to ask about sex and conception around that age. To share the story of their birth with them, I made my own children's book complete with photos of me from the decade before they were born, sometimes pregnant for a moment, but also with photos of them in the hospital when they arrived. I titled it "When You Were Born."

I read it with them. "I took a lot of pills, and shots, at the hospital to try to have you, and they were dangerous, but we so wanted you," I told them. "We wanted you so much, we had to use modern science, and because of modern science, and God, and magic, and our wanting you, you came along."

My book fascinated them. They looked it again, and again. A few months later though, on Easter, they came to me with a burning question: "Does this mean that you are our mom, or not our mom?" they asked.

"Yes, I'm your mom. Science, or DNA doesn't matter. A mother's love is stronger than any of that. And my love for you is stronger than any force in this world."

"You are the babies I had always been trying to have. You are the souls I had been calling. It took me years of calling to get an answer from you, but finally I called, and you heard my voice, and you came to me."

"I am your mom. You are my sons. That is forever."

Two weeks after the boys were born, I took them to Seattle to meet my parents. Dotes got to hold the boys, and we took pictures of them with him, and my mom.

And then, three weeks after that, our dad died at seventy-seven years of age.

Dotes had been in poor health for sometime, and the complications from his stroke twenty-two years before had been great. He often got pneumonia, and there were a half dozen times when the doctors had told us he might not make it. On several occasions, Lynn, Ann, and I had hurried to the hospital, and bid him good-bye for what we always thought was the final time. We'd sing to him, kiss him on his head, and leave with heavy hearts. But Dotes always seemed to bounce back.

He had been declared dead in two wars, had survived a stroke, years in a wheelchair, and it seemed for a while that nothing could take down our old

Marine. It reminded me of the scene in *Little Big Man* where the old Indian thinks he's dying, and lies down, but jumps back up, and says, "I think I'll pick another day." I think Dotes wanted to hold out just long enough for all his daughters to have their families. Lynn, Ann, and I now had two children apiece, and once our entire clan was there, Dotes felt it was time.

Dustin, Billy, and Curtis had all arrived. The boys marched in. The Major marched out.

23

SEND UP A FLARE

Dotes leaves with a twenty-one-gun salute. A band leader becomes a Band-ster. Carrie Underwood is left alone. And a windmill goes flying skyward. . . .

ANN WILSON

After our dad's death, the newspaper did a big story on his big life. They ran a photo of Dotes when he was a big strong Marine at Camp Pendleton, standing at attention, with a little boy asking him, "Where's my dad?" It was perfect. It showed our dad as he had always been, a gentle warrior. We always knew he had been a popular teacher, but after his death we were deluged with cards and notes from his former students. Almost every one said he was their favorite teacher.

The last decade, our parents had lived in a home we called "The Windmill House," across from Nancy's farm, thus named for the windmill in the backyard. And it was there we held the memorial for Dotes, led by his old friend from church Reverend Lincoln Reed. The Marine Corps sent out a full honor guard in formal blue uniforms. They folded a flag and presented it to our mom, and fired a twenty-one-gun salute. Whatever problems our mom had with the Marine Corps in her young life, they disappeared in that moment. She had dreaded this ceremony for all of their early marriage, but when it came late in life, she was nothing but grateful for the respect the Marines showed our family that day.

The rest of 2000, for both Nancy and me, was taken up by the demands of raising young children. I did take on a couple of music projects. I put together another "Ann Wilson Band" for the opening celebration of Paul Allen's Experience Music Project in August, and I also did a few more months with a musical theater group called Teatro Zinzanni, including stints in San Francisco and Seattle.

While in San Francisco, I had a fling with composer Norman Durkee. You can't even say Norman is smart, because that doesn't begin to cover it. He's a genius, but also a whimsical person. He's also incredible ladies' man, and had been married four times, so his reputation preceded him. He took me to amazing restaurants off the beaten track, and told me wild tales of his life that drew me in. Physically, though, the relationship didn't connect. It had been my first relationship in a long time, but it ended when my stint in the show was over.

In 2001, my life took another shift when a company approached me that was beginning to market a weight-loss surgery. It was called the "Lap Band Adjustable Gastric Banding System." It was a non-permanent band that made the size of your stomach smaller, tricking you into feeling fuller sooner. It was an expensive procedure, but one with a lot of promise, and they offered me the surgery, and my sister Lynn as well, if I would act as a spokesperson. They weren't asking me to do television commercials, but they wanted me to make a promotional video, talk about it in the press, and meet other candidates.

I had reached a point where I had tried everything to lose weight. I was tired, and here was another choice. I saw it as a path to better health. I didn't want to take on any more secrets in my life either, so if I agreed to have the surgery I wanted to talk about it. In January 2002, I underwent the procedure.

I became what they call a "Band-ster." The lap band is still controversial because it harkens back to the old-fashioned ideas of willpower, and control, and you have to take the weight off by following rules. If you eat the wrong foods or drink too much alcohol, you won't lose weight. Having the band trains you to eat less, but you are also required to go through therapy because you can't just turn off the feelings.

In the first weeks after the procedure, I was on a liquid diet while my stomach adjusted. I obsessively watched the Food Network, and other cooking shows, when I couldn't eat. It was a way to enjoy the look, and life-affirming qualities of food without eating. It was probably a different kind of eating disorder.

The first solid food I ate after the procedure was a steak with Larry King at a Washington, D.C., restaurant. "Do you think you're going to be able to hold up under the public scrutiny?" Larry asked. I told him I had to get healthier, and that if I could help other people, it would be worth it, too. Larry asked if I was going to make different music because of the lap band.

"It's not like I'm going to write skinny music, if there is such a thing," I said.

"You're a strong broad, you're going to get through this," he said. Hearing Larry King call me a "broad" while I ate a steak, was one of the most surreal moments of my life.

The lap band worked, and I lost sixty pounds. I made a promotional video for the lap band manufacturer, and did a few interviews with the press. Those mostly went well, though I got annoyed that I was always asked how much I weighed before, and how much I weighed now. I knew that if I gave out details, they would appear in a review of our next album. I didn't want to be reduced, as I had in my childhood school weigh-ins, to a number.

I told people I lost four dress sizes. I was also frequently asked, "How bad was it?" It was as if I could quantify the pain of my struggles. I had agreed to this promotion temporarily, but I didn't want the line "Weight-Loss Spokesperson" next to my name. For years I had been known for my band, and I didn't want to only be known now for my lap band. I'm glad I made the decision to have the surgery, but the recovery was tough, in more ways than one.

In early 2002, Nancy had finally softened up on the idea of touring again as Heart. Part of the reason was because, after being off the road for ten years, the expense of fertility treatments, and what Nancy called her "real-estate disorder" (owning several homes), she and Cameron needed the money. Our tour bus once again became a kid zone.

Compared to our other jaunts, this was a relatively short eight-week summer tour, but it felt fantastic to be with my sister again, playing the music that was our legacy. Howard Leese had finally left Heart, finding a gig with Paul Rogers during our hiatus, but we had put together a new band: Ben Smith on drums, Scotty Olson on guitar, Tom Kellock on keyboards, and Mike Inez of Alice in Chains on bass. Mike brought not only his incredible bass playing, but also a legacy of hard rock (he'd also played in Ozzy Osbourne's band), and a sardonic sense of humor. Bill Cracknell, who was such a character the series *Roadies* was based on him, became our road manager. We hired a new manager, too, named Carol Peters. She promised us that she would never tell me to lose weight, or ask us to push our breasts together for photos. Carol is a tiny woman, but forceful, and an embodiment of the old adage, "small hatchet chop down big tree." She has remained our manager and has played an essential role in every chapter of our success since.

Carol had warned me that my lap band surgery might get attention when we were touring that year, but I wasn't prepared for how often it was talked about. It wasn't something I had done for publicity, but it had the unintended result that people were talking about Heart again in the newspapers, twelve years after our last radio hit.

Along with fans at our typical after-show meet-and-greets, the lap band company wanted me to talk with potential candidates in certain markets. It was humbling, but also moving to meet these people with incredible challenges. They weren't necessarily Heart fans. In Houston, one was a scientist that worked for NASA. A select number were what they called "catastrophically obese," which meant they weighed over seven hundred pounds. Many were in wheelchairs. It was very moving to hear their stories, and it made me realize it was not just a matter of willpower. When you weigh six hundred pounds, it's not because you don't want to lose weight, it's because you are seriously ill. As I accepted these people for their struggles, I was less judgmental of myself.

I am a feminist, and a proud one, but this country's obsession with weight is the biggest problem women have ever had. It's bigger than sexism because it spills over into what women think of other women, and what they think of themselves.

Nancy and I have often been cited as women who broke through gender barriers in music in an era when few others did. We never took up that cause on purpose—it was accidental, or at best the fate we were born to. We were naive, young, and unwilling to believe that we couldn't do something just because we were females. I know rock is better for women being in it, but it is a hard life for the female pioneers.

I lost sixty pounds after the lap band surgery, but the real answer for me was to burn more calories than I consumed, and that meant exercise, and watching my food choices. To this day I maintain my post lap-band weight by following the rules.

But the greatest victory I found in my lifelong battle with weight was freedom from the external judgment that ruled me for so long. I go with *my* instinct now, and not my junior high classmates, my mother's, male rock critics, or even standard of other women. A few years after the lap band was installed, and after I'd lost weight, Patrick MacDonald in the *Seattle Times* took another jab at me in a review of one of our shows. He described me as "zaftig," meaning I was Zeppelin-like. By that point, I was long past caring what an overweight rock critic had to say about my body.

I am never going to starve myself again. I am never going to binge and purge to try to make myself pure. Those techniques worked at one time in my life to make me small, but not in the way I wanted to be small. They withered me. I am no longer a heavy person trying to get good—I am just a person, a woman, and a singer in a band, albeit one with a lap band.

I learned that being smaller wasn't worth my soul taking up less space.

NANCY WILSON

It was refreshing touring with Heart again, and my life felt full in every way. My boys were with me on the road those first two years, and when I was off tour, I was working on the score to whatever Cameron's latest movie was.

In 2001, Cameron's *Vanilla Sky* was our second film in a row with Tom Cruise. I found Tom to be a handsome and engaging alpha male. He also reminded me of Roger Fisher, my old boyfriend. Both Tom and Roger had strong jaws, beautiful teeth, wide smiles, and a strong masculine presence. When Tom first met my mother, who was visiting the set, he went up and kissed her. After that day, Mama told everyone she met that Tom Cruise had kissed her.

Tom once took Cameron and me on a tour of the Scientology "Celebrity Center." We were fearful he would try to recruit us. Cameron's hands got sweaty and clammy as we toured the giant building, but Tom never did anything to recruit us. He just smiled, and showed us around.

We had filmed *Vanilla Sky* in New York City. For the scene where Tom Cruise runs during a nightmare, we had emptied Times Square. During a break in the filming, I stood in a silent Times Square. A few months later, 9/11 happened and the movie's nightmare turned real.

Cameron began working on *Elizabethtown* next, and he had high hopes for it since *Vanilla Sky* hadn't lived up to expectations. He worked on the script endlessly, and I worked on the music.

While I was working on that score, we decided to make another Heart album, and in the fall of 2003, we began recording, mostly in Los Angeles. It was our first new studio album in over a decade, and I acted as coproducer with guitarist Craig Bartock, who had joined the band. All of the songs were ours, with the exception of one track by San Francisco indie act Chuck Prophet. I had never been the driving force behind a Heart album, but for this one I was on a mission of God. When we needed some extra guitar muscle, I called up Alice's Jerry Cantrell and Pearl Jam's Mike McCready. Both contributed smoking licks and made the record truly rock.

We made the album *Jupiter's Darling* for a small independent label that later went bankrupt. We traded the big advances we used to get for total artistic control. We didn't expect the album to sell millions, but it did sell over 100,000 copies, and made it to the *Billboard* top one hundred. More rewarding was that some critics, and many of our longtime fans, cited it as one of our best in decades.

Jupiter's Darling came out in June 2004, and we undertook a summer tour to promote it. We played over sixty dates in Europe and the United States. This was my first jaunt as a mother without my kids on the road, and I found that I missed them terribly.

We took most of 2005 off from touring so I could spend more time with my boys and with my mom, who had started to have serious health problems of her own. *Elizabethtown* came out in the fall of 2005. It bombed. My marriage with Cameron had worked best when I could support his career, but as his career stumbled, there were hairline fractures in our marriage.

As adults, we both suffered from a "Peter Pan" syndrome, and neither of us stepped up to the plate in order to gain all the tools we needed. Early in our relationship, he was happy that he'd found someone with a big enough life of their own they didn't mind him retreating into his work. But after we had kids, it became harder to reach each other. We had tried so long to have children, and when we finally had them, I expected us to get closer, but the opposite happened. We were parents first, friends second, and our relationship got lost. We were both scattered and really busy. We always had busy lives, but once we added high-energy twins, it became chaotic. We needed a manual, or a class, because we couldn't figure it out. The balance between collaborator, parent, husband, wife, parent, lovers shifted, and, ultimately moved us apart.

■ ■ ■

As Cameron and I aged, we also both faced the realities of our parents getting older. His father had died years earlier, though his mother remained a constant presence in our lives, so much so that he dedicated all of his movies to her. But my relationship with my own family was transitioning after Dotes passed. My mom had begun to get more forgetful. At first we thought it was just old age, as she turned eighty in 2003, but later that year she was diagnosed as having Alzheimer's. Her health eroded quickly in the next two years. She had been a lifelong smoker, and we knew the Alzheimer's had its grip on her when one day she forgot that she smoked.

By early 2006, she was going downhill fast. We were booked for a show that month that had been planned for a year, a VH1 tribute to us called "Decades Rock Live." We were set to play with a slew of bands who would perform Heart songs. On the bill was Duff McKagan, Rufus Wainwright, Dave Navarro, Phil Anselmo, and the remaining members of Alice in Chains, who had agreed to reunite for the event to play with us, one of the first times they'd performed together since Layne died.

We considered cancelling the show, but Mama's health stabilized, and Lynn promised to tell us if anything changed, so we went to Los Angeles for the rehearsals. Lynn called just after we left the stage. "Looks like she's going, so you should get here," she said.

Los Angeles had some of its worst thunderstorms in history that day, and every flight was cancelled. It seemed there was no way we could get back to Seattle in time. We decided to try to charter a private plane, and attempt to find a pilot who would be crazy enough to fly into a thunderstorm. We found one, but the air traffic controllers wouldn't let him take off. Finally, the storm cleared for a moment, and we launched into the air, and made it to Seattle.

Mama was still holding on when we arrived at the Windmill House with our guitars. Mama was lying on her bed with a picture of the Oregon Coast behind her, and we started singing all the songs she had taught us growing up. We sang her favorites. She loved the Harry Nilsson song "Lifeline" from "The Point," and also "Think about Your Troubles." We sang them all.

She hadn't eaten for a few days, and her systems were shutting down, but she still had a smile on her face. When I was growing up, Mama once told me something about scientific research on music: That when you die, the last thing to go is your memory of music. When all else is gone, there is still music in your brain. Mama couldn't talk anymore, but she was lying there in bed tapping her toe to the music we were playing.

We sang all night long. We were set to fly to Atlantic City that next morning where the VH1 show was to be filmed. It was our highest profile concert in two decades, and though we thought about cancelling, we also knew Lou would want us to go on with our lives. We kissed her head good-bye, and caught the flight east. We told Lynn that if something happened before our show, to wait to call us until we were offstage.

It was hard to focus on the gig, but it went well. Ann sang "Rooster" with Alice in Chains. Gretchen Wilson sang "Even It Up" with us. Rufus Wainwright sang "Dog and Butterfly." Country singer Carrie Underwood sang "Alone" with Ann. It was rewarding to hear young talent like Carrie telling us how we'd inspired her ("You were the first example that I saw of strong women in rock," she told us.), but that night, all the accolades seemed surreal considering the reality we were facing.

After the concert, Lynn called and Mama was gone. The night she died a huge thunderstorm, probably the same one that delayed us in Los Angeles, rolled through Seattle, and dropped hailstones the size of baseballs. The hail hit the windmill behind Mama's house so hard the blades started spinning like crazy. Lynn could tell it was near the end, so she put one of Mama's favorite records on the stereo—a classical piece called "Pines of Rome"—and blasted it super loud. Lynn felt it was the right music to send her off with, as it starts quiet, but gets really big. In the middle of the night, as the music was blaring, the spinner flew off the windmill. And in that moment, Mama passed. That same night, on the other side of the country, we saw the biggest shooting star I had ever witnessed.

One of Dotes's favorite sayings, left over from his days as a Marine, was, "If you're in trouble, or you need to send a message, then send up a flare." I think the windmill spinner flying off, and that shooting star on the horizon, was Mama sending us a message to always be strong. That storm was Mama's final fury, her final flare.

24

I CAN SEE RUSSIA

Nancy tries to fit in at the PTA and at a swank Nashville party. Cameron and Nancy hit a wall. And finally, how a Barracuda bites. . . .

NANCY WILSON

We began a pattern that would continue for the next several years, of touring mostly during the summer, when our kids were out of school. We no longer brought our children out for an entire tour, though, just stints of several weeks at a time. During the school year, we tried to be at home as much as possible to create a normal family life. It was a difficult juggling act. Being a mom was harder than I had imagined, and being a rock mom complicated things further.

Cameron and I had decided to send our boys to a foreign language immersion elementary school, but I started developing phobia about the attitude other moms had toward me. I imagined they viewed me with contempt because I was a fraud and a vagabond. I was shy and nervous around the other moms, and felt out of place. Before any school event, I would spend hours thinking about what to wear. I looked in the mirror, after picking out what I thought was my most "mom" outfit, and wondered, "Who am I?"

Since I worked nights, I couldn't always drop my kids off at school, so we used a nanny. I picked them up, but even with that I worried about the perception of the other moms. It was particularly difficult to figure out who I was because this was Los Angeles, where there is a palpable caste system. Within certain groups, you had more power if you had multiple nannies, but within others, any nanny was frowned upon. I didn't know where I fit in, and just when I began to feel comfortable, we'd go on tour again.

It didn't help when at one parent-teacher conference I was told one of my sons was being disruptive. "He's working on his sense of humor in the class," the teacher said. "And your other son is drumming during classes, even though he's getting straight A's. Can you get him to pretend like he's paying attention?" I replied in the affirmative. But their infrequent bouts of rebellion at this very proper school were something I secretly savored. My sons were proving to be individuals, raging against the machine. They were not followers.

Over time, I got to know a few other parents at school, and realized I was judging myself far more than others were judging me. My fears were mostly internal, part of my lifelong struggle to fit in. One thing that helped was when I became friends with another mother who was a stay-at-home parent and who had sacrificed her own desires to support her husband. And then her marriage fell apart. I realized there was no magic formula for building a marriage.

The tours during the next few summers were some of our best. We went on the road with Cheap Trick, and Journey, and made friends with those bands. But I always enjoyed the offstage jams on the bus, or at parties, even more than our concerts.

As our career had evolved, we found ourselves often being approached by other musicians who told us we had been an inspiration, and many of our songs found second acts in television or film. We hadn't gone into the business for that recognition, but it felt rewarding, nonetheless. Our songs were covered on *American Idol*, *Glee*, and *Dancing with the Stars*. Fergie did a version of "Barracuda" in *Shrek*, and even Eminem covered us. Our songs ended up in video games like Rock Band and Guitar Hero. But it was always the personal interactions with other performers that made us feel best. We did a television show with Katy Perry, who told us the only reason she agreed to be on the bill was because we were on it. Gretchen "Redneck Woman" Wilson became a good friend. Kelly Clarkson called Ann "my favorite singer of all-time." We met Celine Dion in Las Vegas, and she talked to us so sincerely, and so long, she was late for her own concert.

Heart had never been a country band, but people in Nashville always showed us tremendous love. I suspect it might be because we are sisters, and the idea of a family band gets more respect in the Bible Belt. I know they also love the idea of a "little girl with a gee-tar," because even my solo album got airplay there. So when we were asked for the first time if we wanted to attend the Country Music Awards, we agreed. During the telecast, the camera showed us in the audience a few times, which probably made a few country fans scratch their heads.

After the awards, we went to a party held by MCA president Tony Brown in his Civil War–era mansion. Every star in country was present. I was nervous, so I went to the backyard first, where I spied a few of these ancient gray-haired guys with beards and flannel shirts, probably pickers behind the scenes. One said, "Hey little lady, who are you?"

"I'm Nancy Wilson. I'm with a band called Heart. We, uh, we're from Seattle." There was no recognition on these guy's faces. I might as well have told them we were the Von Trapps. But they had some pot. "Hey, little lady, want some?" one old guy asked.

"Okay, if you insist, just a tiny bit," I said. I hadn't had pot for ages, and this was some mellow stuff, like sixties pot. It was exactly the right kind. Suddenly, I was loose and free. I went into the house, and there were a slew of guitars in the center of the room. Our road manager Bill Cracknell told me later that Tony Brown always wanted his parties to turn into jam sessions, but they rarely did. I've never seen a guitar I didn't want to play. I picked one up, and started into Elton John's "Country Comfort." My pot-smoking friends joined in, and so did my sister. I started walking with the guitar, and gesturing to everyone to "come on." Sheryl Crow grabbed a guitar; George Strait, too. Soon enough it was a superstar jam session with Vince Gill, Clint Black, Michelle Branch, Reba McIntire, and many more. I love hootenannies, but this was one of the best.

At home my life was less harmonious. It started to be a crisis. The distance between Cameron and me had only increased with the demands of work, parenting, and financial pressures. The hormones of being a woman and a mother in my fifties, had contributed too, as had losing both my parents. I needed partnership, but I couldn't find any. And he needed partnership in his way, and couldn't find it from me.

I thought we would overcome those challenges, and maybe with counseling we might get some tools. I wasn't ready to give up hope. But Cameron wanted to separate, and that's what we did in 2008. We'd been together twenty-seven years. It was devastating.

It was the end of our marriage, but also the death of my dream of being married to a writer. When I met Cameron, and he wrote that first letter romancing me, I thought my soul mate would make me his muse. But that first letter was one of the only times he ever wrote me. There had been notes on the kitchen counter, or "I love you" in lipstick on the mirror, but I had imagined a very different life than the one I now found. I know some of it, maybe much of it, was my fault.

I had spent years listening to Cameron read me every line of his movies as he meticulously crafted them, and we pored over them together. Those words on paper had moved me, as they had moved millions of theatergoers, with their humor, poignancy, and ever-lasting belief that love could conquer every obstacle put in its way. Ann may have been one of the few who wasn't swayed by those lines. She later told me that Cameron admitted that his male characters were always saved by the female ones.

My marriage dissolved without cute banter from a script, without the poignant turn of a phrase that a John Cusack–type character might have uttered, and without the female character, even the "Beautiful-Girl-in-a-Car," able to save it. Our final days were very unromantic, and much like other stories of divorce. In the end, it looked and sounded very different from the lines spoken in a Cameron Crowe movie.

I moved to a nearby neighborhood with the aid of my girlfriend Julie Bergman, who helped me through the grieving for years to come. Cameron and I quickly became better parents living in different homes than we had ever been under the same roof. He was a great father, and we became first-rate co-parents. The move wasn't as devastating to our kids as I had imagined. They adapted quickly. Much of what I had struggled with was my idea that Billy and Curtis should grow up in a house that looked much like mine did in Bellevue, with Dotes down the hall listening to music, and Mama always there for us. That wasn't to be their life, but there was more than enough love for them.

We were separated for two years before I formally filed for divorce. Perhaps I was holding out hope that we might find our way back together, but it didn't happen. When I filed for divorce, I knew it could get in the press, but I wasn't prepared for what happened when it suddenly became a news story, and everywhere I went people were asking me about it. We were playing a show that night, and I barely made it through.

When I'd walk through an airport, total strangers would shout out, "Will you marry me?" Just like many of the sexist, or sexual, comments we'd gotten over the years, it was too intimate and inappropriate. It was also terribly embarrassing.

When I first auditioned for Heart and sat in with my sister's band back in those Vancouver cabarets, I never imagined that I was signing up for a life under the microscope. Seeing my personal failures highlighted in the press was a price of fame, but it was a steep cost.

■ ■ ■

I learned another lesson about the price of fame in September 2008. Ann and I were in our dressing room getting ready for a show that night. The television was on in the background, and we were watching the Republican National Convention. Like the rest of America, we wanted to see how John McCain's pick for vice president, Sarah Palin, did on the national stage.

As the speeches progressed, I was putting eye shadow on in the mirror, when I thought I heard our road crew playing "Barracuda" at soundcheck. But I wasn't on stage, so this wasn't soundcheck. I looked up, and "Barracuda" was coming from the television. Sarah Palin was walking on stage as our song played.

"*Whaaaaaaaaaat!*"

It felt as if a crime had been committed against us. This was not happening during some tiny out of the way campaign stop—our song was on every single network in the country, being heard by millions. We were suddenly thrust into Republican politics. Our cell phones immediately started buzzing.

Kelly Curtis called first. "Unfortunately, it happens all the time," Kelly said. "You should issue a statement." Just a month before McCain had used Jackson Browne's "Running on Empty" in an attack ad on Barack Obama, and Browne had sued. There had been similar incidents with Van Halen, and even our old tour mate John Mellencamp. Kelly told me Sarah Palin's nickname when she played high-school basketball was "barracuda" because of her aggressive style of play.

Kelly had me call Pearl Jam's publicist, to prepare a statement. "We are fucking insulted by this," I said. My quote went out over the newswires.

The next day, "Barracuda" was played again at the convention. Our "Barracuda" had become Palin's theme song. It was soon being used on newscasts to introduce segments on Palin. We disagreed with Palin on every single one of her policy stances, but that was beside the point. We were musicians, not lobbyists, or spokespeople for any one party. As entertainers, we saw music as a joining force. Onstage we sang, and didn't preach. Now we were singing behind a preaching Sarah Palin, whether we liked it or not.

We had our attorney Don Passman write to the Republican National Committee. Don told us that ultimately there wasn't much we could do. ASCAP had granted a blanket license to the convention. We issued another statement: "We have asked the Republican campaign publicly not to use our music. We hope our wishes will be honored."

I was unnerved. I told *Entertainment Weekly*, "I feel completely fucked over." I clearly couldn't speak about it without dropping the F-word. We issued yet another statement: "Sarah Palin's views and values in *no way* represent us as American women. We ask that our song 'Barracuda' no longer be used to promote her image. The song 'Barracuda' was written in the late seventies as a scathing rant against the soulless, corporate nature of the music business, particularly for women (the 'Barracuda' represented the business). While Heart did not, and would not, authorize the use of their song at the RNC, there's irony in Republican strategists' choice to make use of it."

It seemed like a no-win situation for us. The more we complained the more Republican bloggers blasted us for what they thought were *our* politics. Even a liberal paper, Seattle's *The Stranger*, made fun of our request to the McCain campaign. They rewrote it as an expletive-filled rant titled "Up Yours, You Old Fart!" It was hilarious, but unfortunately it went viral on the Internet with many thinking we had written it.

And then, out of nowhere, something good happened from something awful. There was enough discussion about "Barracuda," that people began asking, well, what *was* "Barracuda" really about? The song had remained popular on album-oriented radio, but its meaning was never discussed. Because of Palin, DJs were calling to ask us to explain what we meant with the song.

It forced us to talk publicly about our personal values, which we had never done before. We ended up on CNN one night with Joy Behar (followed by Ann Coulter, of course).

I wouldn't wish this situation on my worst enemy, but it sent up a flare. It made the song matter in a way it hadn't mattered before. It became a controversy, and in a strange way, even an ugly controversy was renewed purpose. We never addressed it onstage, but each night we went out to take "Barracuda" back. It gave us a reason to rail against something. It also gave cause for some very humorous headlines, like the one in *Slate*, "Will McCain's 'Heart' Stop?"

I'm not exactly sure how long Palin's campaign used the song, because I couldn't bear to watch. Just a week after the convention, Tina Fey skewered Palin with her *Saturday Night Live* sketch, and her comment "I can see Russia from my house." By the time Palin sat down with Katie Couric, it was over for her. Many cited questions about Palin's qualifications as the main reason McCain lost. Palin became a toothless "Barracuda."

Around the time Tina Fey portrayed Palin on *Saturday Night Live*, a spokesperson for the McCain campaign issued a statement about the Fey's imitation. They called the skit "disrespectful in the extreme." Those were just the words I was looking for that night in the dressing room after hearing "Barracuda" coming from the television.

25

HOPE AND GLORY

Ann does a solo album and faces darkness within. Ann kisses a fish on the lips in Canada on the "Zamboni Tour." Nancy catches "the Seattle Music Disease," and her guitar suffers. . . .

ANN WILSON

The previous year, the greatest dream of my childhood came true when I finally met Paul McCartney. It included little of the magic I had imagined when I was a girl because this wasn't the "smile and a wink" Paul of my teenager novels. "Hi Bird, would you fancy a cup of tea?" would forever remain the voice of my fictional Paul, but it was not the voice of the real one.

The meeting came about when Paul was on tour, and playing in Portland. The concert promoter said Nancy, Sue, and I would be able watch the soundcheck. We thought we'd be the only ones, but there were a couple of dozen others who had won the privilege through a radio station contest. Nancy joked that we were "the other contest winners."

Nancy had met Paul briefly when Cameron asked him to write the title song for *Vanilla Sky*. After Paul's soundcheck, Nancy stood and announced, "Come on. I'm going to introduce you."

As we marched to the stage, I could already recognize the glassy look on Paul's face: It was the one I often had in the middle of a long, exhausting tour. Paul was onstage talking to someone else, but Nancy interrupted him. "Hi Paul, it's me, uh, Nancy, remember of Nancy and Cameron?" He looked at her without recognition, but politely shook our hands, and we quickly exited. It was less that we met Paul, or talked to him, because we really didn't, but we did shake his hand.

The concert itself was more a thrill because we escaped into the church of the Beatles—the very thing that had saved Nancy, Sue, and me when we were teenagers. Back then, I had wanted nothing more in life than to meet Paul McCartney in the flesh, but in the end the real Paul meant less to me than the one who had been onstage at the Seattle Center Coliseum in 1966. That Paul had helped forever change how we thought about ourselves, and helped us imagine that we could be musicians.

At our soundcheck meeting, I had said a total of two words to Paul McCartney: "Hi, Paul." There hadn't been the opportunity to thank him for the inspiration, for that essential gift, but he had heard that story a million times before. It was significant only to us, only to the dreamers.

In 2007, while Nancy was living in California, I recorded a solo album, *Hope and Glory*. The album was mostly covers and featured duets with Elton John, Alison Krauss, k.d. lang, Shawn Colvin, Wynonna Judd, and Nancy. It was an honor to work with those greats, but also rewarding in that it gave me a chance to cover songs I had grown up with, like Jesse Colin Young's "Darkness, Darkness," and the Animals' "We Gotta Get Out of This Place."

I recorded *Hope and Glory* with producer Ben Mink, and that next year Nancy and I began working with Ben on a new Heart record. One of the first tracks Nancy contributed was "Hey You." The song had a great chorus, but she hadn't finished it. She had crafted two different endings One was an "I love you" finale, and the other was "Have you had enough of me?" When she and Cameron divorced, she went with the latter.

It had been hard to watch my sister go through such pain. Cameron had been the first real man Nancy had been involved with. Her whole life she had been in love with the idea of love, and to her the divorce was the loss of an ideal as well. Together we immersed ourselves in our new album, with music providing the healing it always had.

By 2009, as we were working on the album we would eventually call *Red Velvet Car*, I was in need of healing myself. Though I had stopped drugs when my daughter was born, my drinking had steadily increased. The lap band actually made things worse because it while it stopped me from enjoying eating as I had before, it didn't stop the absorption of alcohol, so my drinking accelerated. They warn you against overdrinking with lap band, but I ignored those warnings. Over the years, I built up layers of protection around me, and I often built them with wine. I never drank before we performed, so I never felt I had a real problem. Later, I heard from those around me that they were most worried at times when I wasn't working, when those controls weren't in place.

In November, when we were off tour, I collapsed one day, passed out. I woke to find then ten-year-old Dustin over me saying, "Mom, are you okay?" I said I was fine, but I wasn't. I hadn't even had that much to drink, but my body was telling me I had gone too far.

My sisters were alarmed. Lynn and Nancy made an appointment with my doctor, and they went with me. My doctor conducted a number of tests. She calmly showed us my liver results, and tried to explain it in scientific terms. I couldn't understand what she was saying, so she put it directly: "If you keep drinking," she said, "you are going to die."

Within my family, I had always been compared to Dotes because of our body types, or the fact we were the only brunettes in the Big Five. But he and I had both self-medicated, and so did our grandparents. I remember Dotes once getting up and telling me that he couldn't understand anyone who woke up and said, "What a wonderful day with the birds chirping and the sun shining." It was later that I realized he didn't feel that way because he woke up hung over.

In some ways, mine was a classic story: I was a sensitive and shy person, who had gone into the entertainment business. It was an intense industry with many parties, and often I thought I couldn't face things without medication of some sort. Once I stopped drugs, it was easy to think I had gotten past that, but alcohol was a constant, and I was spiraling downward. Nancy was going through her divorce, my daughter Marie had just left home, my parents had died, and I had gone through menopause. Every one of those things seemed intolerable that month, and I drank my way through them all. I went down into the ocean like a plane.

There had been times when people had warned me about my drinking. My mother, Sue Ennis, Michael Fisher, and a few others had shaken their fingers at me. But I've always been rebellious, and if somebody told me to do something, I usually did the opposite. Even after witnessing Andrew Wood, Kurt Cobain, and my friend Layne Staley die, I still didn't understand the power of my own demons. But when you get to the other side of it, and realize you are an Alcoholic with a capital "A," that illusion is stripped.

People in recovery call it hitting rock bottom, and that's what happened to me. There was only one way this situation would turn out if I continued, and that meant not being alive. I had seen rock 'n' roll casualties—we *had* opened up for the Rolling Stones—but I always thought it would never happen to me. I thought I was made of steel, and I could handle anything. Looking at my doctor holding my liver results, and the alarmed faces of my sisters, I realized many of my beliefs were fallacies. In the band, and in the family, I was Atlas holding up the world, and if I went down, much would sink with me.

I found out later my family and crew had already talked about an intervention. They had even built a break into Heart's touring schedule with a stint in treatment in mind. Ultimately, they decided I might rebel if they chose that, and they were right. The motivation had to come from me. It was awful, and it was terrifying, and part of the reason I wanted to stop was simply because I saw the idea of treatment as more humiliation, and something that would take me away from singing, my life force.

By the time I got home, word had spread, and the elves were in action. My assistant, Sherri Anderson, and Dustin's nanny, Roxanne Harris, had already cleaned all the alcohol out of the house. It was probably not an easy task. It was a good call, because in those first tenuous days I might have slipped.

I never went to a twelve-step meeting or into treatment. But I did get support from friends, family, and bandmates who had gone that route, so I knew the language. One of those friends told me that as time went on, the whisper would get quieter. I did go to therapy, which aided in understanding the things that drove me to isolation, and the roots of my drinking.

I'm still cautious. I call ahead before a tour, and have the hotel minibar emptied before I get there. There's always alcohol backstage at any rock show, but it's not in my dressing room and not on my tour bus. I didn't get sober for everyone else; I did it for myself. In that way, the very stubbornness that stopped me from looking at my issues for so long has helped me. I know some around me thought I would fail, but I am stubborn enough to want to prove them wrong. And I remain so.

Sobriety became yet another shift in the way I approached music. My songs have always dealt with my life experiences, but this was a real big one that cried out to be written about. It was part of where the title song "Red Velvet Car" came from: "Maybe you got hit real hard / Maybe you are on the floor / People screaming out your name / And they don't trust you anymore / I'm coming for you."

I haven't had a drink in nearly three years. It has been difficult at times, but it's something I'm very proud of. Sobriety is still a bit like a project for me, like the way I might write a song that has no end. The melody and lyrics are ever evolving, and though a verse might be written here or there, the chorus changes constantly. There is always a conversation about it going on inside my head. I know it is a song I will continue singing for the rest of my life.

We released *Red Velvet Car* in 2010. It became our first top ten album in twenty years, a rewarding sign that we still had a strong fan base four decades after our start. It was one of our best-reviewed albums in years, with *Rolling Stone* raving, "these barracudas still draw buckets of blood." That review also read, "Heart's finest moment might be right now, as the Wilson sisters keep making good music years after their classic-rock peers have faded away." This from the same publication that once called us "cock rock without the cock." Things had shifted in music, and in rock 'n' roll journalism, and we were no longer lampooned for the very idea that we wanted to rock. That subtle change might be Heart's greatest blow against the empire.

Red Velvet Car felt like Heart had "re-upped," a term that Dotes always used when a Marine enlisted for another stint. Nancy's powerful "Hey You" became one of the singles, but the album also included "Sunflower" which she had written as a birthday gift to me. I turned sixty that year. I was newly sober, and with a hit record. There were very few sixty-year-olds who ever hit the top ten, which was a particular joy I had never imagined when I was younger. Heart had become one of only a handful of groups to score top ten hits in four different decades, a feat in the modern music business that was nearly impossible. It felt that week as if I had re-upped in life, and in music.

We promoted the album at first with what we called our "Zamboni tour of Canada." We played some of the same hockey rinks we had in our first few years, and in the dead of the winter. But Canada always treated us well, as if we were hometown girls. Our shows sold out, and the tour showed up on the *Billboard* charts for the hottest that season, just behind Lady Gaga and Rihanna.

In many cities we were treated like royalty, not just a touring rock band.

In Newfoundland, we were "screeched," a ritual where visitors are forced to kiss the lips of a fish, eat a fish gizzard, and throw back a shot of "screech" rum. I substituted juice for the rum. That night there was a huge dinner, and a sing-a-long. Nancy and I won everyone over with our version of "The Great Titanic." It was one of the first songs we learned to sing, but it was particularly important to Newfoundland, which was near where the ship sank. In Vancouver, members of their First Nations held a ceremonial dance dressed like eagles, ravens, wolves, and whales for us. One of the dancers looked exactly like a Native American Mick Jagger, complete with oversized lips.

One of the strangest experiences of the tour came in Calgary, of all places, the very city where I had been were fired from Lucifer's in 1975. In the years since that gig, we always had successful shows there, with generous and adoring audiences, and Lucifer's had long since closed. This time we were playing the decidedly upscale Southern Alberta Jubilee Auditorium, and it was one of the best shows of the tour.

Calgary city officials came before the show to give us the honorary Calgary "White Hat," which is bestowed on visiting dignitaries. We were asked to recite an oath: "Heart, having pleasured ourselves in the only genuine cowtown in Canada, namely Calgary, Alberta, and having been duly exposed to exceptional amounts of heartwarming, handshaking, foot-stomping, down home, country-style western spirit do promise to share this here brand of western hospitality with all folks and critters who cross my path." We repeated the oath, stumbling over the phrase "having pleasured ourselves," and they put oversize cowboy hats on us for a photo op.

In a town that almost ended my career, and that of Heart, where we had nearly been poisoned by Pine Sol–laden food, where we had died in a way, and also been reborn as we left on a train to open for Rod Stewart in Montreal, we were now honored guests. We had "pleasured ourselves" in Calgary, and Calgary, apparently, would never forget. Nor would we.

▪ ▪ ▪

In June 2011, U2's massive "360-degree" tour came to Seattle's Qwest Field, and Bono's assistant called to invite Nancy and me. It was the single biggest tour in rock history, and when Bono calls, you come.

We had first met Bono in 2004 when we played in Dublin. He came to our show, and backstage afterward we sat down and talked about the craft, not the business, for hours. It was the kind of deep conversation you can only have with another singer. He wanted to talk about how I connected with the audience with my voice, how certain songs were written, why I sang a song a specific way. He brought us a dozen white roses that night, and we kept them until they dried up. They came in a bucket and even after the roses were gone, we traveled with that bucket in our dressing room, and referred to it as if Bono was still a presence in our lives, which he was. "Can you hand me that mascara, right next to Bono's bucket?" Nancy would ask me. It became sort of a holy relic.

When we walked into Qwest Field in June 2011, staring at the "Claw," U2's giant scaffolding, I wasn't expecting to do anything other than say hi to Bono because it was right before showtime. But Bono immediately embraced us as if minutes, rather than years, had passed since we'd last seen him. There were a handful of people in the corners of his dressing room, and I immediately recognized Eddie Vedder, Matt Cameron, and Mike McCready of Pearl Jam, and greeted them, too.

Bono is one of the most powerful human beings in the world, but the reason he's a great lead singer is because he knows how to tell a story. He worked his small audience backstage by telling us about his long recovery from his back injury. "It was a pretty close call," he said. A piece of a disc had ripped through one of his ligaments, and it was threatening his spinal cord. "I could have lost the use of my left leg," he said.

The operation was a success, but he spent eight weeks in rehabilitation, which was a mental challenge unlike any he had faced. He turned to classic books he hadn't read since childhood, including T. E. Lawrence's *Seven Pillars of Wisdom*, the story of Lawrence of Arabia. Bono said Lawrence's perspective on Arab independence had given him resolve that anything could be overcome. He explained to us how the title of the book was Lawrence's loose interpretation of the "seven pillars" of Biblical verse. And then Bono recited from memory the dedication poem that starts Lawrence's book: "I loved you, so I drew these tides of men into my hands, and wrote my will across the sky and stars to earn you freedom."

It was a surreal moment. I felt Bono coaxing himself open, as if we were his bridge to begin to communicate with the sixty-five thousand waiting in the audience. A roadie opened the dressing room door, announcing it was showtime, but Bono held up a finger to indicate that he wasn't ready. He hadn't finished his story on Lawrence.

Eventually, Bono stood up, put on his leather jacket, gave an Elvis-like shoulder shrug, and walked onto the long ramp to the stage. Our backstage enclave was ushered toward the mixing board, to watch the show. Eddie Vedder then lit up some of the most powerful marijuana I'd ever smelled, and I tried not to breathe until the fumes passed my airspace.

In the tiny mixing board area sat one person, who I realized was also probably in the dressing room shadows as Bono told us his stories of Lawrence, and overcoming impossible odds. It was Steve Jobs. I had never seen him in person before, and I was struck by how thin he was, a matchstick of a man, but with a presence nonetheless. I knew he was ill—he would die just a few months later. But as U2 began to play, the expression on Jobs's face shifted, and a huge smile came upon him.

The show was transcendent. I had never seen rock be so big and so intimate all at once. "Where the Streets Have No Name" was my favorite moment. It seemed as if the whole glory train of rock 'n' roll was bursting out of the tunnel.

As I watched Bono's performance I kept thinking about the words we had exchanged before and in fact every time we talked together. Bono always wanted to chat about how it is the lead singer's job alone to make sure there is a connection with the audience. It was a huge responsibility he said, whether you are in a bar playing to a tiny crowd, or performing to sixty-five thousand people.

▪ ▪ ▪

In the summer of 2011, we accepted an offer to open up for Def Leppard on their world tour. I had totally missed Def Leppard in the eighties, and I only knew them as a big metal band. My initial thought was that by touring with them, we'd have something to aspire to. They seemed to represent the empire we had raged against. The tour would also take us to Australia for the first time, and that was a place Nancy and I had always wanted to visit.

As the opening act, we found ourselves on a stage Def Leppard had constructed, and at first I had trouble getting used to their eighties "ego ramps," that made you stand even higher on the stage. Our staging was lights, and nothing else, as we wanted our songs to be the show. Their set had the giant ramp, flame machines, fireworks, smoke machines, and the massive production of a Broadway show. I assumed we would rule the night with our simple sincerity.

Sometimes that happened, but other times it was impossible. There were shows we went out, and hit it as hard as we could, and Def Leppard flattened us. It was like "Bambi Meets Godzilla." There is no arguing with butt rock. At a lot of dates though, we got better notices than they did. I loved a headline in Milwaukee: "Heart out-throbs Def Leppard," but it was apples and oranges, really.

I had also been naive about the amount of partying there would be on the tour. I had expected, because these guys were in their fifties, they had been tamed. Once I saw the reality of it, I said, "Holy shit, how am I going to live through this?" Their attitude about drinking was that it was just part of the experience. The tour was like sharing a bunk with Keith Richards for six months: charming, exhausting, and toxic. I came out of it sober, but it wasn't that much fun sitting there with my soda water, while everyone else partied down.

I'd injured a knee during the tour, and Def Leppard's Joe Elliott told me to have it taped up in their "health" room. The room had a massage table, candles, and incense. But it also had cartons of cigarettes at the ready, and a full bar set up. That was their idea of healthy.

Def Leppard were good people, though, and I felt a real connection with Joe Elliott. He would come offstage from the ego ramp, and immediately turn into a sweet and thoughtful guy. A few times we also talked about how difficult it is to be a lead singer. "This is hard stuff," he said. "There's the wall of expectation. Do you flip the bird to the crowd, and refuse to play the hits they want to hear, or do you give it to them? If you don't do 'Barracuda,' or 'Pour Some Sugar on Me,' they are going to boo." Joe felt as trapped as I did by past hits.

The U.S. tour initially had been scheduled to end in Seattle, where we could go home to our own beds. But Joe Elliott's father died in the middle of the summer, so the tour was extended. We knew, and understood that as much as anyone. The finale was in San Antonio, and we ended our set with a desperate version of the Who's "Love Reign O'er Me," and the emotions overtook Nancy. She grabbed her guitar, and smashed it to bits—Nancy was as exhausted as I was with the big production tour we'd been on for most of the year. We had long ago moved away from eighties bombastic excess and wanton destruction. But in San Antonio we'd reverted to our more barbaric selves. Nancy's guitar lay in pieces on the stage after the show was over. It was the perfect punctuation for the end of a tour that celebrated the past.

26

GLIMMER OF A DREAM

Heart receives a Rock and Roll Hall of Fame nomination. Nancy's romantic life takes a surprising new twist. A new album springs forth, and a boxed set. And Ann and Heart go full circle, back where it all began by a cottage near a creek. . . .

NANCY WILSON

In the fall of 2011, we were nominated for the Rock and Roll Hall of Fame. It was quite an honor, and would have seemed impossible to us when we first started, when we were driving around Canadian back roads, or playing Michael J. Fox's high school prom. We didn't make the final list of inductees for the year, but getting nominated, and being on the short list, was a step toward that recognition, and one we were grateful for.

In early 2011, my romantic life also took an unexpected turn. I'd casually known Geoff Bywater for a few years, as he worked in music production on television shows for Fox. Heart's manager, Carol Peters, arranged dinner with him. I thought, "What can be wrong with that?" I knew it was time for me to get out there.

I went with Carol to meet Geoff at a restaurant. It was an edgy dinner because he felt nervous and I was so anxious I nearly bolted. He really liked me, but I was scared and decided it was too soon. Geoff was divorced himself, and was a great father to four wonderful children.

Geoff was persistent, and in the fall of 2011, we went out again a few times, usually with mutual friends. Every date we had was plagued by my nervousness, or the awkwardness that we always had chaperones with us. Then, on what was our fifth date, it was just us. Something shifted, and a deep and beautiful conversation ensued. At the end of the night, there was a kiss. That kiss changed everything.

I discovered in that one kiss something about myself that I had lost. I found that I could be an adult with another adult, and that I could move on. I finally gave myself the permission to let the past be the past. In Geoff, I found a trusted friend, and he helped me close the book of guilt and wrong I had been carrying around. Together we opened a brand new book with that kiss.

I never thought I would be in love again. I never thought I would be in another relationship. My life had become centered around Heart, my sisters, my friends, and my children. Though my friends and family described me as the "most hopeless romantic" they'd ever known, that part of me had gone missing for a few years. It came back with Geoff.

After that magical date, Heart left for Australia for the long last leg of our tour with Def Leppard. Over the next month, Geoff and I wrote love letters back and forth electronically. We talked on the phone a few times but it was through written correspondence, like lovers in the Victorian times, that we formed our true bond. We decided to go steady, and he mailed me a bracelet. I mailed him a sunflower that I painted. I later printed up and bound all the letters, texts, and emails that we had exchanged into a book. We wrote six-hundred-and-three love letters in one month.

As Geoff and I became serious, I let Cameron know I had someone in my life. Cameron had moved on into a new relationship, as well. I told him I was committed to being better at communicating with Cameron in our original family group. Cameron supported me, and that freed up my heart and improved the bond of our co-parenting.

In early 2012, Geoff and I became engaged. We moved fast, but it felt like a wave overtook us, and at our age, you really know what you want. On April 28, 2012, in a restaurant in Mill Valley, California, we were married. Ann, Lynn, my two sons, and my dear friends Sue Ennis and Kelly Curtis watched me start this new chapter. Geoff's children were there, and his friend Sammy Hagar who owned the restaurant.

Love heals everything. It's a lot like music.

In 2011, Ann and I also began working on a new Heart album, which we decided to title *Fanatic*. Ben Mink came aboard as our producer once again. We were on the road a lot that year, so we cut some of the record in unusual places, like hotel rooms. Ben would book the corner room on a top floor, and we would sing and play at full volume. Only occasionally would we get a complaint from the front desk. It showed how far the music industry had changed from the days we were with Mushroom in Vancouver, thirty-five years before, when you needed a giant, acoustically perfect studio to make a record.

We also did a few sessions in traditional recording studios, not just hotel rooms. In early 2012, we were working on final vocals at the Village in Los Angeles when we got a message that Elton John was down the hall, and he wanted us to come say hi. I was always nervous around Elton, but he was down-to-earth and warm, and we'd become good friends. Around that time he had been asked by a publication what he thought about Heart, and Elton said: "I have been a huge fan of Heart their whole career. I love that they rock, and the sound of Ann's voice always sends shivers down my spine. I am happy to say that they have become great friends. I absolutely adore them." We adored him, too.

We walked into Elton's studio, and just he and producer T-Bone Burnett were there. We sat on the couch, and they played us four tracks from Elton's upcoming album. Elton wanted us to return the favor by playing our album. "Our stuff is nowhere near ready to be heard," I said. I could just as well have said, "We're not worthy."

But Sir Elton John insisted. We told him we'd send him a copy, once it was all done. But Elton would have none of that, so we cued up the few tracks that were close to being done. To watch Elton John be the first person to listen to *Fanatic* was a memory I will never forget. Here was the same Elton John I had seen in Vancouver in the early days of Heart, when I had purchased that counterfeit scalped ticket to his show, and climbed a fence to sneak in. Here was the same Elton John who wrote the songs that I taught Kelly Curtis to play on guitar when I was a twelve-year-old guitar instructor. Here was the same Elton John who wrote all those great songs with Bernie Taupin, the same Bernie Taupin who penned "These Dreams," my song, and Heart's first number-one hit. And here was that same Elton John closing his eyes, tapping his feet, and listening to our new album.

"*Fanatic* is fantastic," Elton said—Elton John, Captain Fantastic himself.

ANN WILSON

At the same time we were working on *Fanatic*, we were also compiling our first boxed set, *Strange Euphoria*. It included three CDs, one DVD of a 1976 live performance from Pullman, Washington, and even a bonus CD of five Led Zeppelin covers offered through Amazon titled *Heart: Zeppish*. I was a bit wary of putting out the Zeppelin CD, since we didn't want to get swallowed up as a band that covered Led Zeppelin all the time, but that bonus CD gave us a chance to release some of the material we'd recorded with John Paul Jones. That seemed like kismet.

We'd been working on *Strange Euphoria* for over a decade, imagining it, drawing up song lists, and refining the design. When it was done, the fifty-one tracks offered our first full career retrospective. We had decided to include several previously unreleased songs that challenged some of the basic assumptions listeners had about Heart. Songs like "Strange Euphoria" and "Boppy's Back" had humor and lightness to them, which was always a big part of us but rarely made it on record. Musicians constantly cut up behind the scenes, and we have lots of outtakes of Nancy and me cracking wise and being funny. It felt liberating to put some of those tracks on the set and to give a wider spectrum to our songwriting process.

The set also included the very first record we ever made, *Through Eyes and Glass*, cut when we were teenagers backing a country musician. Copies of the few forty-five singles that were sold in the day have gone for hundreds of dollars on eBay. Hearing that song again made me think about how seriously we took our music. Even as kids, we were railing against people who were posers, just faking it. More than a little of the Heart catalog was shaped by our early experiences growing up in the First Congregational Church, where we learned about righteousness. That personal authenticity has always been ground zero for us.

The title song "Strange Euphoria" was always one of my favorites. We wrote it with Sue in the seventies, when we were all feeling euphoria after some herbal help. But the title also summed up the feeling that music has given us from the start, a euphoria that can't quite be explained—an absolute crazy high.

There were many moments in 2011 that felt like we were cycling back full circle to our early roots, and deciding to write this book was part of that, of course. I had always thought one day we would tell our story, and in a 1979 interview with *Picture* magazine, I even predicted it. "I hope I never grow up," I said, "but, if I do, I hope I have enough money to travel so I can try and get young again. I'll probably write down what happened to me and publish it. I think people would find it interesting to know what went into Ann Wilson."

We mixed part of *Fanatic* in Studio X, the studio we once owned. Again, we were back where we began because we had recorded so many of our early hits—*Little Queen*, *Dog and Butterfly*, and *Bebe Le Strange*—in that building. The millions we invested in the studio remake had served it well, and to hear our new songs in that space was thrilling, and an emotional renewal. I could still remember the controversy, back when Mushroom had placed an armed guard outside of the studio as we finished and mixed *Magazine* in a marathon session, probably prepared to shoot me if I messed up a single note on purpose. Heart was a unified band then with a singular mission, and it felt like us against the world, which, of course, it was.

Over the years, we lost touch with some of the early band members. There have been twenty-seven members of Heart over the years, besides Nancy and me, and not all of us were close, though many became extensions of our family. Howard Leese played with us for twenty-four years, and we always stayed in touch with him. Though Howard wasn't in the very first Vancouver incarnation, he was running the tape machine at Mushroom that day when I cut our very first demo, and from the moment he joined the band the next year he was an absolutely essential part of Heart. When Heart went on hiatus in the nineties, Howard had to find other work. He was quickly snatched up by Paul Rogers of Bad Company, and has played with him ever since. He deserved to be picked up quickly because he is such a fantastic player.

Ben Smith has had the second-longest tenure, playing drums with us for over twenty years and counting, and he's the only non-Wilson to be both in Heart and the Lovemongers. Guitarist Craig Bartock has also been with Heart for ten years and counting, which rivals the tenures of Denny Carmassi and Mark Andes, from the eighties.

When we played the Backstage with John Paul Jones in the nineties, Roger Fisher, Michael Derosier, and Steve Fossen all came to the show and visited with us. Since I had gone to see Led Zeppelin with those guys, it seemed appropriate,somehow. Fossen and I always got along well. I played with Steve for so many years, starting back with Hocus Pocus, and we had an intuition with each other, onstage and off, and a shared sense of humor.

Our dealings with the men in Heart with whom we'd had relationships have always been more complicated and filled with a wide range of emotions. Nancy's ex, Roger Fisher, went on to have seven children. When Roger lost two of his children, one as an infant and another as a young adult, it was a heartbreaking turn of events for us as well. When his daughter Alisha, who had been born when we all lived together in Vancouver, died a few years back, it was a deep grief we all felt. because she had been part of our extended family.

For years after our break-up, I had almost no contact with Michael Fisher. Though we never married, we had a complicated split, with many painful emotional and financial details. I heard he had married a couple of times and had many children. He continued to work in the music industry, developing state of the art speakers, doing what he did so well, and providing PA systems to venues.

One day in 1991, when we were working at Bad Animals, I was walking into the studio, carrying Marie in my arms—she was a baby then—and there was Michael walking out. I hadn't seen him in over a decade.

"Hi," he said. "Who is this?"

"This is my daughter, Marie," I replied.

Michael wanted to know how I'd gotten Marie, whether I birthed her or not. I told him I had adopted.

"Wow," he said, looking at Marie. "I had no idea. That's so great. She's beautiful."

We only spoke for a few minutes, but Michael told me he had several children—he would father eleven in total. I know both he and Roger are good parents.

The last time I saw Michael was just a few months after that random studio run in. Once again, I was walking into a venue through one door, and he was walking out another, carrying part of a PA system. We just shot a look—in true Ann and Michael form—and it was a soul-melding look across a room. No words were spoken. No words needed to be spoken. The silence was molten.

In the past few years, we have rekindled a friendship through email, like many old friends eventually do. Michael and I sometimes discuss parenting issues through e-mail. I feel that he is a wise and confident patriarch. After all the time that has gone by it feels like once again I am saying "hello" to a person I was once so close with. I was twenty-eight years old when we broke up, and he was only a couple of years older, so we were both kids. I hold Michael no ill will for the actions of his youth, or for his fiery passion. There was power in that passion, and it fueled many of my songs, it fueled Heart, and it fueled me for a time.

This thing we all built together—all twenty-seven members of Heart—has had a life beyond anyone one of us. But as different players have moved through the band, the thing that has remained constant is Nancy and me. We have tried to remain true to the thing we created so many years ago. The words we come up with, the feelings we share under the name of Heart, are just as sincere as they were in the *Dreamboat Annie* days. To us, and we can only hope to our fans, they are just as meaningful.

In May 2011, Nancy and I traveled to Vancouver with this book's cowriter to go back and visit the places we'd lived and worked in our early days. We'd been in Vancouver for many shows in the subsequent decades, but we'd never returned to our old haunts, and I couldn't remember the addresses. I emailed Michael Fisher, and with his encyclopedic memory, Michael provided the exact locations.

Once we began driving into Vancouver, I hardly needed an address because I could smell my youth. In downtown, we passed the former clubs where we'd made our mark: the Cave, the site of Heart's very first show, and Oil Can Harry's, where I'd had the surreal experience of singing "Stairway to Heaven" while Robert Plant walked through the club. Vancouver was now a thoroughly modern city of skyscrapers, with none of the hippie vibe it had in 1971. I could still remember the excitement I felt moving there as a young woman, as if a whole new world was opening up. I still have "landed emigrant" status in Canada, a nation that became my second home for six years. I could legally move back today if I wished.

Once we left downtown, and headed over the Lion's Gate Bridge toward West Vancouver where many of our rental homes had been, time seemed to stand still. We passed a grocery store. "That's where I shopped for the entire band, with five dollars, trying to buy enough food to keep us alive for a week,"

I announced sentimentally. In the parking lot of that Safeway, I had backed into a pole, and damaged the bumper of Heart's van. I had been afraid to go home and tell Michael Fisher, thinking he'd go crazy at the damage to our hard-earned new investment. But Michael had forgiven my fender bender. Perhaps he had a sixth sense that soon after our van would come to a far worse fate when it collided with the moose that nearly killed me.

Within moments we were driving up the hill toward Inglewood Avenue, taking the same route I took as a young woman when I went to Vancouver to be with Michael. Had I really hitchhiked from the bus station, getting a ride from a stranger? Had I really walked the last few blocks up what now seemed like a steep hill, carrying my guitar, and a backpack full of my clothes? Had I really been that young, that innocent, that full of possibility, that possessed by longing?

The big Tudor house, once full of naked hippies, was gone, and two modern homes had replaced it. We peeked around one, and I saw the spot overlooking Lassen Creek where Michael's round house cottage had stood. The cottage had been demolished, but a gazebo had been built in its exact location.

Lassen Creek was idyllic the day we visited. Forty years had passed since I had first arrived, but other than the new homes, the setting was the same. One of the only changes was that Sarah McLachlan now lived across the road, in a regal gated mansion. That the home of the woman who started Lilith Fair is fifty yards from where I wrote all our early songs seemed like sweet justice.

And though the visit brought back a flood of memories of my early romantic life, of the start of Heart, of our five-year plan, my strongest memory was of the music. It had been sitting outside the cottage by the creek, where I had written those *Dreamboat Annie* songs that in the decades since had taken on a life of their own. I had stood in these woods, with a soul full of love, and played my flute, accompanied by the sound of the gurgling brook. In that earlier version of Ann, those songs had existed only as a glimmer of a dream in a young girl's imagination. I had sung their words countless times onstage, but for a moment that day in Vancouver, they came to my lips as spoken words, without melody, a credo of sorts: "Cold, late night so long ago, when I was not so strong, you know."

I hadn't written the songs back then, even though many came straight from my life, from my diaries, from my phone calls with my mother, from my nights of passion with the first man I loved. I hadn't written the songs back then because I never do.

The songs had written me.

The year we started working on *Fanatic*, I turned sixty-one. My daughter, Marie, had a baby the year before, and I became a grandmother. My passion for music remained, and remains, as alive, and as young, as my granddaughter, Niobe. Almost as soon as *Fanatic* was done, the songs to follow started to write themselves in my head, and I don't think that will ever stop.

When *Fanatic* was completely done, and I began typing up the official song lyrics to submit to our music publisher, I discovered themes that seemed to reoccur in all our work. The strongest thread was the wild romantic heart in flames, something that has been with me from the start, but if the songs weren't about adult love, they were about the love between friends, or family.

Some of those familial themes were probably were ingrained in me even before I ever wrote a single song, and they showed up again on *Fanatic*. In "Dear Old America," struggle of growing up in a military family was apparent. The lyrics went, "When I get back, I'm gonna own this town / Shine that medal and wear that crown / Fall on my knees and kiss the ground / Dear Old America." Even years after Dotes and Mama had passed, the legacy of our youth and of the Marine Corps echoed in everything we did, along with our dad's post-traumatic stress disorder. Just because the person is gone, does not mean the bell stops ringing. In that way, songwriting is a bit like therapy too, just as it is part of the ritualized passing down of the family story.

When I was writing some of the songs for *Fanatic*, I felt as if I was shaken to my core, wide open to the muse. It was as if I'd been struck by lightning, just like when I was a young girl. That certainly was true of "Rock Deep (Vancouver)," a song we wrote after our visit back to Inglewood Avenue. "Seattle in the rearview mirror," it began, and then chronicled our early story. "I still can see you sleeping," the third verse went, "in a bed of moonlight seeping / and I remember crying / 'cause I knew the sun was rising."

The final verse grabbed an image similar to the photograph on the cover of *Dreamboat Annie*: "A young girl with a burning heart / stares down at the big ships anchored far below / and she knows where she is going / 'cause her very soul was glowing / and in this gentle harbor / she don't need to go no farther / rock deep."

To me, this last album feels more Wilson/Wilson than ever. The bond between Nancy and me grows deeper each year. We are more experienced women, and grown-up women, and mothers, and I am a grandmother. But at our core, we are as we have always been: Fanatics about love, art, truth, and the belief that we can do anything together we set our minds to. We write our own story our own way.

I remain a fanatic about music, about the power of love to heal, about Heart. When I'm onstage and I look over at my sister, I see not only a mature woman with a guitar, I see the child within Nancy, and the child within me. I see both of us on the floor with our heads propped up on our hands, in front of a tiny black-and-white television, watching the Beatles, and imagining a future that at the time was beyond imagination for girls of our generation.

But ultimately, I am more a fanatic of Nancy Wilson than anything else. I always have been, and always will be. I need only look over at my sister—onstage, or off—and know she is a fanatic of me.

EPILOGUE

From the White House, to the Rock and Roll Hall of Fame, to a piecrust stage again, all in one season. . . .

ANN WILSON

This book was first published in September 2012. The notation "bestselling author" was something we never thought would end up on our resume, but it happened. The response from readers was gratifying, but the attention had another unexpected outcome: Don Smith, who had taken me to the Junior Prom, and who I had heard through the grapevine had died, turned out to be very much alive. Don savored the book, and loved being included.

The original lineup of Heart also weighed in. Howard Leese loved it, and Steve Fossen said he enjoyed it. Michael Fisher took issue with the story of how the "Round House" by the creek went from a place he and I lived, to a band house. His memory was that neither of us felt good about it, but it was a necessity at the time. Michael and Roger also announced they were planning their own book, titled *Bros*. I very much look forward to reading their take on their extraordinary lives.

The original lineup of Heart was on our mind that season because just before Christmas of 2012, when we heard that we had been inducted into the Rock and Roll Hall of Fame.

NANCY WILSON

We found out about the Hall of Fame when we were coming back from the White House. So much of 2012 was surreal, but this was the most surreal moment of all. Within just a few short days, we met President Obama, made Robert Plant weep, and were admitted to the elite eagles nest of the Rock and Roll Hall of Fame.

We met Obama at the Kennedy Center Honors, where we were asked to do a song to honor Led Zeppelin. The day of the show, we walked into the White House, as the Marine Corps band was playing, and saw eighteen individual Christmas trees. It was something out of a dream, and I couldn't help but think of our mother, who had brought us up for a moment just like this.

We snaked through lines of security, and slowly made our way towards the reception with the President. As we approached the hall, we could see the other Kennedy Center honorees around the President, including David Letterman, Buddy Guy, Dustin Hoffman, and Natalia Makarova. In line with us were many celebrities, including Jack Nicholson, Stephen Colbert, and Alec Baldwin. We got right to the door of the reception room, and then we were stopped by security. A velvet rope was put in place, and it was announced that it was full. We had arrived at the White House, but we were again outsiders.

We did get to meet the President later. As we approached, my mind was racing about what to say. I practiced many witty comments, but when my moment finally came, and I felt his earnest handshake, all I could say was, "Thank you for your leadership." I was back in high school social studies, the ultimate nerd again. "I'm doing my best," President Obama said. To Michelle, I said, "You rock!"

She looked as surprised as I was to hear those words come out of my mouth.

ANN WILSON

That night we had our moment at the Kennedy Center Honors show, and we took it. We performed "Stairway to Heaven" with a gospel choir, string section, and with John Bonham's son Jason, on drums.

Going onstage, playing in front of the President, First Lady, and the members of Led Zeppelin was one of the most sublime moments of my life. Even on a normal night, you look down at your audience at your own risk, because as a singer you are leading the charge. You must stay exactly in the moment, and in the song. This time I looked out, and in my view was Yo-Yo Ma, President Obama, and Jimmy Page.

I'm a bit of Zeppelin purist, so I wasn't initially sure about the choir, as I didn't want it to be overreaching, but in the end it came out velvety and great. We couldn't see the Zeppelin guys that clearly from the stage, but watching the television broadcast later, the cameras seemed to catch Robert Plant's face full of deep emotion. This could have been for any number of reasons, but Robert's beautiful tears that night became famous.

Then, there was a big dinner with all the honorees. Jack Black kept coming up to me, and making jokes, telling me that the best way to sing is to never warm up because "it's bad luck." He said he'd seen too many excellent rehearsals followed by lousy performances. I was seated next to Kid Rock at the dinner, and despite the fact that we have political differences, he was interesting, smart, and funny.

Jimmy, Robert, and John Paul were at the table next to us, and were very gracious and warm. We were good friends with John Paul Jones from working with him on *The Road Home,* which he produced and played on. Plant was not the smoldering God I had met earlier in my life, but his heart seemed light, and I had never seen him look so happy. He said, "I want you to meet my girl," as he presented Patty Griffin. I said, "Congratulations.

How long have you been married?" "Oh no," he said laughing, "She's just my girl." Plant told me that he hated it when other people did "Stairway," but he had really liked our version. I thought to myself, "Okay, I can die now."

It was the excitement surrounding that Kennedy Center performance, and the raves it earned that shaped our summer 2013 "Heartbreaker" tour. Jason Bonham's band would open, we'd follow with a full-on Heart show, and the night would end with thirty minutes of Led Zeppelin songs with Jason on drums. I had initial reservations about this idea for the tour, but the response to Kennedy Center show kept growing. Still, I felt we shouldn't sign on without the blessing of Led Zeppelin. Jason asked them directly. "Do it," they said. "It'll be great." The hammer of the Gods had sounded approval.

NANCY WILSON

From the moment the Hall of Fame show was being discussed, there was tension about who would speak, who would play, and how it all would go. The Hall of Fame inducts the version of the band that made the first album that qualifies, and even though we've had thirty players in Heart over the years, the inductees were to be our original lineup: Ann, Roger, Steve Fossen, Howard Leese, Michael Derosier, and myself.

By email, there was much posturing about what would be played, with whom (the Hall of Fame encourages other musicians play with you, so we picked Soundgarden's Chris Cornell, Alice in Chains' Jerry Cantrell, and Pearl Jam's Mike McCready, the Seattle super group of all-time), and when to rehearse. We settled on doing "Crazy on You" with the original lineup. Even before rehearsals there were disagreements. The original lineup guys wanted to walk in after we were in the room. It was all posturing, all macho. It was as if we were all moving back together once again to live in Michael Fisher's tiny "Round House" by Lassen Creek in Vancouver.

Finally, on April 17, I walked into a rehearsal studio near Los Angeles and saw the original band, including two of my old boyfriends. My husband Geoff was with me, and that changed the dynamic. Still, it was strange seeing those guys after, literally, decades.

They were already cranking on "Crazy on You" when we walked in. It sounded just like we did years ago, which is different than Heart plays that song now. It was a more innocent sound.

Roger strode up immediately, and we hugged. "Wow, forty years," he said, referring to when Heart began. I said, "What's forty years between friends?" He was trying to pin my eyes, but I wasn't interested in a heavy moment. Derosier didn't get off his kit to greet me, so I blew him a wide air kiss. The atmosphere seemed tense.

The exact dynamic was in the room from decades before, but the difference now was that Ann and I just owned it. We used to be the chicks in the band, but now we were Heart.

The other guys had been on the radio in the weeks before the Hall of Fame induction, insinuating that maybe it was time for a Heart reunion that included them, something we weren't considering. We wanted to be sensitive to their hopes and dreams, but we are already part of a band called Heart that we love, and we have a vision for it. It would make no emotional or musical sense otherwise. We were at this time to honor and share the achievements everyone who had ever been in the band, but we were not interested in being "chicks" in a band again.

Ever.

ANN WILSON

I walked into the rehearsal a little bit before Nancy. Steve was mellow and funny. Howie was lovely, and sweet as ever. But Michael Derosier seemed shutdown. Roger was a ball of energy, though, and came up to me to talk about our book. He wanted to know what I meant by calling him a "stallion." "Rog, you were always the guy with the penis that was out, the naked guy with the guitar. I said you were sexual. Surely, you can't be insulted by that?" He said he wasn't, but seemed confused. Again, I sensed the distance between our minds.

We were doing a rehearsal at the Nokia Theater the next day, and there Derosier came up to me. "We've got to talk," he said. I said, "Is this really the right time? We're doing camera blocking. There are people everywhere. Is this the right moment to air dirty laundry?" But he said we needed to talk right then. We walked over to seats in the bustling hall.

He softened. Derosier said he wanted to tell me that if I'd heard about him saying some nasty things over the years, that I needed to understand what it was like for him to lose everything he once had as a young man. He lost a lot when he lost the opportunity to be in Heart. Heart had been the best time of his life. It made him bitter, he said. He wanted me to know he wasn't intentionally mean, but he'd been in despair. My heart swelled, and I remembered the deep, funny, handsome young man who drummed for us in the seventies. It took a lot of guts for him to open up to me like that, honest and face-to-face, and I respected him for it. It was the most emotional moment of the whole Hall of Fame experience in a way.

The next night, as the show itself began, we were at tables in front of the stage, watching the other inductees. First was Randy Newman, then Carole King doing a beautiful version of "So Far Away" for Lou Adler, and then Public Enemy. Flava Flav grabbed the microphone during their induction, and went completely off his rocker. Most of that got edited out of the broadcast, but watching it, I thought, nothing that anyone in our band might do could be more show-offish than this.

After Oprah inducted Quincy Jones, who gave a shout-out to Seattle, and Jennifer Hudson killed on the Donna Summer songs, it was our turn. Chris Cornell introduced us with a heartfelt speech where he called us his "hometown heroes," and told a story about how he once was loading equipment in an alley, discouraged after a bad gig, when I drove by him, in a sports car. He saw it as a sign to keep going. It was a touching speech, but in a way, I felt detached, like I was afraid to feel all the emotions that were coming at me from so many directions that night. I felt like a spectator at our own coronation.

When Chris finished, we came onstage: Nancy, myself, Roger, Howard, Steve, and Derosier. Despite all the rehearsing we'd done, we hadn't talked about how this moment would go. I assumed Nancy and I would speak last, and that's how it appeared later in the edited broadcast of the show. It was a very uncomfortable moment, but finally Howard grabbed the microphone and thanked the fans. We gestured for Roger or Steve to talk, but they declined. Finally, Nancy did.

She gave a beautiful speech, about how when we were growing up there were only four jobs available for women: "Teachers, mothers, nurses, or waitresses." We became both musicians and mothers in an era, "when women normally did not rock, and were not expected to be leaders," Nancy said.

"We're not finished rocking, yet," she continued. "We are looking straight into the face of the future, and we say, turn it up!"

When Nancy was done, I took the microphone. "I had the wrong gender, looks, DNA, and hometown for music business success in the era we grew up in," I said. "But aren't the sweetest parts of music always what's wrong? I got a chance to sing, to find my voice onstage, and I took it, and I still take it every night, in front of every audience. And I will never, ever, take it for granted."

Roger then grabbed the mic, talked a bit, and it was done. Then we were playing "Crazy On You," for the first time in thirty-three years as the original line-up of Heart. It sounded all bash-y, and crash-y, and Rog was running around like a chicken with its head cut off. Nancy stayed as far away from his hyperactivity as she could. "Crazy On You" was crazed, and fast. Our guitar brother, Jerry Cantrell, was the rock of Gibraltar though, solid and heavy, and if he hadn't been there the whole performance might have ended up in hyperspace.

Next, it was just Nancy and me on "Dreamboat Annie," and our portion of the night ended with the ultimate Northwest lineup of all-time—Mike

McCready, Chris Cornell, and Jerry Cantrell—all ripping through "Barracuda." It was ten tons of rock.

When the show was over, we all parted ways. There was no goodbye with the original members. Everyone just drifted apart.

I know Michael Fisher was there, because he wrote me after, but I never saw him. I never even glimpsed Michael Fisher once during the several days of rehearsals and the event itself. Something tells me he thought it best to step back.

The whole experience felt happy, but kind of brittle, to be honest. All those years later, seeing those guys again, being onstage with them, it all came back clear as day. We truly have moved on. Nancy and I are in our own musical and emotional world, now. That isn't to say that one is wrong, or one is right, just that we are on different paths, even though we now share a plaque on the wall in the Rock and Roll Hall of Fame.

NANCY WILSON

I'm in the Rock and Roll Hall of Fame, but so are two of my old boyfriends. I did think briefly, "Way to go, Einstein," that maybe I'd had better ideas in my life than going out with two guys in the same band. Not many women, or many men, can say they are in the Hall of Fame, with not one but two of their former loves. Joni Mitchell can say that for sure, so maybe I'm in a better company than I think.

We never had a proper goodbye with the other guys after the induction ceremony. I did see Roger leaving, and went to yell out to him, but he was moving too fast in the other direction. My last glimpse was Roger crossing a street, with a small blonde on his arm, carrying a guitar case. He looked so much like the same guy I used to cross the street with, and from a distance that small blonde could have been me. But in a flash, he blended back into the crowd and was gone.

I was most excited about going through the induction, and being escorted across the street, in the other direction entirely, by my husband Geoff

Bywater, a steady prince. And next to me was also my ever-present sister Ann.

You move on. Some things change, and some things stay the same for your whole life.

ANN WILSON

Just days after the Hall of Fame, we were back on the road again with Heart, our current Heart. Our first gig was an odd one for newly inducted Hall of Fame honorees—we played a private party for a hundred people at Sammy Hagar's bar in Cabo San Lucas, Mexico.

It was a fun, loose gig, and we ended, already thinking about the summer "Heartbreaker" tour, with a power encore of three Led Zeppelin songs. That blew the roof off the party. The crowd started went wild, kicking off their shoes, and knocking tables over. It felt like we were back on the Canadian prairie, playing in a small club, back forty years ago, when the Rock and Roll Hall of Fame didn't even exist. It was like we were back at Lucifer's, before a crowd that loved us, but a crowd that also destroyed the venue. Only this time around, Sammy Hagar owned the club. Sammy didn't care if a chair was busted. On a good night, he might break a few himself.

We were thrilled to be back with our own band, even though we were playing on a tiny piecrust of a stage. That night, that little stage in Cabo felt as long and as wide as all the roads we'd gone down over the years to get there. That tiny space felt endless.

ACKNOWLEDGMENTS

The Medal of Honor goes to Seattle's own Charles R. Cross upon the occasion of his commitment. He went with us to the heart of our story and helped us tell it with honesty and pride: a true human being and rock fanatic. Thank you, C.

Love and gratitude to the rest of the Big Five, those with us and those forever in our hearts: Lynn Wilson, Lois Dustin, and John B. Wilson USMC (ret.).

Many thanks to Sue Ennis, Kelly Curtis, Michael Fisher, Roger Fisher, and Mike Flicker. To Carol Peters and her team, including Sue Wood, Sacha Guzy, and Megan Brody, we appreciate everything you do for Heart.

To the book people, thank you for helping to make this a reality: Carrie Thornton, Calvert Morgan, and everyone at HarperCollins, and Sarah Lazin and Manuela Jessel at Sarah Lazin Books.

The authors would especially like to thank the following people who sat for interviews for this book, or provided photographs, documents, or research materials: Dick Adams, Sherri Anderson, Mark Andes, Burl Barer, Duane Baron, Faith Bentley, Julie Bergman, Mark Bowman, Denny Carmassi, Michael Castanada, Frank Cox, Art Crowder, Kelly Curtis, Mick Echoe, Linda Elves, Sue Ennis, Roger Fisher, Michael Fisher, Mike Flicker, Steve Fossen, Geoff Foubert, Don Grierson, Rolf Henneman, A. C. Ice, Mike Inez, Eric Johnson, Roger, Keagle, King County Library System, John Kohl, Howard Leese, Ron Nevison, Pat O'Day, Don Passman, Kim Pedone, Neal Preston, Marcia Resnick, Roger Ressemeyer, Lisa Richards, Mary Roberts, Barry Samuels, Seattle Public Library, Norman Seeff, Neal Skok, Ben Smith, Mark Sullivan, Suzie Walsh, Lynn Wilson, Sue Wood.

HEART IS

- **Ann Wilson** (1972–present)
- **Nancy Wilson** (1975–1995, 2002–present)
- **Ben Smith, drums** (1995–1998, 2002–present)
- **Craig Bartock, guitars** (2004–present)
- **Debbie Shair, keyboards, synthesizers** (2004–present)
- **Dan Rothchild, bass guitar** (2012–present)

Former band members

- **Steve Fossen** (1967–1982)
- **Roger Fisher** (1967–1979)
- **Don Wilhelm** (1967–1969)
- **Ray Schaefer** (1967–1969)

HEART IS

- **Gary Ziegelman** (1969–1971)
- **James Cirrello** (1969–1971)
- **Ron Rudge** (1969–1971)
- **Ken Hansen** (1969–1971)
- **Debi Cuidon** (1969–1971)
- **David Belzer** (1971–1974)
- **Jeff Johnson** (1971–1974)
- **Mike Fisher** (1972–1974)
- **John Hannah** (1974–1975)
- **Brian Johnstone** (1974–1975)
- **Howard Leese** (1975–1998)
- **Michael Derosier** (1975–1982)
- **Mark Andes** (1982–1992)
- **Denny Carmassi** (1982–1993)
- **Denny Fongheiser** (1993–1995)
- **Fernando Saunders** (1993–1995)
- **Scott Olson** (1995–1998; 2002–2003)
- **Jon Bayless** (1995–1998)
- **Scott Adams** (1995)
- **Frank Cox** (1995–1998)

- **Mike Inez** (2002–2006)
- **Tom Kellock** (2002–2003)
- **Darian Sahanaja** (2003–2004; 2007)
- **Gilby Clarke** (2003–2004)
- **Ric Markmann** (2006–2009)
- **Kristian Attard** (2009–2012)

Grateful acknowledgment is made to the following for permission to reprint copyrighted material:

"Magic Man" by Ann Wilson and Nancy Wilson. Copyright © 1976 by Andorra Music. Copyright Renewed. All rights for Andorra Music administered by Universal Music Corp. (ASCAP). Used by Permission. All Rights Reserved.

"How Deep It Goes" by Ann Wilson. Copyright © 1976 by Andorra Music. Copyright Renewed. All rights for Andorra Music administered by Universal Music Corp. (ASCAP). Used by Permission. All Rights Reserved.

"Heartless" by Ann Wilson and Nancy Wilson. Copyright © 1977 by Andorra Music. Copyright Renewed. All rights for Andorra Music administered by Universal Music Corp. (ASCAP). Used by Permission. All Rights Reserved.

"Barracuda" by Ann Wilson, Nancy Wilson, Michael Derosier, and Roger Fisher. Copyright © 1977 by Strange Euphoria Music, Know Music, Of The Roses Music, and Universal Music—MGB Songs. Copyright Renewed. All rights for Strange Euphoria Music, Know Music, and Of The Roses Music administered by Universal Music Corp. (ASCAP). Used by Permission. All Rights Reserved.

"Mistral Wind" by Ann Wilson, Nancy Wilson, Susan Ennis, and Roger Fisher. Copyright © 1978 by Strange Euphoria Music, Know Music, and Universal Music—MGB Songs. All rights for Strange Euphoria Music and Know Music administered by Universal Music Corp. (ASCAP). Used by Permission. All Rights Reserved.

"Dog & Butterfly" by Ann Wilson, Nancy Wilson, and Susan Ennis. Copyright © 1978 by Strange Euphoria Music and Know Music. All rights for Strange Euphoria Music and Know Music administered by Universal Music Corp. (ASCAP). Used by Permission. All Rights Reserved.

"Break" by Ann Wilson, Nancy Wilson, and Susan Ennis. Copyright © 1980 by Strange Euphoria Music, Know Music, and Sheer Music. All rights for Strange Euphoria Music, Know Music, and Sheer Music administered by Universal Music Corp. (ASCAP). Used by Permission. All Rights Reserved.

"Even It Up" by Ann Wilson, Nancy Wilson, and Susan Ennis. Copyright © 1980 by Strange Euphoria Music, Know Music, and Sheer Music. All rights for Strange Euphoria Music, Know Music, and Sheer Music administered by Universal Music Corp. (ASCAP). Used by Permission. All Rights Reserved.

"Two Black Lambs" by Ann Wilson, Nancy Wilson, and Susan Ennis. Copyright © 1997 by Skivvey Shirt Song Service, Beatie Boots Music, and Sheer Music. All rights for Skivvey Shirt Song Service, Beatie Boots Music, and Sheer Music administered by Universal Music Corp. (ASCAP). Used by Permission. All Rights Reserved.

"Hey You" by Nancy Wilson and Ben Mink. Copyright © 2010 by Know Music and Zavion Ent., Inc. All rights for Know Music administered by Universal Music Corp. (ASCAP). Used by Permission. All Rights Reserved.

"Red Velvet Car" by Ann Wilson, Nancy Wilson, and Ben Mink. Copyright © 2010 by Strange Euphoria Music, Know Music, and Zavion Ent., Inc. All rights for Strange Euphoria Music and Know Music administered by Universal Music Corp. (ASCAP). Used by Permission. All Rights Reserved.

"Dear Old America" by Ann Wilson, Nancy Wilson, and Ben Mink. Copyright © 2012 by Strange Euphoria Music, Know Music, and Zavion Ent., Inc. All rights for Strange Euphoria Music and Know Music administered by Universal Music Corp. (ASCAP). Used by Permission. All Rights Reserved.

"Rock Deep (Vancouver)" by Ann Wilson, Nancy Wilson, and Ben Mink. Copyright © 2012 by Strange Euphoria Music, Know Music, and Zavion Ent., Inc. All rights for Strange Euphoria Music and Know Music administered by Universal Music Corp. (ASCAP). Used by Permission. All Rights Reserved.